To
Ralph Tyler

With best wishes for your
success in developing the
behavorial sciences.

Moe Stein

THE
THEMATIC APPERCEPTION TEST

An Introductory Manual
for Its Clinical Use with Adults

THE
THEMATIC APPERCEPTION TEST

*An Introductory Manual
for Its Clinical Use with Adults*

REVISED EDITION

by

MORRIS I. STEIN, Ph. D.
University of Chicago

1955

ADDISON-WESLEY PUBLISHING COMPANY, Inc.
CAMBRIDGE 42, MASS.

To My Parents

CONTENTS

PREFACE

This manual was prepared on the basis of research and clinical experience as an aid in teaching the clinical use of the Thematic Apperception Test. Its purpose is to introduce a technique of analysis and interpretation that has proved useful in practice.

One of the fundamental assumptions underlying the technique presented here is that the principles involved in analyzing and interpreting TAT protocols are, in large measure, no different from those employed in studying behavior. This implies that the method will have to be modified and refined as we continue to make progress in our knowledge of the fields of personality and psychopathology and, of course, as we continue to learn more about the test itself.

Although the method presented has been found useful in working with children's protocols, the author has limited himself to a discussion of those pictures that were designed for adults, since most of his experience has been with this group.

The author acknowledges his indebtedness to Henry A. Murray and Eduardo Weiss, in whose seminars he not only found the stimulation to investigate problems in the field of personality but also the ideas that were to prove most fruitful in this regard.

Appreciation is also expressed to Gordon W. Allport for having read this manuscript and to Robert W. White and Eugenia Hanfmann for having read the manuscript of the first edition and for the many valuable suggestions they offered. To Nevitt Sanford the author is thankful for permission to use his definitions of needs and press.

To Jacob W. Getzels, Kenneth Fisher, Murray Horwitz, Robert A. Harris, and Pauline B. Hahn the author expresses his thanks for advice and assistance while the manuscript for the first edition was being prepared. To Patricia Hanson the author gratefully acknowledges his appreciation for taking care of the many details involved in preparing this manuscript for publication.

M. I. S.

Chicago, Illinois
July, 1954

FOREWORD

If there is a distinction between art and science, it is clear that the employment of projective techniques is still nearer to the former than the latter. At present their most effective use demands lengthy clinical experience, broad understanding of humanity, empathy, psychological-mindedness, and insight. As our comprehension of projective approaches to the study of personality increases, the direction of improvement of our procedures will undoubtedly be from art toward science, toward greater precision and quantification, toward greater uniformity among interpreters. Eventually we shall probably attain reliable and valid methods without sacrificing human relevance, without dissecting the total, live personality into its dead members — eventually, but not yet.

For a long time to come the most effective use of projective techniques will call upon both art and science, compounding clinical impressions with experimental controls. Such is the method described in this manual. It increases the usefulness of the Thematic Apperception Test since, even despite our present great limitations of knowledge, it makes possible a precision in personality diagnosis which is practical in the busy life of the clinic, which does not require unreasonably long hours for test interpretation. Still, in accomplishing this, it does not unduly sacrifice breadth and vigor in viewing psychological dynamics, and it maintains congruence with an inclusive theory of personality.

The history of the TAT has been remarkable. First it was described in a brief article of eighteen pages outlining the fundamentals of the procedure but giving no detailed, standardized method of interpretation, for indeed none had then been evolved. After that little was written by the group which developed the instrument, although its use spread quickly. Now, a number of years later, those who were associated with that original group are beginning to report the results of their work in the intervening period, a period during which many others have tried to discover the best way to utilize the technique — a matter on which there has been little general agreement.

Here, then, is outlined a method coming from one who has worked at the Harvard Psychological Clinic and resting on the Murray need theory with its thematic analysis of needs and press — a theory of personality which has never gained the attention it deserves. Not only does this book show how these concepts can be applied in clinical practice, but it outlines simply, and in many instances for the first time in print, the chief problems which confront the analyst and interpreter of the findings from this test. Incidentally, one of the primary lessons taught by this manual is how completely adequate projective testing rests on understanding of personality dynamics which can be gained only from intimate, firsthand association with diagnostic and therapeutic work. It reveals the falsity of the all-too-prevalent concept that any psychometric technician can "administer and score" the test and then hand his results over to someone else to integrate into the total clinical picture as he sees fit. Such usage renders the TAT a pallid and impotent instrument indeed.

This manual is a product of both the clinical experience and the research concern of the author. He recognizes that there is rapid change in the use of the TAT and associated procedures, realizing that his own contribution represents only the most recent addition to this flux. Emphasizing the value for TAT interpretation of what has come to be called clinical intuition, the author hazards a detailed presentation of his own "intuitive" analysis of a protocol, submitting it to microscopic scrutiny. In doing this he opens himself to attack from all sides, for it is unlikely that any other single clinician would agree on all aspects of his analysis. His boldness is not linked with dogmatic insistence that his approach is the only possible one, and it enables him to demonstrate many of the general principles involved in analyzing the TAT.

For teaching, this book with its case material should be of value in courses on the dynamics of personality, abnormal psychology, and psychopathology, as well as in those courses which are devoted primarily to studying the TAT. Clinicians who are doing research in the TAT also should find much of worth in these chapters, because of the many hypotheses proposed and employed which merit more minute and careful experimental investigation than they have yet received. In the rapidly expanding literature on the TAT, this manual will make its contribution because of its practicality and common sense. It maintains a happy balance between the undue rigorousness which limits the significance of results and the arty impressionism which blurs their meaningfulness.

JAMES G. MILLER
University of Chicago

May 1948

INTRODUCTION TO THE FIRST EDITION

In clinical practice, where the task is either the diagnosis of a single problem or the assessment of the complete personality, the clinician is concerned with two major areas — intelligence and personality. Psychometric tests usually provide for an evaluation of intelligence but the majority of techniques at hand for the investigation of personality (paper and pencil tests) are largely unsatisfactory. With the advent of projective techniques, new and more fruitful tests have become available for the study of personality.

Among the projective techniques, the Rorschach has achieved greatest prominence to date. It is a relatively simple task for psychologists trained in psychometric techniques to accept and learn the fundamentals of the Rorschach test. In the Rorschach, as in intelligence tests, there are responses to be scored according to very definite criteria. Furthermore, some interpretation of the Rorschach record can be made after a psychogram is drawn and various ratios calculated. However, problems do arise where deeper interpretations are indicated. At such times, only those who are trained and experienced in the theory of personality and in the analysis of psychological dynamics can abstract from the Rorschach record all that it contains.

However, since the Rorschach yields data primarily on the structure of the personality, many psychologists have been aware of a need for a test that will yield content material. In many instances the psychologist who gave his patient only a Rorschach felt that he had the skeleton of the patient's personality but not the flesh with which to embody it. As a result, more and more psychologists have been turning to the Thematic Apperception Test (TAT), developed by Morgan and Murray,* as another aid in the investigation of personality. But here they encounter additional barriers. They learn that those who have developed the test and worked with it the most analyze TAT protocols according to a "need-press" system which they, as practicing psychologists, find to be too time-consuming and painstaking a process in daily clinical practice, although it proves to be valuable in academic research. Furthermore, they also find that some psychologists achieve remarkable results without recourse to need-press analysis or need-press terminology. This is confusing and for most clinicians who have just begun working with the TAT, it has remained an esoteric technique.

---

* Morgan, C. D. and Murray, H. A., "A Method for Investigating Phantasies: The Thematic Apperception Test." *Archives of Neurology and Psychiatry*, 1935, **34**, 289–306.

It is the purpose of this manual to aid the psychologist in breaking down the wall of secrecy that surrounds the TAT and to indicate how it can be used in clinical practice. It is not claimed that the psychologist will become expert at TAT analysis after reading this manual; that will come only after much experience with the test. Furthermore, the manual is not intended for beginners in psychology or for beginners in the study of personality; it is designed as a manual for those who have had some training in the analysis of personality and who are adequately oriented toward clinical practice.

There is no bibliography, but the psychologist who is interested in the literature on the test is referred to Mayman's book in Rapaport's " Diagnostic Psychological Testing," Vol. II,* and Tomkin's book, " The Thematic Apperception Test."†

The psychologist who is interested in a revised need-press technique of analysis which may be utilized for research purposes is referred to the work of Aron.‡

---

 * Rapaport, D., *Diagnostic Psychological Testing*, Vol. II. Chicago: The Year Book Publishers, Inc., 1945.

 † Tomkins, S. S., *The Thematic Apperception Test*. New York: Grune and Stratton, Inc., 1947.

 ‡ Aron, B., *A Manual for Analysis of the Thematic Apperception Test*. Berkeley, Calif.: Willis E. Berg, 1949.

INTRODUCTION TO THE REVISED EDITION

In 1948 the first edition of this manual appeared. Those who have used the manual for training purposes have generally been of the opinion that it would be of greater value to the student if not one, but several protocols were analyzed. To meet this need, this second edition has been prepared. This manual has also been expanded to include the TAT pictures that are administered to women.

There are three additional goals that I have had in mind in preparing this manual. None of them have I made explicit in the body of the manual itself but I would hope that after reading through the cases here the reader might be stimulated to think about them.

Techniques such as the TAT have been called "projective techniques." This term does complete justice neither to the original psychoanalytic meaning of projection nor to the value and significance of the techniques. L. K. Frank, who is probably responsible for christening the techniques as projective techniques and who provided much valuable stimulation for work in this area, once suggested to the author that he thought his original article should be regarded as a railroad timetable — good up to a certain time and no longer. To be sure, this remark should not cause us to overlook the many significant insights in this article, but it certainly should be applied to the use of the term. What term should replace it is of relatively little significance* just so long as students and clinicians adopt the attitude that techniques such as the TAT, Rorschach, etc., are not to be learned as projective techniques but as a means through which the psychologist communicates with the patient and collects data which are to be analyzed in terms of the available body of psychological knowledge. This includes the data from the theorizing and researches on perception, thinking, learning, personality, etc.

By presenting a variety of cases in this manual I hope that it has the indirect effect of stimulating thinking with regard to research or clinical analyses of normal individuals. It is only natural that since clinical psychology stems historically in large measure from psychopathology, clinicians should be more sensitive to the "catabolic" characteristics manifest in psychological tests than to "anabolic" ones. But as the psychologist is called upon to predict behavior as well as to diagnose his patient or subject, the need for attending to the integrative or construc-

---

* "Unstructured tests" is a possible substitute but it is unlikely that this or any other name would be immediately successful in overcoming the cultural lag with which names will be met.

tive aspects of personality is paramount. I have not spelled out in detail what the nature of some of these characteristics might be, for such a task would require more elaborate documentation and discussion than is possible here. I do hope, however, that as the reader compares and contrasts the cases he will observe how they differ in terms of ego-strength, self-concept, intensity of drive, thought processes, interpersonal relations, etc., and derive some clues for future work in this area.

Included among the cases are three that have undergone different types of therapy: insulin shock, client-centered, and psychoanalysis. These cases were not selected because they are illustrations of the therapies that the patients had, and the reader is cautioned not to make any generalizations as to the effects or values of the therapies from the before and after protocols of single cases. These cases are presented to illustrate how individuals who have been exposed to therapeutic experiences react to the TAT. It is hoped that these records will stimulate thinking with regard to the objective measurement of the therapeutic process. Such hypotheses will have to include some measure of the status of the patient before therapy as well as the changes he has been able to achieve after therapy.

As in the first edition, it is not claimed that the psychologist will become expert at TAT analysis after reading this manual — that will come only after much experience with the test. Furthermore, the manual is not intended for beginners in psychology or for beginners in the study of personality; it is designed as a manual for those who have had some training in the analysis of personality and who are adequately oriented toward clinical practice.

It was very tempting to take advantage of the opportunity presented in preparing this edition to discuss personality theory. However, this, I felt, would be going beyond the scope of a "manual" and therefore I omitted such discussion. Nevertheless I should like to point out that the theory, if it were presented, would be personalistic in nature — an integration of dynamic and psychoanalytic theories of personality and the data and theories of general psychology.

This manual is limited only to the TAT. In the body of the book there are few references as to how the TAT fits into a psychological test battery that might include a test of intelligence, the Rorschach, the Sentence Completion Test, etc. It is not my intention to give the student or the clinician the impression that the TAT could or should be used by itself. To be sure, there are persons who believe they can get all the information they desire from a single test. I would like to indicate, however, that in my own experience using the TAT as part of a battery has been most valuable. To discuss how all tests would be integrated in a case study is a project reserved for the future.

PLAN OF THE MANUAL

Each of the sections in the manual has been selected with a definite rationale. For introductory purposes, each of the pictures is described and the problems or personality factors most commonly elicited by each of them are then discussed briefly and presented in the context of stories as told by patients. There are several reasons for following this procedure.

(1) To acquaint the reader with the kind of material that he might obtain from the test.

(2) In interpreting a TAT protocol, interindividual comparison of the stories can frequently be utilized to determine significant material. Knowing the common responses, the psychologist is in a better position to evaluate the obtained material.

One important caution must be emphasized in this respect. The psychologist should not exaggerate the importance of interindividual comparisons, because the intraindividual material is of primary significance in this test.

(3) Furthermore, a knowledge of the data usually obtained from each of the pictures will aid the psychologist on those frequent occasions when he does not have two hours at his disposal to administer the complete set of pictures. There often arises the problem of investigating a specific area in which the patient is experiencing a good deal of conflict. The psychiatrist, or any member of the clinical team, may be very anxious to obtain information only about this specific problem and the psychologist has a very short time at his disposal. Due to the exigencies of the situation, the psychologist should feel free to select from the set of TAT cards those pictures he believes can give him the most information in the available time. For example, if the psychiatrist is interested in the family situation, Pictures #1, #2, and #6 would certainly be those to be selected, amongst others. The psychologist must, however, be extremely cautious when using the cards in this fashion. Patients may give banal and evasive stories to those pictures which the psychologist has selected because they may be aware of the psychologist's motives. Hence they may not be sufficiently cooperative to speak their minds freely. It is a common experience that significant data may be revealed concerning a specific area by pictures that have rarely revealed data concerning that area. Psychologists should, therefore, be aware of the dangers to which they expose themselves when using a short form of the test.

Following the description of the pictures and common themes, there is a section on administration which is designed to meet the conditions that may exist in many clinical situations.

A technique of clinical analysis is then presented which is based on the following two hypotheses:

(1) People reveal their personalities and problems in talking about others and in structuring unstructured situations.

(2) The same set of principles which is utilized in analyzing and interpreting daily behavior may be utilized in working with TAT material.

To help the clinician in sharpening his attention for the factors to be looked for in the clinical analysis, I have included the definitions of needs and press. Scoring a few protocols according to these definitions, although laborious, would provide valuable training.

Finally, a series of protocols is presented and analyzed to demonstrate how the technique of clinical analysis may be utilized. For didactic purposes the cases are thoroughly analyzed so that the beginner may follow all the steps in the development of the final interpretation. In an effort to cut down on repetition, where a point is explained in one case it is not discussed further in the next.

The manual does not include a bibliography. But the student who is interested in such is referred to Watson, R. I., *The Clinical Method in Psychology,* New York: Harper & Brothers, 1951, and the section called " The TAT Newsletter " in the Journal of Projective Techniques. Since 1951 the Journal of Projective Techniques has collated a bibliography on the TAT for each year.

CHAPTER 1

THE TAT PICTURES AND THEIR COMMON STORIES

The TAT consists of thirty pictures.* Since experience has shown that subjects find it easier to project their needs, feelings, experiences, etc., when they have characters with whom to identify, the majority of these pictures depict life situations involving one or more persons. However, the pictures without people are not without significant value. Of these thirty pictures, ten are administered to all subjects — boys and girls, adult males and adult females. The remainder of the pictures are divided so that ten are administered to adult males, ten to adult females, ten to young boys, and ten to young girls. In this fashion, each individual is tested with a complete set of twenty pictures. On the back of each picture there is a number and a letter. The number refers to the order in which the card is to be presented to the subject and the letter refers to the age and sex group for which it is best suited: B — boy, G — girl, M — adult male, F — adult female.

Since this manual is concerned primarily with the testing of adults, only the pictures administered to adult men and women are described, together with sample stories. When pictures are administered to both males and females the stories obtained from men are preceded by the letter M, and stories obtained from women are preceded by the letter F.

PICTURE #1   A young boy is contemplating a violin which rests on a table in front of him.†

The main character in the stories commonly ‡ told to this picture is the young boy who has been forced, usually by his parents, to practice or study the violin. The hero's reactions to their demands (passivity,

---

* The cards are printed by the Harvard University Printing Office, Cambridge, Massachusetts.

† The description of each of the pictures is taken from *Thematic Apperception Test Manual* by Henry A. Murray, M.D., Harvard University Press, Cambridge, Massachusetts.

‡ The common responses that are presented in this manual are based on clinical experience. More thorough investigation of the common stories to each of the pictures is a problem for future research. A study by Ruth Markmann (*Prediction of Manifest Personality Trends by a Thematic Analysis of Three Pictures of the Thematic Apperception Test,* Radcliffe College, unpublished thesis, 1943) is representative of the type of material that such investigations might yield. The following is a distribution of common stories based on a study of 88 normal adult males. Since in some stories there is more than one theme, the total number of cases indicated below adds up to more than 88.   (*cont.* p. 2)

compliance, counteraction, aggression, escape into fantasy, etc.) are also included. These stories are frequently told by patients whose parents have dominated them. The hero's reaction to the situation described in the story usually reflects the patient's reaction in similar circumstances.

Other common stories discuss the boy's aspirations, goals, and fantasies of achievement. These stories are usually told by patients who are ambitious.

> (M) He is looking at it, looking at it, and doesn't want to practice, or is it he is forced to practice and doesn't want to concentrate on whether he should. Outcome, he'll have to whether he likes it or not.

(a) The child becomes a great violinist or learns his music thoroughly through his own effort and active and constructive work. (17 cases)

(b) The hero dreams of becoming a great hero but active striving is not considered or incorporated in his plans of action. (16 cases)

(c) The hero wonders about the construction and history of the violin and how one makes music. (13 cases)

(d) The boy is forced to practice by his parents and although he has thoughts of rebellion and rejection, he turns in the end to compliance, which brings him some form of success. (12 cases)

(e) The boy is forced to practice but he objectifies his autonomous thoughts in behavior. The violin may be broken, music disliked, or the task-setting adult may be the object of the hero's aggression. (12 cases)

(f) The hero is forced to practice and his passivity is manifested in a half-hearted deference and compliance. The hero puts little effort into his work so that he does not learn how to play well. (12 cases)

(g) The hero's interest in the violin is the result of a previous interest of his father, or some other individual who serves as an example for the hero to follow. This story is seldom found in pure form but overlaps with an achievement theme or a curiosity theme. (11 cases)

(h) The ambition of the hero to play is begun and fostered by gifts or aid from a nurturant person. (9 cases)

(i) No particular sequence of needs and press. The subject is primarily concerned with the description of the inner states and conflicts of the hero. (8 cases)

Other articles regarding norms which may be of interest to the reader are: S. Rosenzweig, "Apperceptive Norms for the Thematic Apperception Test, I. The Problem of Norms in Projective Methods," and S. Rosenzweig and E. E. Fleming, II, "An Empirical Investigation," *J. of Personality*, 1949, **17**, No. 4. (I should like to call the reader's attention to a footnote on p. 487 of this second article, which refers to the first edition of this manual: "Stein, on the basis of his 'clinical experience,' describes the common stories for the TAT pictures used with male adults. The difference between his account and the kind of empirically derived and detailed norms here presented is recognized in his own discussion. It is nevertheless noteworthy that the two sets of findings seldom contradict each other.") The reader is also referred to Eron, L. D., Frequencies of themes and identifications in the stories of schizophrenic patients and non-hospitalized college students, *J. consult. Psychol.*, 1948, 12, 387–395.

(M) Well, well, the picture itself, ah, looks like a boy who was a small boy who had just finished practicing his violin lesson. Let's see, and was thinking perhaps some day, he would be a great violinist himself, and oh, perhaps he has been put to the job by his parents but doesn't like it too well. He likes it fairly well but doesn't like to practice and he puts it down, starts to daydream about how he will practice and be great some day. I suppose later on he starts, gets back to reality and starts practicing again and finally does become competent.

(F) The child was told by his mother that he had to practice the violin. The child walked into the room, took the music down and the violin on top of it. Instead of picking up the violin and playing, he just sat there and stared at it thinking about other things that he would rather be doing. Right now he is having a mental conflict whether to pick up the violin and play or get out of it. Probably will pick up the violin and start practicing.

(F) Well, I think this boy is definitely an artist. He has ability. He has practiced and studied for many years and I think he's contemplating the violin as one of his most cherished possessions. He is dreaming of the future and what he is going to do with his violin and what he is going to accomplish with it. And I think that some day he will become a famous violinist. Was it deliberately made to look like Yehudi Menuhin?

PICTURE #2   Country scene: in the foreground is a young woman with books in her hand; in the background a man is working in the fields and an older woman is looking on.

Either the young woman in the foreground or the man in the background may be selected as the main character in the common stories told to this picture. The stories usually refer to the hero's or heroine's reactions to an uncongenial or unstimulating environment, or to problems arising as a result of difficult relations with members of the family. From these stories we usually learn how the patients regard their environments, what their levels of aspiration are, and what their attitudes toward their parents might be.

(M) This farm girl is very interested in books because she is carrying some in her hand. She seems to want to get away from the toil and labor in the background and go and read her book. She seems to be looking toward a nice quiet place where she might get a little enjoyment out of reading and a little relaxation from the toil and farm work. The man in the fields seems to be working very hard and the girl thinks that if she had a better education she might not have to work as hard as that. There is the girl's mother standing on this side. She doesn't seem to be very well. In fact, she looks sort of pregnant. Perhaps the girl by reading those books will open up a brand new life in the future for herself. The mother and father probably want the girl to work and she doesn't want to work. Instead she wants to read her books as I said before and learn to do something greater than just an ordinary farmer that has to slave and struggle all his life. This story probably has a good ending because she reads the books and sees different things that are going on in the outside world and she runs away from home.

(M) The painter is trying to give a picture of farm life in all its glory, honest, hard-working, intelligent people, the salt of the earth, all of the glory and none of the hardship of farming and probably too is trying to show by the girl, in the background, with the books, aspiring to something better than what they are, the American dream of opportunity. You can imagine, say the father, or the man who owns the farm coming out west when he was a young man, claiming some land and settling down, raising a family, growing old, and being a grandfather in the house of his son. One of the younger sons marries a girl close by and settles down on his father's farm to work it and in turn they have a family. He's probably never had much of an opportunity to do, oh, to have an education or to read books, appreciate any of the arts or sciences, but he still wants his daughter to have the advantages he missed. I suspect the mother is not quite as enthusiastic, very often they aren't, but the father still has his way in sending the daughter through school. She, I would say, is very enthusiastic, hard-working, very pleasant personality, very appreciative of what her family is doing for her. I expect she will marry, above her class, will live in the city and think back about her days on the farm when she was a child.

(F) This girl just finished teaching school in a little country house. On her way home she's been thinking of wonderful places she'd like to go, things she'd like to do and then she has come now to her home which is a peasant's village and she sees the beautiful country and fields and people she loves. She realizes that although she has these dreams she would never pick herself up and go and (long pause) and then she knows she will continue to dream but these dreams will never become an actuality. She (long pause) continues on her way home, puts her books down and her dreams vanish as she begins to help with the dinner.

(F) The girl feels that she's in, she's getting an education at the expense of her mother and father. Perhaps she ought to be there helping them. Mother looks as if she knows this conflict is taking place and is afraid, feels sure the girl will give in to her. But she ignores the father completely. Conflict between her and the mother. See mother looking at the father and saying I have him under control and it's just her I have to control. She has a proud look on her face. I suppose girl sees the father as too compliant to mother and she feels that no doubt he has lost his own initiative by doing this and doesn't want this to happen to her. Wants to go out and gather from ambition and become more than slave to mother's wishes. She looks like she's getting ready to cry about it. Guess she has some safety there and don't know if she'll have any if she goes out into the world. I believe that if she knows that all this is going on it's good. She knows that mother knows she'll give in — more safety with mother, mother is a strong creature in family. But it's hard to tell with a female, they're highly irrational, unpredictable. She looks so sad she'll give in to her mother.

PICTURE #3BM On the floor against a couch is the huddled form of a boy with his head bowed on his right arm. Beside him on the floor is a revolver.

This picture lends itself to stories involving depression, dejection, and suicide. The boy is commonly seen as having been wronged or as having done something wrong. We are then told how he resolves his predicament. These stories often reveal the types of situations which the patient finds frustrating and his reactions to them. There are two perceptual distortions which occur occasionally and which should be noted: (1) the boy may be seen as a girl; (2) the revolver may be seen as a toy or anything which makes it appear as a less aggressive object. The first distortion is found most frequently in the protocols of patients with strong feminine tendencies; the second in those of patients unable to express their aggression overtly.

Father didn't let him go to the movies. He's been punished for breaking the object in the corner. Probably wishes he was dead — " When I grow up I'll show my father " (that's the way I always thought). Well, that young boy seems to be sad about something and wants to be alone and he is up in his bedroom and there is some object on the floor. There is something he has been trying hard to do and he's failed and he doesn't know what to do about that. So I think he is crying it out by himself.

She really looks like she is in trouble, she certainly feels bad about something, guilty, feels guilty about something, doesn't know what to do, how to face it, outcome is very hard to decide, only thing is she'll have to stop crying and face it. She may have committed some crime, I know that I felt that way, it still means you have to take the consequences or take the coward's way out.

This young man is in Serbia or rather in a Balkan country. He had been, he had been, as young and sensitive and, and inclined toward melancholy and other aberrations but now, let's say he is in Yugoslavia. The Germans had overrun the country. His father, who had been a very prominent man such as a lawyer, or a politician has been captured or probably killed by the Germans. His fortune has been lost and his friends have all died in the, oh, I forgot to mention he is Jewish, of a Jewish family. His friends have died in the struggle. The rest of his family are someplace else, probably a worse place such as France and he's making feverish attempts to release his father, to get his father released but without success and now he has returned from an exploit in which he went to the headquarters of the Germans, walked in, shot the man, lieutenant or general or whoever was there, and ran through the streets quickly and ran home. And now he hears the German policeman come and he knows what they will do to him and there he has just put a bullet through his own head. I guess that is a pistol.

PICTURE #3GF A young woman is standing with downcast head, her face covered with her right hand. Her left arm is stretched forward against a wooden door.

Stories to this picture involve situations of despair and grief. The heroine may be troubled by a conflict with her boy friend, husband, or family. She may have committed some wrong and feels guilty about it, or plans for some way out. The heroine may also be grieving after the death of a loved one.

This is a young girl, about 24 or 25, unmarried (long pause). Had been doing something secretly, either politically or socially or economically; working at a vocation of which her father and brother wouldn't approve, that is, the whole family wouldn't approve. The father and brother are bawling her out. She tried to justify her position and words got more heated and more furiously and finally she couldn't argue with them logically any more and began to cry. They saw that they had broken down her defenses. They kept at it more and more until she got up walking out of the room still sobbing, grabbing onto the door for sheer physical support. She sees no way out of the conflict. She's sure of her convictions, knows they won't give her away, no hope of reconciliation, not at present. She'll walk away and because she is so sure of her convictions will probably leave home and living her life independent of her family.

(What might she have been doing that caused all this?) She was working for a labor union and her father was a capitalist. She might be dating a Negro boy and her family is middle-class white Protestant. Or she might want to get money to go through school and is working as a waitress in a cocktail lounge, her family being of the upper class.

This looks like the woman who something terrible has happened to her. Something she feels very ashamed of — oh, probably she, she probably thought somebody loved her who didn't — was much more involved in the situation than the guy and she was more generous than he and was laughed at. He took it very casually. She was so involved in it herself she can't find what's left of herself outside of her shame. She comes back home — knowing it will be empty, at least the door will be closed. Nobody will see her. Until she can rearrange her life, her feelings, build up her outside — uh, she'll go out again. She feels the solid door, yes, shut out, try to shut out her devastated memories. A devastated picture of herself. That's all for her. Poor kid! (How does it turn out?) She'll be O.K. She'll probably go through it alone. Probably won't even talk about it to anyone. It happens to everybody. She'll be O.K.!

PICTURE #4 A woman is clutching the shoulders of a man whose face and body are averted as if he were trying to pull away from her.

Men and women tell stories to this picture which are usually concerned with a conflict situation between the couple in the foreground. In the stories told by men, the man may desire to leave the woman because he has a plan which he wishes to put into action but the woman wants to keep him with her. The conflict may be stated in general terms as an " argument " or the story may involve the " eternal triangle " with the seminude figure in the background as the man's mistress or girl friend. These stories frequently reflect the patient's difficulties in marital adjustment, his attitudes toward women and sex. In the stories told by women the plots are generally the same — the man wants to leave the woman in the foreground for another woman or because of some plan that he has in mind. The techniques used for controlling the man or dealing with the situation are often described. As with men, the stories told by women reveal information related to heterosexual adjustment.

(M) Well, he's got some plan in mind. She got some hold on him. She's in love with him and vice versa. There's some relation between the two pretty strong probably love. And he's going to do something that's a bit rash, and she's trying to restrain him, using any method she can. His mind is mainly centered on this driving idea at the time. And she doesn't share that idea. She's trying to hold him back into the world that she likes and she's known him in most of the time. And the outcome is that he'll win out. He'll do what he wants to do. His drive is stronger than her hold on him. So, therefore, he'll do it.

(M) He had an argument with his wife. He wants to leave and she's begging him to stay. She loves him something awful. The picture in the background shows that he's probably going to his mistress. She tells him she was faithful for five years while he was overseas. She's the clinging vine type. He is probably not satisfied. He is probably not satisfied with her and that's why he has a mistress. He looks like the love them and leave them type. She keeps trying to be passionate but he can't, she seems to be afraid to give.

(F) He's strong silent man, huh. He's being asked to do something against his principles by this rather exotic looking creature. Until he met her, he probably had been in love with some sweet thing from his home town. He might be on a ship where these two people have met. She looks like adventurous type. His appeal lies in the fact that he has principles which she can't overcome. His face too is full of seriousness. He's afraid of what might happen if he does listen to her. Little gal back home doesn't have to offer what she has to offer. That's probably why he's on ship anyway. These two more mated than appear to be. He knows it and she isn't so sure of it. He knows nothing else but this girl, if he'd listened to her, all else would leave. Ending says, hell with it all, and goes with the girl, come what may, stronger than the both of us. Stern, unrelenting look won't last very long. The little gal in the background is going to be left in the background, won't bother her much either. She didn't understand his restlessness, the other one will.

(F) This is a toughie. Oh, dear! (Sighs) This man has been unfaithful to the woman he loves — not his wife. He's been caught in the act — and because he feels so guilty is trying to rush away. She is trying to hold him back and be understanding. Like the average man he is trying to run away from a situation in which he has been wrong. Eventually the woman will forgive him and he'll come back to her.

PICTURE #5 A middle-aged woman is standing on the threshold of a half-opened door looking into a room.

In stories to this picture the middle-aged woman is frequently described as having surprised one or more individuals in an activity which they prefer to keep hidden from her. Or she may be inspecting the room for any of a number of reasons. These stories usually reveal the patient's attitude towards his mother or his wife, or her mother or herself, and/or the situations about which the patient is curious.

(M) She opens the door and has a look of surprise on her face. You can see by her way of dressing that she's old-fashioned and her husband isn't. He's probably on the couch with a blonde. She is thinking back of the faithful years of service to him and her children. She'll surely think of a way to kill him. She'll close the door without his knowing it and put poison in his food tonight, or if she is ever-loving she'll think of a way to win him back.

(M) This woman is looking to see if there is anyone in the room, living alone, looking around before entering reminds me of myself, reminds me of a lonely old maid, could visualize a million morbid things — her employer is dead, spying on her husband, walked in unexpectedly and saw her husband, could be a mother watching her children at play.

(F) The young daughter is entertaining the boy in the parlor and the mother came down to peek and see what's kept him so long and why she hasn't gone to bed. The youngster will become very annoyed and say goodnight and go to bed. A look of half annoyance and half of curiosity is on the mother's face. The lamp is lit. That's what makes it night. That hall from which the mother is entering is dark.

(F) This is interesting. Sort of a faded woman, married a long while to a man who she assumes has taken her for granted for so many years. She is the type who will keep a fine house. If she is a mother, will be an understanding one, but all the little things, love, have been lost in her life. And suddenly it's spring. She's probably married to a studious, quiet, reserved man who never expressed appreciation or deep love for her and she's kept a garden and opened door to study, and this beautiful morning there are flowers for her and suddenly everything is right. He will not have to speak again but there they are and he realizes her love for beautiful and she will understand him. There'll be nothing said that every — when he comes home. She and he will know that she's pleased with this simple gift.

PICTURE #6BM A short elderly woman stands with her back turned to a tall young man. The latter is looking downward with a perplexed expression.

The elderly woman and young man in this picture are usually seen as mother and son. The son may be seen as asking his mother's permission to do something that he had planned for a long time. He may want to leave home to undertake a job in another city, to get married, or to enlist in the armed forces. His desires usually conflict with his mother's. In most stories we are also told how the conflict is resolved. These stories reflect the patient's attitude toward his mother and the factors which may have caused friction at home.

Another common story to this picture is one in which the young man brings sad tidings to the woman. This story is found most frequently in the protocols of veterans who had promised their buddies who died on the battlefield that upon return home they would report the circumstances of their deaths to their families.

> John, after finishing college, felt that he must get away from the town he lived in in order to achieve success. He found that the hardest part in doing so would be to explain to his mother and when he did come to tell her she was very much upset and reasoned with John. She tried to show him ways and means of how he can achieve his success by staying home. He tried and found it was successful and became a farmer in his community.

> This picture shows great sadness. There has been some kind of bad news because the woman is turned in a typical motion of sorrow. The man in the picture is grim faced or sorrowful looking. He's thinking deeply perhaps of a tragedy. A death, it's obvious that he brought the bad news. He has his coat on and his hat in his hand. He doesn't feel too happy about having brought the bad news. The woman will just take it the best she can which most people do. The young man will never forget having to tell the woman.

PICTURE #6GF A young woman sitting on the edge of a sofa looks back over her shoulder at an older man with a pipe in his mouth who seems to be addressing her.

The couple in this picture are usually seen as engaged in some conversation, discussion, or argument. The relationship between the two may be casual or it may be more serious. The girl is usually startled by the actions or motives of the male and tries to deal with them. Attitudes toward men, the woman's role, and heterosexual situations are revealed.

Hmmmmm. This man invited his secretary or co-worker to visit him at his apartment under the pretext of business. When she got there she took off her coat and conversation was purely social for a few minutes, and she sat down on a couch. She never considered him as anything but another person, liked him and respected him. At first he was sitting across from her, and then made some sort of proposition at which she was taken completely surprised by. He got up and crossed the room, stood behind her, arguing with her. She still couldn't stand it, couldn't conceive it. She'll probably get up, put on her coat, and go home, disliking him intensely.

All kinds of implications in this picture. Somehow I don't have a clear idea of what is behind it. Not much feeling for it except that man surprised woman. Has a quizzical, humorous type of face. Pipe denotes complacency. He's much more interesting than she to know. He has kind of face I like. She looks like very concerned about her own beauty and looks beautiful but without much type of understanding of his type of humor. See that married young when beauty all important thing to him. His face is ruggedly handsome. He seems to have grown into interesting type of maturity. Her face would imply that she has stopped learning, keeping pace with him except to keep herself beautiful. I would say he's a very successful man. He's able to provide her with lovely things that she wants most. Perhaps question has come up, he's going to press her into an answer. He's going to shock her out of her complacency to see if there's anything behind that mask of satisfaction. She realizes that this is a moment probably been building up for some time, and for the first time she's a little afraid, not physical fear. It's fear that she's failed him somewhere along the line. In spite of the rather smiling countenance that he has, she realizes that answer is of vital importance at this moment. Personally I don't think she will make the right answer. I can see him going in a different way — very much alone. He will realize that beauty is an ephemeral thing and not enough.

PICTURE #7BM   A gray-haired man is looking at a younger man who is sullenly staring into space.

The younger man is frequently seen as having come to the older man for advice or the two men are discussing a problem of mutual interest. These stories frequently indicate the patient's attitude toward adult males and also some of the problems about which he may be concerned. At times the stories to this picture reflect the patient's attitude to therapy.

Father and son are having a serious talk. The son had done something that he shouldn't have done. The father is giving him advice. I think the son will take the advice and everything will be all right. He was fooling around with the wrong girl.

This is a doctor and a patient. The doctor has just told the man of the coming operation and the young man is shocked and very sad about the thought of an operation, which he dreads. The doctor answers him that nowadays modern science and all that will be lamp of life for him, and that he wouldn't have to be afraid of dying from the operation or of being maimed. After explaining to him and showing him textbooks of different cases and various things, he succeeds in showing the boy that he'll be all right, and the boy isn't afraid anymore.

PICTURE #7GF An older woman is sitting on a sofa close beside a girl, speaking or reading to her. The girl, who holds a doll in her lap, is looking away.

In the stories told to this picture the older woman is usually seen as the mother who is either talking or reading to her daughter. The mother may either be trying to explain something to her daughter or is reading to her. The stories usually reflect significant information regarding mother-daughter relationship, attitudes toward the mother, and/or attitudes toward the self.

This is the story of a mother and daughter — reading probably Tolstoy's stories or something, something quiet and moving stories, legends of Christianity or something like that. While the mother reads in complete communication with her daughter — reads to her child — all her feeling for her daughter is richly surrounded with the guides — with the directions of sureness — the daughter takes it not as a part of the mother but as something that a — she has to take, and try on, and fit in to the other parts of herself, and try to — something she'd like to be, something she'd like to equal, aspire to, and which is — which is for the future — which doesn't fit in with her daily life yet; which she is storing away. Trying to fill in the terrible vacuum of childish uncertainty. But she can't explain herself and can't even acknowledge herself — let alone talk to her mother about; to her the world is still something she can go out and grasp when she is grown. The mother knows she can — will if she can give the kid just this security of reading with her, of giving her these aspirations — just this one kid. That's probably as much as one person can do.

This child's father has just been killed. Or not necessarily father — sister, brother, grandmother, some relative close to the child — could even be a maid. And the mother is thinking how the best way to break the news to the child without making it a traumatic experience, so she can understand it. So she tells the child about God's way of doing things, about a life hereafter, makes death into something beautiful instead of something to be feared. And the child is thinking about this person, and can't quite understand what death is or that she won't see the person anymore. She don't realize the impact of what the mother has said until a few days have passed.

PICTURE #8BM An adolescent boy looks straight out of the picture. The barrel of a rifle is visible at one side, and in the background is the dim scene of a surgical operation, like a reverie-image.

In the stories told to this picture the main character is usually the adolescent boy. The scene in the background is utilized as a representation of the boy's fantasy or wish to become a physician. Or the boy may have shot the figure on the table and he is now awaiting the outcome of the operation. The first theme reflects the patient's ambitions and the second, his aggressive tendencies. In aggressive stories, the patient may reveal the individual against whom his aggression may be directed.

This is a story of a young fellow — don't know exact age. Has many ideas, wants to be a doctor, wants to be a great hero, save people's life. He has gone through school, works not too good, more sensitive than most children, lets imagination run free. Grows older, 14–15, had few friends, because he differs from others. People change their minds. They feel that he has something. They feel that they have confidence in him. He may become a good doctor. At age 12, 13, 14, 15 someone got him a microscope. He is interested, wants to become a surgeon, work hard, get to some place. He probably will, lots of people become doctors. He will be a good one, study a lot, and reach his goal. He is going to have some struggle, though. He is not too sure if he wants to, if he wants to become a doctor, because it might turn out that scientific work is different. The heroic idea will always be in back of his mind. He really gets into medicine, some ideals will be lost, but he will make a good doctor.

There has been a shooting. The young man, the boy in the foreground, did the shooting — got a look of regret on his face. Probably thinking of why did he do it. Probably sorry now that he got back his sense. Background is a doctor and an assistant operating which is probably to remove the bullet. The young man is now thinking about what will happen if he dies and I hope he doesn't die. Being that very young, 14 or 15, in the event that the wounded man dies he will be sent to a corrective school which may straighten him out. From his dress and appearance he seems to be a good boy. If the full facts are brought out it might be that he had a justifiable circumstance for shooting the wounded man whoever he may be.

Bob, who was a good scholar in school, was very playful at home. One day he found his father's shotgun. Like all boys he was told to keep away from certain destructive toys. He started to play with the gun and accidentally pulled the trigger not knowing the gun was loaded. Shot his father although no charge was placed against him, the thought has remained with the boy ever since.

PICTURE #8GF   A young woman sits with her chin in her hand looking off into space.

The woman in the picture may or may not be identified. When she is, she may be regarded as a housewife or as having some occupation. She is usually resting from her work, contemplating her present life situation or fantasying about the future.

Not an artist model, is it? Don't think so. Seems to be very poor environment. Hard-working woman, guess she — working and getting nowhere. Takes time off to think what it's all about. It's a young woman. She got a nice face on her, not old looking, kind of young looking. May have a husband and two or three children, has to scrub, wash, and clean and farm to take care of. May be happy, just taking time off.

This girl has gone to school which opened up complete new worlds to her. Now that she's finished school, that is, the University, and she has to decide on a vocation or get married, she's just sitting there in her chair, sitting backwards in her chair, her head in her hands, wondering what she should do, which of these new worlds she should explore. Her mind is wandering, projecting herself to many situations one after another. She'll probably continue sitting in the chair, just thinking for hours until there is some interruption. As time passes she'll make up her mind about what she wants to do.

PICTURE #9BM   Four men in overalls are lying on the grass taking it easy.

The men are seen as either resting and dreaming after a hard day's work or they are taking a short rest before returning to their work. It is usually the more energetic individual who concludes his story by having the men return to their work.

> During the days of the depression it was a common thing to see groups of men lying in a park huddled against one another just dreaming of things they might have done if they were wiser. Although they are broke at present they continue to dream of things to come.

> This could be 3 or 4 hikers definitely or hoboes. They have been doing some strenuous work of some sort, either hiking or construction workers of some sort. Being that they are not settled down in a really permanent overnight position, they are just taking a rest. Like most people they will probably rest up in a little while and get on with what they are doing.

PICTURE 9GF   A young woman with a magazine and a purse in her hand looks from behind a tree at another woman in a party dress running along a beach.

The woman running along the beach is usually seen as running away because she is involved in some kind of situation with a man. Typically, the young woman behind the tree merely observes what is going on or gains some satisfaction from the proceedings. The stories may reflect attitudes toward other women, sibling rivalry situations, or heterosexual relationships.

> This girl is a waitress — she works in a restaurant drive-in near the lakeside. There's dancing in the evening and she hates it. She sees those fancy people coming to dances, dressed up, with cars, rich. One night the guys get real high and they go out swimming, they don't come back, and after a while one of the girls whose guy is out swimming gets excited and starts worrying, goes tearing down the beach looking for the guy. It's dark. She can't see him anyway, and she goes frantically up and down the beach yelling. But our gal, the waitress, doesn't give a goddamn. She watches from behind a tree and thinks it's too bad these people don't know any better than to go fooling around drunk at night, while she has to work for a living staying on the job until four o'clock.

> Girl in evening gown, running away. Don't know where she's running, may have been to dance. It's summer time. She's running along beach, may have had a misunderstanding with escort. The other girl was not invited, this is going to be a long story, is

reading a book. No, looks like a pocketbook and towel. She was on the beach, saw other girl come running so she hides behind the tree. She can't be running from danger, she's just eavesdropping, otherwise wouldn't be so calm, hiding behind the tree to see what it's all about. Maybe they were two sisters, one invited to prom, the other wasn't, hides behind tree to see what is going on.

PICTURE #10   A young woman's head against a man's shoulder.

The man and woman are frequently seen as expressing their affection for each other. The stimulus for this event may be a happy occasion or some unfortunate circumstance. The themes usually indicate how the patients regard their present marital relationships, what their attitudes toward their parents' relationships are, or what expectancies they have regarding their own future marital adjustment.

(M) She looks pretty sad. He looks like he's trying to be comforting. Therefore, something has happened. By her head on his shoulder, by his arm around her, he's going to try to comfort her now. She'll get over it pretty soon, I guess. Maybe some bad business about one of their children or something. One of their children might have got hurt or something.

(M) This picture shows a couple, a married couple on their 25th anniversary. They are shown embracing each other and it appears that memories of the past 25 years are going through their minds.

(F) This is beautiful. —— I can see two people finally coming to that one moment when they understand, complete, love at that moment, nothing to do with physical, it's mind and heart, it's there through a great tragedy. Each thought they lost everything, maybe a child. Of course, in each of them there is a physical love, with this loss of a child for whom they'd almost forgotten each other. In their efforts to prove that the child loved one better than the other in conflict, and with loss of child, they turned to each other and once again laughter, understanding, and depth of emotion, that never existed before. A third person in there and the fact that two left, they are completely one, nothing can change that. Her greatness will affect his terrific ambition and strength. She will need his strength and he will need her greatness. They supplement and complement each other. That's the way it will be from now on.

(F) This is the story of two people, a man and a woman who come together out of fullness rather than emptiness of their lives. There was great understanding between them made especially rich by the fact that he comes and goes and is often away. Each can live alone in their own strength and so doubly enrich their own feelings for each other.

PICTURE #11   A road skirting a deep chasm between high cliffs. On the road in the distance are obscure figures. Protruding from the rocky cliff on one side is the long head and neck of a dragon.

In the common stories told to this picture the obscure figures (animals or men) are seen as being attacked by the dragon and their techniques of defense are usually described. Or the man in the picture may be an adventurer or a scientist who is exploring unknown regions. The first type of story usually indicates the patient's fear of aggression and his means of coping with it; the second type reveals the patient's curiosity or desire for dangerous or novel experiences.

(M) There is a path, wall, and bridge. The thing to figure out is what this is. Looks like an animal chasing a man and there is another prehistoric animal. Long neck, webbed feet coming down the side. These animals are also running for their lives including the man in front of them. They get away in the end.

(M) This man one day thought he'd go hiking. He lived near this big set of mountains and so he started out, walking around the mountains and decided to go up to see the view down below. He came across one path that interested him. He decided to take it. Went up the hill, it was rocky and he slipped and fell to what looks like a bridge. From the other side of the hill an animal walked on the path — it was enormous thing, six feet high. It startled him and interested him. He stayed at a safe distance. Out of the side of the mountain came an animal with a long neck. Two animals looked at one another as if they were going to have a big battle. The strangeness of the animal with the big neck scared him so that he started to run. He ran over the bridge, found a path, ran till he was out of breath. Started again, the path ended and he got killed falling off the cliff.

(F) What is it? (Anything you want it to be.) Maybe I need glasses (long pause). This is taking place in a mountainous region not inhabited by human beings. There are nature-made roads, stones and bridges naturally made. Up, up in a hole in one of the mountains maybe like a cave it has some sort of a webbed foot, long neck, long beak, lizardous animal looking for prey. Along the mountain bridge we have a four- or six-legged animal walking also in search of prey. This latter animal is unaware of the presence of the former and while he is gazing down at the ground this lizardous animal is about to descend out of his cave and attack this six-legged animal. Somehow he must have some poison on his tongue or hidden pocket which shoots people because the shape of his mouth and feet do not permit him to successfully attack this six-legged animal, so he will probably descend from his cave and attack the animal and devour it.

(F) I think this man is traveling in the wilds of South America. No, it cannot be, that bridge looks built. I've got an idea. This man is an explorer. He is exploring an unknown part of the continent that has been developed by prehistoric man. There are still some prehistoric animals alive. A dinosaur. He's scared and wants to get out as fast as he can. I don't know what he's on. It can't be a horse. He is running from the animal. He'll go back to civilization and report what he has found. Of course he won't be believed until some other man finds it. There is definitely a civilization because a bridge has been built. I wish I could be more lucid about what he is leaning against. He's running there for protection.

PICTURE #12M   A young man is lying on a couch with his eyes closed. Leaning over him is the gaunt form of an elderly man, his hand stretched out above the face of the reclining figure.

The young man on the couch is usually the main character in the stories told to this picture. He may be asleep and the elderly man is coming to awaken him; he may be hypnotized by the elderly man; he may be sick and the elderly man has come to inquire about his health. Stories to this picture frequently give us insight into the patient's attitudes towards various adult males in his environment. They also indicate the role of passivity in the patient's personality and at times his attitude to therapy. On a deeper level of interpretation, homosexual tendencies may be revealed.

This scene shows an old man leaning over a fellow holding his hands over him. Evidently it may be a priest that's giving the man his blessing, from the way the man has his hand raised over his head, he isn't giving him any food or any type of help, yet he does seem to be poised in a sort of a helping way. I think that evidently the man is in sickness, and this priest or whoever he is, is taking care of him. The man may get well.

It looks like a hynotist putting a patient to sleep. The patient looks like he has just gone into a very deep trance. It seems to be very successful. The patient will, in the trance, tell the hypnotist a few things that he probably don't know himself and he might eventually be cured from what was bothering him.

This young fellow lying on the bed and there is a man standing over him with his hand raised. It looks like he is about to waken the boy. The young man fell asleep while he was still in some shop and the man is coming along to wake him up and get him back to work again, and I can't see by the expression on his face whether he is angry or not. He is just standing over him just about to touch him. He is probably the boy's father, and get him awake and start him back to work. I imagine they get along all right. The boy is doing what any other boy would if they had the chance to grab a little nap. The father gets along all right with boy otherwise he wouldn't be in that attitude, of waking him as he is. He would be grabbing him and shaking him a little bit rougher. They get along all right. Well, I suppose so.

PICTURE #12F   The portrait of a young woman. A weird old woman with a shawl over her head is grimacing in the background.

The two women in this picture are frequently seen as related to each other in some way — the woman in the background may be a living person or some dead person. The two women may be in conflict or the older woman is advising the younger one. Another common theme is that the two women represent two aspects or facets of the younger woman — the younger woman representing the present and the older woman the future, or the younger woman is the self and the older woman her conscience.

Young girl, and old witch — or might be a grandmother, I don't know what she is doing there, woman behind her — is not even looking at her, she's looking someplace else. Might be living in some — might be grandmother. Can't make anything out of that. Nice looking girl. But grandmother looks like a horror.

This is the story of a woman who is trying to make up her mind. She's divorced, she's got kids, she's living alone with the kids — and she's haunted by the thought of her own mother who is now a nasty evil old dame — brought up her own kids with malice and cruelty. This lady is trying to see herself in a relationship to her children, and trying to think of what they'll think of her when she's an old woman, when they are bringing up their kids — she thinks of all the reasons that people have children, something to own, something to love, something to hate, something to dominate, something to bring out — to let out your tenderness on so — she wonders how she, how she'll be measured by her own kids and is worried that she probably herself will never be free of the imprint of her own mother who's always lurking there, sneering — and whose image — she — she finds too often in herself.

PICTURE #13MF   A young man is standing with downcast head buried in his arm.   Behind him is the figure of a woman lying in bed.

Sexual plots are most frequent in the stories told to this picture.   The young man is usually seen as contemplating or having had sexual intercourse with the woman on the bed.   The woman may be the young man's wife, a girl friend, or a prostitute.   These stories usually reveal the patient's attitude toward men or women and sex.

Another frequent theme amongst men is that the woman lying on the bed is the young man's wife, who is either sick or dead.   The young man's feelings are then described.   This theme usually indicates the male's hostile attitude toward his wife or women in general.

(M)   This boy has just awakened after sleeping with a young prostitute all night.   He has just gotten up and dressed.   He's a young school boy and now he's going to school.   He doesn't know if he'll be able to make it.   Now he's afraid of venereal disease and diseases in other ways from the woman.   He doesn't know what to do, if he should leave right away or stay there and find out from her if she was diseased or not.   But he takes his books and goes to school.   On the way he stops at the doctor's and finds out that he's not diseased and neither is she, and he's much happier, but he resolves never to go out with prostitutes again.

(M)   Take it from the angle of sex.   That is the only way you can take it.   The young fellow is a sex maniac, sex crazy.   He had this girl come up to his room.   Only a single bed there so I imagine it is his bed.   Imagine she wouldn't give in so easy so he goes crazy and killed her.   Arms flung out so I imagine she's dead.   The young man is sort of remorseful about what he had done and hiding his head in shame.   He'll be hanged anyway.

(M)   This is a bedroom scene, a young girl is lying on the bed, apparently she is dead from the looks of the card.   There is a fellow standing up fully clothed with his arm thrown across his face and an attitude of grief.   Apparently the girl is dead for some reason or other.   I guess he has been reading a book or studying the book on the table.   Well, maybe the girl had been sick, maybe she is sick instead of dead and the young fellow doesn't know what to do.   He will probably call a doctor and have him come up and look at the girl and find out what is wrong with her.   They are probably husband and wife.   The doctor will come in and cure her and they will live happily ever after. I imagine they are in love or he wouldn't be feeling bad the way he apparently is.

(F) This boy is a college student. He hasn't had much experience with sex. He met this girl whose moral standards are different from his own and they proceeded to her room. His passion became overwhelming and the conflict which he had had and which up to this time was latent was overpowering and he proceeded to have sexual relations with her. In the morning he awoke, got up, got dressed and immediately he realized that he was no longer what he considered pure and had terrific guilt feelings and there was no question about it, he thought he had done something wrong. He thought he had done the most evil thing that he could possibly have done. He, his hand is over his face in anguish while she continues to sleep. He'll pick up his books which are on the table and go back to school. Probably for the next day or two days he'll be overcome with remorse but once the guilt subsides he'll probably go back to the girl and continue to have sexual relations with her.

(F) This can be a very gory one. Rape. (pause) He's very sorry so he strangled her. He doesn't know whether he's sorry he raped her or sorry he strangled her. The result is, he'll pay for his crime.

PICTURE #14MF The silhouette of a man (or woman) against a bright window. The rest of the picture is totally black.

It is usually said that the figure at the window is spending a sleepless night. He is at the window thinking over the various problems on his mind, contemplating the universe, or a scene outside, or he may be considering suicide. The stories reflect the patient's problems, desires, and ambitions, or suicidal preoccupations.

(M) The man has just spent a very restless night in his room and couldn't seem to sleep very well. He had been depressed and his mood was apparently as dark as the room was and it is daylight and the sun is just coming up and he has just opened the window. It seems to give him new hope.

(M) The silhouette picture of a man. Looks as if he's about to jump out of a window. That's all I can see. He's halfway out of the window now. Might be that the man was lying on the bed there. He'll jump.

(M) There's a young fellow standing in the window looking up at the sky imagining some planes go by. He's hoping he'll be up there in one of the planes. He feels like it is the life for him. We all want to be pilots or even mechanics sometime. It's just his dream maybe, like most of his dreams it is shattered and nothing comes of it because he took sick and won't be able to do it.

(F) I think this is a boy who left home, went to a large city to make his way, become successful. He's come to his room, he doesn't have any friends. He's not making any headway. Just wondering if it's worth leaving home for. Leaving the people he knows and says it doesn't matter, he'll become successful and he'll go back home.

(F) This boy is an artist or writer. He wants very much to create. He is not particularly worried about the possibility that he might not be able to create because he has never tried to create anything which he really considers great art. He is living alone in an apartment which overlooks a body of water, could be an ocean, a sea or a lake, it's quite high up. Having this apartment located in this particular place is extremely important to him because he can look up at the stars and feel that he is close to them. During the day when he is trying to create he looks out over the oceanside at the beautiful scenery which inspires him. Tonight he is in a particularly good mood, standing at the window looking at the stars and dreaming of eventual success and being a great artist or a great writer. After standing at the window for a while he will probably close the window and go to bed.

PICTURE #15MF   A gaunt man with clenched hands is standing among gravestones.

The gaunt figure is usually seen as praying over the grave of a deceased person. His attitudes and feelings, both past and present, toward the deceased are described. Frequently the person who is said to be deceased is the one against whom the patient has a good deal of aggression in reality.

(M) The man is standing by the grave of his wife. He seems to be in great despair. Apparently he didn't know till now how much he had loved her. Since they had been married a long time, probably thirty or forty years. He is very much disturbed in his mind and eventually he will follow his wife to the grave.

(M) This is a picture of a man in a cemetery — an old man — probably praying over some loved one that's passed away. The man was probably overcome with grief when he lost this person, and he can't seem to get over it, so he's going there to pray. It could be his mother or wife. It could be anyone.

(F) This is a very beautiful woodcut incidentally. Well, this man reminds me of Scrooge since Christmas is coming. He is repenting for his miserliness and cruelty all his life. He is coming to the cemetery where people who died because of him are buried. His time is coming and he is suddenly aware of a fear of God. Still he does no good with his life. In spite of his repentance I doubt if he'll do anything charitable in the last years of life. He'll die the same way he lived.

(F) This reminds me of Henry James. The man whose grief in the graveyard is opening key to the vision of his own wasted life — yes — do you know Henry James? I can see this man's grief. He realizes, asks himself what there could be in his relationship to his wife that could have caused her such agony. He feels that, well, well, that the richness of his feelings for his wife are now replaced by intensity of his grief. At least glad for that, he isn't left empty.

PICTURE #16　　(Blank card)

Since the patient is free to construct his own picture, there are countless stories that may be given to this card. Frequently patients choose to speak about problems that are uppermost in their minds or they tell stories which reflect their attitudes toward the psychologist who is administering the test or the therapist who is treating them.

(M) Heart trouble as my doctor seems to think — and I do myself, has a great deal to do with sex problems. It's really because I don't know too much about sex, and then again because I know so much about sex, but I couldn't succeed in satisfying myself with women. I couldn't get enough women to satisfy myself with. All-in-all it's not too hard a case to figure out, although there are lots of things in my background that will have to be probed into yet. I, myself, think I'm doing very well, and I think the doctor does too. My paintings succeed in being a great help to the doctor, and I find a lot of enjoyment in painting them. I hope I will be cured soon, and I think the doctor's helping greatly. As to the real problem of my case, I'm not quite sure, but I've got my own ideas, but at the moment I'm not as self-conscious or having the problems I had before.

(M) The card I have now is a blank card, evidently no picture was put on it. I have difficulty in making up a story on a blank card. Maybe it should show a picture of some fellow at the Veterans Administration just trying to figure out what he is best fitted for. It is very tough under the circumstances to make up a picture of a blank card. He may be thinking of many things — maybe of being a writer, maybe of learning a trade, maybe of getting into a business and earning a living that way. There's so many fields for a fellow to get into today if he can only find out what he is best suited for, and can stick to what he starts out with. It is necessary for success but it does take a lot of spirit and a lot of guts in spite of all the help that men get from the outside it is up to himself to succeed. That's about all I can say. The outcome will lead to whether I succeed or not, and it's up to me to show that determination and spirit to find what I'm best suited for. After all no one can exactly guide me in that I realize, and try to make the best of things in the field that isn't above my ability or below my ability.

(F) This is a picture of a . . . this is a picture of people sitting around a council table, a round table and there is a girl standing at one end of the table speaking. In the picture everyone is listening to her with attention. There are pictures on the wall and heavy leather chairs; there is a secretary sitting in a room taking notes; there is a blackboard with figures on it; there is a telephone in the room; there is a bookcase; there are thick rugs on the floor.

This is a girl who has achieved what people have been trying to achieve since the 1700's. What she has done is to set up a counseling program for management. She has gotten management to understand the worker as an individual and make them feel that they are consciously responsible for the welfare of the worker. These people sitting around the table are representatives of labor, of management, of the unions. This is the final session of a series of meetings that they have been having. They have worked out a satisfying plan of operations of this factory, one of which gives benefits to the worker as well as management, satisfaction in the way of production to management. The animated look on her face is due to the fact that she has finally achieved her life goal, so to speak. The plan will go into effect after the meeting breaks up, and with this experience behind her she will continue to other plans where she will try to do something.

(F) I think of stories in books and plays on TV and especially the murders, the mysteries. It's a man walking along a path and there are two branches. Over one branch where the path divides is a river and the other leads to railroad so he sits down to decide which one to follow — the railroad or the river. The railroad will lead into a town, then he'll have to get a job, it'll be confining to him, he'll have to get along with other people and compromise. If he follows the river he'll come to a farmhouse, do work, fish and swim in the river, it's pleasant. Thinks it could go on forever. So he got tired of thinking and fell asleep, dreamed about going into town and getting a job in a store, and the store was held up later in the afternoon. He and the owner of the store were there, the owner refused to give the robbers money so they started to shoot, threatened to shoot. The man trapped them and got the gun away, became a hero. Then they took them to the police and the next day reported for work and the owner told him he couldn't work for him anymore. He asked, " Why, I saved your life." The owner said, " I don't want to be reminded of unpleasant memory. Don't want to be grateful for saving my life." He woke up and took a nap again. Dreamed about the road to the river. Walked along the river, stopped, went swimming, then went to a farmhouse, knocked on the door, no answer, he pushed the door open, found food on the table, helped himself to it. No one showed up so went to sleep on the couch. In the morning he heard noise and there was a man and the local police. Seemed that someone murdered the farmer's family, he went to the police, his car broke down and it took him so long. They accused him, started to take him to jail and he woke up. He took the railroad to town. Decided that any road he took would have its problems.

PICTURE #17BM   A naked man is clinging to a rope. He is in the act of climbing up or down.

The man on the rope is usually seen as demonstrating his athletic skill and physical ability before a large audience, or he may be seen as making an escape. The first type of story reveals the patient's desire for recognition, his level of aspiration, or his exhibitionistic tendencies. The second may indicate the problems or situations with which the patient cannot deal adequately or his reactions to emergencies. Patients may comment upon the fact that the man is nude and this may be disturbing to some of them. Patients who are concerned with masturbation may reveal their preoccupation in stories where the hero is seen as both going up and coming down the rope.

This fellow is in a building, working in a building. All of a sudden a fire starts. Then everyone is trying to get out of the same exit. He finds a rope, ties it around himself, and slides down.

John is quite an athlete. He isn't much good in school but he likes sports. The teacher asked for volunteers to climb the rope in the gymnasium. John volunteered. He is at the top of the rope and all the other students are applauding him.

Well, this man sure is strong. Look at his muscles. Oh, I wonder why he hasn't any clothes on. He is in the circus and he is climbing up the rope and now he is coming down again. He has a lot of fun whenever he climbs up and down like that.

PICTURE #17GF   A bridge over water. A female figure leans over the railing. In the background are tall buildings and small figures of men.

The female in this picture may be waiting for a loved one to return. In some stories he may be a member of the crew in one of the ships that is seen as unloading. In other stories the woman is engrossed in her thoughts and has come down to the bridge to think. She may also be quite depressed and contemplating suicide.

> This is a story of a girl against the world — and she stands on the strong steel bridge in a bright strong sun, a big stone building behind and keeps watch, while her friends are smuggling from their ship, from their boat into the warehouse — and the strength of the society which doesn't belong to her; yet she is living, she is a living human being, she can defy it. Live against it as the men live against society in their smuggling.

> This is a sort of fantastic sort of picture. Outer space they talk about. Oh, it's a bridge, dock workers down here. Look like bringing in cargos or something. Woman on the bridge apparently going to jump off. Find it hard to be interested in this. Except that the boss looks like a real tough individual. What is the moon doing, whether it's beautiful or not it doesn't make any difference to woman because she's going to jump. From the attitude this is a nefarious business going on down here. Even if she jumps it won't make any difference. They'll continue with their unloading. They won't be a bit touched.

PICTURE #18BM   A man is clutched from behind by three hands. The figures of his antagonists are invisible.

Patients frequently are concerned with their inability to develop an adequate rationale for the three hands that appear in the picture. In the common stories the man in the picture is seen as either drunk or having been in an accident and the hands belong to the people who are helping him. Or the hero is being attacked from the rear and the hands belong to his attackers. These stories reveal the patient's anxieties concerning aggression that may be directed against him or the patient's attitude toward alcoholism or drug addiction.

> This card shows a drunk being grabbed by a pair of hands. It looks as if this pair of hands just for the heck of it intend doing

the man harm. Probably drag him into a ditch and hurt him. I think perhaps he will be beaten and robbed and wake up and find himself in a ditch.

This man was working hard all day. He felt pretty low and decided to join the boys at the bar. He got drunk and his friends are taking him home. He'll wake up the next morning with a terrific hangover and his wife will bawl him out. He better keep away from the stuff if he wants to keep peace at home.

PICTURE #18GF A woman has her hands squeezed against the throat of another woman whom she appears to be pushing backwards across the banister of a stairway.

The woman against the banister may be frequently perceived as a woman or a man and at times it is a younger person. The woman who is standing upright may be trying to help the other person or the two people may be in the midst of a severe argument. Murder and/or strangling may also be referred to.

There's the husband who came home drunk. He comes staggering into the hallway — and hollers for his wife who's the housekeeper. She holds him up. He's almost unconscious and she looks into his face and wonders whether there's any way to live with a man that — she gives him her protection and care and love, and always patience — and he returns it with only at the times when the world outside will allow it. When he's not so beaten down and so frustrated and belittled by his work, his boss, his being robbed of any dignity in his life, that he has to rebuild himself in the tavern before he can face himself — and she thinks of the man he could be — and the woman she could be if he could live his life at his best — at his fullest level — instead of always climbing from the bottom to the middle and back again — and never finding himself — living out his whole life in someone else's basement. Never their own lives.

Well, there's a — might be a mother and child. May have fallen down the stairs and she's probably just picked him up. Trying to see if he's all right. Evidently very worried about it. Seems to be quite limp in her arms which caused her to worry. That's all, I guess.

This woman standing above other as if imploring person to " look at me, I mean what I'm saying. Can't you see it. Don't you know I'm telling the truth, you must feel it " and she's utterly sad whatever event has occurred. Is it a man or a woman? Contours more like a woman. She's probably another woman, another sister or daughter that I know whatever is disturbing this other person I know what I'm talking about, can't you believe me. I've had same feeling before. But there's nothing good about it — if you rebel. Look at me, look what I am. If I had had someone to tell me the truth I wouldn't be what I am at this moment. Somehow I feel the other woman will listen to her. In her face she sees such complete truth and such baring of her soul. Looks as though proud silent woman and now tells other woman what makes her mystery and other like running away from husband and living in a shabby rooming house. For the first time she stands completely revealed before other woman, she can't help but believe and I think she will make the right decision, that would be to face life the way it is, not the way she hopes it would be.

PICTURE #19 A weird picture of cloud formations overhanging a snow-covered cabin in the country.

Patients frequently have difficulty in developing stories to this picture because they regard it as " weird." Nevertheless, in most of the stories the common theme is that the cabin is snowbound but the inhabitants are comfortable. The condition of the inhabitants and how they hope to cope with their predicament are usually described. These stories frequently reflect the patient's desire for security and the manner in which he hopes to deal with the frustrating circumstances of his own environment.

(M) The warmth of the house contrasted strangely with the cold outside. It gives me a feeling of comfort and security. The light cast forth strange shadows, creating grotesque-shaped animals in the snow. But the people in the house are unmindful of these shadows as they serenely went about performing their chores. The mother and the two children are calmly awaiting the arrival of the father. In spite of the desolation life was going on.

(M) It is a hut in Alaska where several fellows are staying. Within it is warm and cozy and they are quite comfortable. They are grouped around the table playing poker. The wind is howling without but as I said all is warm and cozy inside and they will bed down for the night in about fifteen minutes.

(F) Well, a little house way up in the country in the middle of winter. The people inside are snowbound and I feel there's something morbid on the outside of the house. The trees seem to be very gruesome looking. Something on the top of the house — seem to be two staring eyes. The people in the house are warm and comfortable. But I think the food will run out and all are going to die. The occupants are a grandmother, mother, and a few children. No husband. He's gone to war and gotten himself killed. We'll get rid of him. All are going to die. How blithely I say that. The father is not there to protect them. Let's say that.

(F) A small town was stricken by a flood and this house was completely uprooted and is being thrown back and forth among the waves. The waves have stopped temporarily but it is still stormy. The house inside is warm and comfortable which seems like a sort of paradox. The house will continue to float on the waves after the storm lets up and after the waves and water disappear will settle down and it will always be a miracle in this town how this one house or why this one house was left completely intact and unhurt by this terrific flood when everything else in town was practically demolished. Many people will wonder if it was because the owner of the house was a man who was close to God — preacher, priest, or rabbi.

PICTURE #20   The dimly illumined figure of a man (or woman) in the dead of night leaning against a lamppost.

The figure at the lamppost is usually seen as ruminating over various problems that are uppermost in his or her mind, awaiting a girl friend (or boy friend), or waiting to attack a victim. These stories frequently reflect the problem with which the patient is preoccupied; heterosexual problems and attitudes, and aggressive tendencies in the patient's personality.

(M) Scene in Central Park. The young man is waiting under a lamppost in the center of Central Park looking up into the tall skyscrapers surrounding the park and the hotels and apartment houses of the rich. He dreams of the day when someday he might be as rich as they are and he might be able to have the things they do.

(M) I can see a picture, seems to be taken at night. There are stars up in the sky. There's a lamppost with a bright light coming out of the lamppost. There is a sort of a man leaning against the lamppost. His hand is in his pocket, which is generally that of a picture of a gangster. He seems to be waiting for someone. He is blotted out so it is very hard to see the character of the man. Seems to me that trouble will be brewing there. He seems to be waiting for something and he seems to be very serious about what he wants. This is all I can see in that picture. The outcome would probably be death.

(M) In this picture there's a man that's leaning against a lamp-post, he looks like he's out of a job and he's disgusted with everything and doesn't want to face his wife or his mother and the outcome of this picture is that he will do something drastic like going away or killing himself.

(F) Well, this is a story of a young girl who has an appointment and she's keeping this appointment outside because it seems to me that, that it involves some kind of situation that has to be settled. She's going to meet a man, I'm sure. She's a nice person but there's a problem there. He is going to come and they're going to talk this whole thing out. I have a feeling it's going to be quite successful. No feeling of sadness to this thing. What the problem is I don't know. But anyway it's going to work out okay, I'm sure. They're probably going to have words about things. Certain unpleasantnesses first, but it's going to work out okay, I'm sure of that. And uh, well, that's all.

(F) This is a man who is terribly much in love but unable to support a wife. Not only unable to support a wife but the girl he has fallen in love with is extremely wealthy girl whose parents judge suitors for their daughter's hand according to their economic status. He has just come from the girl's home where he has seen beautiful furniture, clothes, butler, maids, car and realizes he will never be in a position to give her these things. He has already made his choice — knows he never wants to give her these things. He stopped under a lamppost thinking about it — does he have the right, does love give him the right to deprive her of the things she is accustomed to. Another problem is will she ever be able to make the adjustment although on a verbal level she says that immaterial things are so much more important. He's standing there thinking about it. He will probably walk through the streets of the city all night, thinking about this problem.

CHAPTER 2

ADMINISTRATION OF THE TAT

The amount of material obtained in a TAT story is a function of the patient's mental set while taking the test. It is therefore of primary importance that the rapport between the psychologist and the patient should be at its height when the test is begun. The psychologist must constantly bear in mind that the patient should feel psychologically at ease throughout the testing. Otherwise the patient will find it exceedingly difficult to give free rein to his imagination and to verbalize his fantasies. The techniques involved in establishing rapport for this test are no different from those employed for other clinical procedures.

Administration Time

The test is administered in two sessions of approximately one hour each. At least one day should intervene between sessions. Pictures 1–10 are administered during the first hour and pictures 11–20 during the second. By dividing the pictures in this fashion, the effects of fatigue factors, which might operate to decrease the patient's productivity, are kept to a minimum.

Instructions

With the patient's mental attitude at its best, the psychologist gives the instructions to the test, as follows:

"I am going to show you some pictures, one at a time, and your task will be to make up as dramatic a story as you can for each. Tell what has led up to the scene shown in the picture, describe what is happening at the moment, what the people are feeling and thinking, and then give the outcome. Speak your thoughts as they come to your mind. Do you understand? Since you have fifty minutes for the ten pictures you can devote about five minutes to each story. Here is the first picture."

The instructions for the second session are as follows:

"You remember that during the last session you told stories to pictures. I now have some more pictures to which you are also to tell stories. Only this time I should like you to let your imagination go in making them up. You remember that I should like to know what happened before the scene that you see in the picture, what is going on at present, what the people are thinking, how they feel, and finally what the outcome will be."

Picture #16 is a blank card and is accompanied by a special instruction:

"For this card, I should like you to imagine a picture, describe it to me, and then tell me a story about it as you have done for the other cards."

The psychologist should and must feel free to adjust these instructions to the patient — to his personality and intellectual level. Furthermore, the psychologist must grow accustomed to the instructions so that he can deliver them with ease. Regardless of the language upon which the psychologist decides, he must indicate to the patient that he is interested in a dramatic story, and that he wants to know the past (the events leading up to the scene depicted in the picture), the present (the actions, thoughts, and feelings of the people involved), and the future (what the outcome will be).

Clinical experience has shown that it is not advisable to stress the matter of "imagination" in the instructions to the first series of pictures, since clinic patients feel threatened by the unstructured character of imaginative activity. Those patients who are particularly anxious about their fantasies may become completely constricted and produce unimaginative stories which are frequently worthless.

Techniques for Recording Protocols

A record of the protocol may be obtained in any of the following ways. Each of these has its advantages and disadvantages, so that the clinician must select the one which best serves his needs.

1. *Manual recording*. This requires no equipment other than pencil and paper. The psychologist writes the story as the patient tells it. Since patients will frequently talk more rapidly than most psychologists can write, some of the important data will be lost. However, it is possible to cut the amount lost to a minimum by developing a shorthand technique of one's own, by using one of the standard shorthand systems, or by simply asking the patient to slow down a little so that the psychologist can keep up with him. The main disadvantage of this technique is that it is quite wearing on the examiner. This method is suited for all types of patients and has the advantage that the clinician can be constantly aware of the patient's behavior during the test.

2. *Self-recording*. After administering the instructions, present the patient with pencil and paper and ask him to write his stories. The main advantages of this technique are that it is not as wearing on the psychologist as the previous technique and leaves him free to do other

work.   But these advantages are frequently overshadowed by many disadvantages:

(a) This technique usually forces a patient to assume a mental set that will aid him in producing a " literary masterpiece." He therefore reads and rereads his protocol, changing and altering his production to suit himself.   Thus the many important nuances of a rough production are lost in the polished product.

(b) The psychologist loses valuable material that is frequently gained from observing a patient's behavior while taking the test.   Slips of the tongue, inflections of the voice, pauses, hesitations and the like, which are important data for interpretation, are lost if this technique is adopted.

(c) Subjects of low intelligence level are frequently completely inhibited by this approach since they are quite sensitive about spelling errors and their inability to write well.

(d) A patient's productions may grow shorter and shorter as he approaches the last of the cards, because of the increasing effect of fatigue factors.

(e) Patients' handwritings vary a great deal and frequently are illegible, so that it is impossible to read and analyze the stories.

3. *Stenographic aid.*   After giving the instructions, the psychologist introduces the stenographer to the patient and explains to him that the stenographer will take down his stories as he tells them.   It is wise for the psychologist to make notes on the patient's behavior while he tells his stories if this technique is adopted.   The main disadvantage of this approach is that the stenographer may frequently have an adverse effect upon the patient.   The patient may feel inhibited in the presence of a third party or he may try to impress the stenographer with his ability as a storyteller.   It may help at times to have the stenographer sit behind a screen but care must be taken that the patient does not grow suspicious of the screen and who may be behind it.   Should he feel deceived, then all efforts at developing adequate rapport will fail.

4. *Machine recording.*   There are various portable machines available through commercial channels for the recording of speech.   Many of them come equipped either with desk or hand-held microphones. While this technique has the advantage of making the recording of the protocol less wearing on the examiner, he should be aware of several pitfalls:

(a) The psychologist who utilizes mechanical recording devices must be constantly alert to the setting of the volume control.   This must be adjusted to the patient's voice level, which may vary throughout the test.

(b) Material may be lost when the patient turns away from the microphone, when the apparatus becomes faulty, when the patient talks too rapidly, or when the patient has a speech defect.

(c) Many patients are " mike-conscious " and are therefore inhibited in the presence of a microphone. This may be overcome by permitting the patient to make a practice record and then listen to the record as it is played back. This may aid the patient in overcoming his fear of recording and it will also show him the level at which he should speak for best results.

(d) It is expensive.

(e) There is often much delay in getting the records transcribed, thereby delaying the analysis.

The psychologist using this technique should make notes about the patient's behavior throughout the course of the test.

5. *Hidden microphone.* A microphone is placed in such a fashion that it is hidden from the patient and still picks up all that the patient says. The microphone is connected to a speaker unit which is placed in an adjoining room in which a stenographer records all that is heard. A high-fidelity microphone should be used, because imperfections in the mechanical apparatus may result in many distortions. It is also wise to have a signal system (flash-bulb arrangement) between stenographer and examiner so that the stenographer may indicate whether or not the patient is talking too rapidly for accurate recording. The main disadvantage of this technique is the expense that is involved in obtaining the necessary equipment and the difficulty of having two rooms properly set up.

Role of the Psychologist during Test Administration

The role of the psychologist while the patient tells his story to each of the pictures is essentially neutral. The psychologist must indicate to the patient that he is vitally interested in everything the patient has to say but the psychologist must not betray his own feelings with regard to what the patient has said. That is, if the patient tells a very aggressive or morbid story, the psychologist should not indicate either verbally or behaviorally whether he approves or disapproves of what the patient has said.

The following are some of the occasions when the clinician may be forced to make certain comments:

1. When the story is primarily descriptive, the clinician should say something like this: " You did a very good job describing the picture but now I want you to make up a *story* about the picture. A story with a plot in which you will tell me what happened before the scene that you see in the picture, what is going on at present, what the people are thinking and feeling, and finally what the outcome will be."

2. When the patient has forgotten to tell about the past or present

or the future or when he has not adequately described the thoughts and actions of a character, then the psychologist may ask for these. He should, however, preface his remarks with a favorable comment upon what the patient has done. For example: "You did a good job in telling me what the boy is doing, but can you tell me something about what led up to the situation that you described and then what the outcome will be."

The psychologist must exercise a great deal of caution in phrasing his remarks to the patient. All remarks should be geared to the patient's intellectual level and emotional state. Should the psychologist overstep his bounds he may affect the results by inhibiting the patient, or by forcing the patient to construct his stories according to the style suggested or implied by the psychologist.

3. Should the patient, prior to starting the test, ask for an example of a story, the psychologist should suggest that the patient begin without an example and that he will probably find the telling of stories easier than he anticipates.

4. Should the patient be unable to determine what various objects in the cards are (e.g., the gun in Picture #3, the house in Picture #19, etc.), and ask the psychologist to define them, he should say: "It can be anything you want it to be."

5. When the psychologist finds that the stories are too short or too long, he might suggest: "Your stories are good but let us see if you cannot make the next one a little longer (or a little shorter)."

It is suggested that all comments asking for additional story material should be reserved primarily for the first two pictures. The patient should then be permitted to tell several stories without interruption. In these stories the psychologist should note whether the patient returns to his original approach (e.g., omitting a discussion of the past) or whether he has altered his approach; then any further material that is desired should be probed for in the inquiry.

However, there may be many unforeseen circumstances in which a patient may have certain questions. In answering these questions the psychologist will have to use his own discretion but he should bear in mind:

(a) That his remarks should be geared to the patient's intellectual level and emotional state.

(b) The remarks should be made in such a fashion that the patient cannot learn what kind of story would please the examiner.

(c) The psychologist's comments should in no way imply that there are "correct" or "incorrect" answers.

(d) The psychologist should never indicate by his manner or in his answer how he regards the patient's question or that the question in any way reflects upon the patient's ability to tell stories.

(e) The psychologist should always bear in mind that all of his comments will have an effect upon a patient's productions. He should therefore consider the effect before making a remark.

Recording of Psychologist's Comments

All comments and remarks made by the psychologist should be noted in the protocol at the point at which they occur. The comments should be put in parentheses to indicate that they were made by the examiner. The following is an example of how this should be done. The story was told to Picture #1.

> This child must have been forced to take up violin lessons. He doesn't seem interested in the violin. He put it down. He must be daydreaming. He doesn't show any interest in the violin so I guess he didn't learn how to play it. It must have been forced on him——. (*Good. You told me about the past and what the boy is doing. Now can you tell me what the outcome is?*) He doesn't care for the violin. He'd rather daydream or think of something. Thinking of going out to play.

Timing Responses

The psychologist should note the time that elapses from the moment the patient is presented with a picture until he starts his story, and the total time that the patient uses for each story. As yet there are no norms that can be utilized for purposes of determining " shock " (long delay) or impulsivity (quick response). Until such a time as norms are available, it is suggested that the psychologist should make his judgments on the basis of intra-individual comparisons or on the basis of norms which he has developed in his own experience.

For accuracy a stopwatch should be used for timing the delay before a patient starts each of his stories and the total amount of time that passes before completing the stories. If no stopwatch is available, a scheme may be devised for timing, such as tapping dots at a constant rate of speed . . . . . , or drawing a line, ————, to indicate the patient's delay before telling his story. It is obvious that these techniques are useful only for timing first responses. Time taken for the whole story can be estimated by the number of words spoken by the patient and his rate of speech.

Recording Notes of Patient's Behavior

Additional notes concerning the patient's behavior while taking the test should be noted and inserted in parentheses at the point at which they occur. These include notes of behavioral manifestations and reactions, such as tics, restlessness, laughter, smoking, etc. Pauses may be indicated by horizontal lines, the length of the line serving to indicate the length of the pause (——,——) .

Inquiry

Valuable data can frequently be obtained from the patient by means of an inquiry. There are two main forms of inquiry: the intermittent inquiry and the final inquiry.

Intermittent Inquiry

The intermittent inquiry is conducted during the course of the story. In the intermittent inquiry the psychologist questions the patient about any of the material that he feels is lacking to make the story complete.

For example, if a patient says, in a story, that the hero did not get along with his friends, then the clinician may ask: " How does he feel about not getting along with his friends?," or he may say: " Tell me some more about the friends with whom he cannot get along."

This technique should be handled only by the most skilled psychologist and then only with extreme caution. The following is an example of how too many direct questions may interfere with the test results. The patient who told the story had suicidal tendencies. Until Picture #14, the stories were long and full of valuable material, but because the patient was pressed too far on this picture, he became anxious and all the stories that followed were descriptive and contained little material of any significance.

PICTURE #14

This guy is an astronomer and he's looking out of the window and he's watching the stars and seeing how beautiful they are and watching the falling stars and thinking about his work in a dairy and ends up with his making a great discovery and becomes a famous astronomer. (What sort of a person is he? What is he thinking about? What is his life like?) Well, his life is, er, oh! he has a wife and child and he's very happy and, er, he's, er, there is nothing very unusual about him. I'll tell you what's wrong with the thing. This here is trying to get me to talk about myself and I sort of feel, er, well, I, I don't know to talk about it outright but not in this way, er, because (You feel that it is unnecessarily indirect, that it will——) No, no, not only that, it's, I, I don't know why I sort of object to it. I, I can't get a good logical reason why, though. (Patient laughs.) (You feel that there might be something about it, something, er —) Listening to this I mean it's obvious that's a dark room and, er, looking out of the window and, er, you talking to me about suicide and, er, I mean, I am purposely scared away from saying that I am going to jump out of the window.

Final Inquiry

Since the intermittent inquiry is so difficult to conduct, it is wiser that beginners limit themselves to a final inquiry. The final inquiry is conducted when the patient has completed his stories to all twenty pictures. The psychologist then returns to each of the pictures about which he desires more information. The patient is reminded of the story that he told to the picture (a summary of the plot will usually suffice) and then he is asked to fill in the desired details. It is also advisable, although not always necessary, to ask the patient the source of each of his stories — whether they are from books that he has read, past experiences, experiences of his friends, movies, etc. The fact that a story has been based on a movie or a book does not detract too much from its importance in the individual case since the patient has no doubt selected only certain details and has distorted or overemphasized other details in the story that he tells the psychologist. These distortions are quite relevant to the individual case but are difficult to evaluate unless the psychologist is acquainted with the objective material upon which the story is based.

In the final inquiry it is frequently valuable to ask the patient to select those pictures he likes best and those he likes least and then to ask him to give his reasons for his various choices.

If the patient is to be seen at a later date, then additional material may frequently be obtained by asking the patient to recall as many of the twenty pictures and as many of the stories as he can. The pictures and stories that are omitted, recalled, or distorted, and the reasons for these, frequently reveal valuable data to the examiner.

Other Uses of TAT Stories in Diagnosis and Therapy

Experience has shown that in both diagnostic and therapeutic work, it is useful to repeat the stories to the patient and to ask him for his free associations to them. In addition, TAT stories may be used as the basis for more elaborate and lengthy discussions during which the psychologist may attain more insight into the patient's problems, feelings, and sentiments. To get at significant material, word association tests may also be constructed on the basis of critical words or critical situations as revealed by the test.

CHAPTER 3

TECHNIQUE OF CLINICAL ANALYSIS OF THE TAT

The validity of a clinical analysis and interpretation of the TAT depends, in large measure, on the background and training of the psychologist and his understanding and appreciation of the principles of dynamic psychology. The psychologist must bring to the fore his full store of psychological knowledge to abstract from the TAT all that it contains. In working with a TAT protocol the psychologist should attempt to discover the factors which are pertinent to the development of a patient's personality and the factors which are operative at the present time. This point cannot be overemphasized because it describes the attitude which the psychologist must assume in his diagnostic work — a problem which confronts him daily. By "diagnosis" is meant to determine the crucial factors in the personality and how they are interrelated in the total personality picture.

Diagnosis and Classification

Diagnosis is frequently confused with classification. Those who insist upon classification simply tag their patients with labels or pigeonhole them in categories but overlook the dynamic factors involved in each case. It is unfortunate that there are some psychologists who are so concerned with whether or not a patient is a schizophrenic, for example, that they tend to overlook the more important factors involved in the etiology of the disease and the features of the patient's psychological make-up which are particularly relevant at the moment. This trend in clinical practice has forced psychologists to probe for the precise pathognomonic "signs" in their test materials that would indicate at a glance the exact Kraeplinian tag with which the patient should be labelled. Unfortunately the important data are lost by following such a procedure. Only when the dynamics in a case are the same as those found in classical psychiatric types is it possible to suggest the proper Kraeplinian classification.

The diagrammatic presentation that follows may make our position with regard to the function of the TAT in diagnosis and classification somewhat clearer. For illustrative purposes brief excerpts have been selected from the stories told by one patient to four of the pictures. The interpretations, for which these selections served as the raw material, are then indicated by means of arrows. For didactic purposes the interpretations are presented on two levels of generality. Finally, since the combination (or syndrome) of the four final interpretations

PATIENT'S STATEMENTS CULLED FROM DIFFERENT STORIES:

PICTURE #1	PICTURE #6	PICTURE #14	PICTURE #20
The boy looks at the violin and wants to play it but is afraid that he cannot do it.	The boy tells his mother that he cannot work any more because the boss is making it too tough for him.	He got out of bed to look out the window because he cannot sleep. He has too many problems on his mind.	The man wants to accept the offer of a job but thinks his heart condition will interfere with his work.
↓	↓	↓	↓
lack of confidence	finds it difficult to cope with his environment	preoccupied with problems	heart condition
↓	↓	↓	↓
insecurity	uncongenial environment	anxiety	somatic symptoms

Classification: Psychoneurosis: Anxiety state *

* This classification has been chosen for demonstration purposes only. It is obvious that the syndrome indicated above may also be found in other classifications.

is similar to that found in a clinical group known as psychoneurotic, the last row of arrows converges upon that classification.

By adopting and maintaining this diagnostic attitude, the psychologist will not only gain a complete and thorough appreciation of the dynamic factors involved in the individual case, but he will also unearth valuable material which he can relay to the therapist who can utilize these data effectively in treatment. The problem of selecting the correct Kraeplinian classification is of relatively minor importance.

Before describing the technique of clinical analysis and interpretation, the problem of blind analysis will be discussed.

Blind Analysis

Before reading a TAT protocol, it is suggested that the psychologist should know no more about the patient than his age, sex, occupation, marital status, whether he has any siblings, and whether his parents are living or dead. With only this information at his disposal, the psychologist proceeds to analyze the dynamic factors in the protocol " blindly." For purposes of this manual, " blind analysis " means analysis without knowledge of the complete case history. When doing a blind analysis, the psychologist should be primarily concerned with diagnosing the case as suggested above. He should not set up as his major goal the prediction of the precise nature of the manifest symptomatology. Thus in any one case the TAT may indicate that the patient is a dependent individual who is extremely intrapunitive but it will not indicate that the patient has developed a gastric ulcer. To attempt to determine the precise manifest symptomatology in each case will cause the psychologist to err in many instances.

For clinical purposes, a blind analysis is recommended for several reasons:

1. It yields an independent judgment on the case uncontaminated by other data that might be available.

2. It frequently provides the psychologist with clues concerning critical areas which a patient may either consciously or unconsciously conceal from the psychologist during the interview.

3. In practice, where the psychologist works cooperatively with a psychiatrist and social worker, the data obtained by the other disciplines are frequently unavailable at the time when the psychologist prepares to analyze the TAT protocol. By becoming adept at blind analysis, the psychologist will be able to meet these emergencies without too much difficulty.

When a complete case history is available, however, the protocol should be reread.   This procedure has great value because:

1. It will give the psychologist added experience regarding the ways in which the dynamics of various problems reveal themselves in TAT protocols.

2. It will highlight factors that may have been overlooked in the original blind analysis.

Assumptions Underlying the Technique of Clinical Analysis

The technique of clinical analysis and interpretation of a TAT protocol is based upon two fundamental assumptions:

1. People reveal their personalities and problems in talking about others and in structuring unstructured situations.

2. The characters, the situations, and the problems described in the stories are the same as those observed and encountered in everyday life. Therefore in analyzing and interpreting a TAT protocol the psychologist should adopt the same set of principles that he employs in analyzing and interpreting situational behavior and the patient telling the story should be regarded as participating in or having participated in the situations described.

Common Errors in TAT Analysis and Interpretation

The psychologist should, however, be forewarned of two common errors in TAT analysis and interpretation:

1. There is a tendency for beginners to project their own needs and personalities into their interpretations.   This may be overcome by approaching the TAT material objectively, by making judgments only

when they are substantiated by two or more stories and by knowing oneself so well as to realize the areas in which projections may occur.

2. There is a tendency to make too literal interpretations of the stories. Such interpretations will frequently be inaccurate because the objects in the picture upon which an individual chooses to project his feelings, attitudes, etc., are rarely as valid as the feelings and attitudes themselves. For example, we cannot assume that a story to Picture #1 involving a discussion of the boy's desire to play the violin reflects the patient's musical interests or aspirations. The patient may have projected his aspirations, which really lie in an entirely different area, upon the violin because it was the only object available in the picture. This fallacy may be overcome by concentrating primarily upon the dynamics involved in the stories, by knowing the common stories to each picture, by reserving judgments about specific factors until they are corroborated by two or more stories, and by then giving preference to those stories in which the objects, people, etc., referred to are not suggested by the pictures themselves. (For example, if the patient says to Picture #1, " the boy wants to play the violin," to Picture #6, " the son is leaving his mother to play in a symphony orchestra," and to Picture #20, " the man is going to a concert," then we may postulate an interest in music.)

With these precautions in mind, the psychologist is prepared to begin his study of the technique of clinical analysis and interpretation. The various categories are listed below and then each is discussed individually. To save time in daily clinical practice, it is suggested that the psychologist should become so well acquainted with these categories that he can select the significant data in TAT stories without referring to the manual on each occasion.

Factors Involved in the Technique of Clinical Analysis and Interpretation

  I. The Hero
 II. Environmental Stimuli
     A. General setting
     B. Specific stimuli
        1. Living beings
        2. Inanimate objects
        3. Social forces, pressures, and ideologies
III. The Hero's Behavior
     A. Needs as manifested in
        1. Activities initiated by the hero with regard to objects or situations
        2. Activities initiated by the hero with regard to other people
        3. The hero's reactions to the activities initiated by others

IV. Cathexes (positive and negative)
 V. Inner States
VI. The Manner in Which the Behavior Is Expressed
   A. Fantasy
   B. Pre-motor level
   C. Inhibited behavior
   D. Motor level
     1. Gestures
     2. Active reaction
     3. Passive reaction
     4. Energies directed externally
     5. Energies directed internally
VII. Outcomes

I. THE HERO

The first step in analyzing a TAT story is to select the hero. In general, it is assumed that the patient has identified with the hero. Therefore it is also assumed that the press that impinge upon the hero are the same as the press that affect the patient; the hero's needs are the same as the patient's needs; the objects, activities, and sentiments which the hero cathects are the same as those cathected by the patient. The same assumption is made for each of the items that is suggested on the following pages.

At times a patient may speak of two or more individuals in a story and it is not immediately obvious which of them is the hero. This can usually be decided by comparing the data from the story in which this occurs with the data from other stories. Consequently, if the heroes in most of the stories are submissive, then it can be assumed that the character in the questionable story who is submissive is the hero. Another possibility in two-hero stories, in which the characters described have contradictory personality characteristics, is that the patient is revealing the contradictory facets of his personality.

Finally, there are occasions when the patient may not identify with any of the characters in the picture, but he will describe a situation in which his attitude toward the person depicted is revealed. For example, the patient may not identify with the woman in Picture #5 but will discuss and develop a story about the woman in which he will reveal his attitude toward his mother.

In TAT stories the hero may usually be identified by any one or a combination of the following factors:

a. The first character about whom the patient chooses to speak.

b. The character who occupies the patient's attention throughout most of the story.

c. The character who initiates the important activities.

d. The character about whom the story revolves.

e. The character who is being acted upon by most of the other individuals.

f. The character who is most like the patient in terms of age, sex, physical appearance, or psychological make-up, as determined by an analysis of the stories or biographical data.

When a psychologist is called upon to observe an individual in a social situation and then to diagnose that individual's personality on the basis of what he has observed, he usually finds valuable clues in the individual's physical bearing, manner of dress, and expressive movements. Similar clues can be found in TAT protocols in the patient's description of the hero. The psychologist may interpret these TAT clues according to the theoretical principles that he follows in interpreting situational behavior.

> The man is dressed in a clean white shirt, his suit is pressed and his hair is combed carefully. He is at attention while speaking to the man.

II. ENVIRONMENTAL STIMULI

In a study of situational behavior, it is obvious that the observer must attend to the environment in which the subject behaves and to the specific stimuli which impinge upon him, as well as to the main character himself. In a TAT story this material is available in the patient's description of the situation in which the hero is participating. The patient's description of the environment in a TAT story has an added feature which observers at times find difficult to infer from the behavior of their subjects in practical situations — how the subject regards his environment. By virtue of the fact that the patient must structure the situation in which the hero functions, he tells us how he regards his environment. Furthermore since the test is unstructured — within the limits of the objective features of the pictures — the environmental factors about which the patient chooses to speak are usually the same as the external factors which have had important effects upon him in reality or about which he has been or is presently concerned.

A. THE GENERAL SETTING

The environment described in the story should be analyzed according to the general setting in which the behavior occurs and according to the nature of the specific environmental stimuli.

Is the environment one which fosters the hero's development or does it handicap him?

Does the hero find the environment congenial or disagreeable?

Is the hero in harmony with his environment or is he at odds with it?

Does the hero find the environment satisfying or repugnant?

Does the hero find the environment pleasant or painful?

Are there any barriers, physical or psychological, which hinder the hero in his activity?

Does the hero find the environment to be one of plenty or one of scarcity?

These are several of the questions the examiner should ask himself in analyzing the general aspects of the environment.

Having decided what are the nature and tone of the general setting, the examiner should then focus his attention upon the specific factors that are operative.

B. SPECIFIC STIMULI

The specific factors that stimulate the hero's activity may be subdivided into three categories — living beings, inanimate objects, and social forces, pressures, and ideologies.

1. *Living beings*

Stories describing interpersonal situations, in this instance those situations in which the other characters act upon the hero, should be analyzed for the motives and purposes of these characters as reflected in their behavior. For this purpose the press (represented by the letter *p*) analysis suggested by Murray * is valuable. It is not suggested that the practicing psychologist should attempt to label all the press as they occur in the protocols. This procedure is too time-consuming. Practice with such a procedure while studying the test is valuable, however, since it will sensitize the psychologist to the significant data in the protocols. The definitions of the press variables presented below are condensed from Sanford's † unpublished manual.

(1) *p Acquisition.* A person wants to dispossess the hero (of money, property), to rob or to swindle him. Or a competitor in business threatens the hero's financial security.

> He was a senior in college. Then he found out that one of his best friends had stolen something from him.

> They are on the defensive because they are afraid that someone will come and take what they have.

---

* Murray, H. A., *Exploration in Personality.* New York: Oxford University Press, 1938.

† Sanford, R. N., *Thematic Apperception Test — Directions for Administration and Scoring.* Cambridge: Harvard Psychological Clinic, 1939 (mimeographed).

(2) *p Affiliation.*

(a) *Associative.* The hero has one or more friends or sociable companions; or he is a member of a congenial group.

> They have been fanatically and fervidly in favor of war and they have been dished out broadsides right and left in their college. They are roommates.

> Jimmy had a gang.

(b) *Emotional.* A person (parent, sibling, relative, erotic object) is devoted to the hero. The hero has a love affair (mutual) or gets married.

> He tried to explain the history of his courtship and told her how he met Betty and how her family disapproved of him completely and especially of his family. They have been seeing each other regularly and decided to elope.

(3) *p Aggression.*

(a) *Emotional, verbal.* Someone gets angry at the hero, or hates him. He is cursed, criticized, belittled, reproved, reprimanded, ridiculed. Someone slanders the hero behind his back.

> The mother doesn't look happy. The fellow looks kind of mad, and the mother looks mad. They probably had a pretty big argument.

(b) *Physical, social.* The hero is in the wrong (he is an aggressor or a criminal) and an individual defends himself, retaliates, pursues, imprisons, or perhaps kills the hero. The State, the police, a parent, or some other legitimate authority punishes the hero for misconduct.

> He can't be blamed because nobody knows exactly what has happened or rather his shouting out, shows that he can be, that he did know something about it and that he did it, so he is taken into custody and after a short trial he is sent to the death house in the prison and killed.

(c) *Physical, asocial.* A criminal or a gang assaults, injures, or kills the hero. Another person starts a fight and the hero defends himself.

> They went out on round-up and when they had gone out 50–60 miles they stopped for lunch. There had been a little plan to get rid of him so they push him after they had all gotten on their horses they pushed him off his horse, grabbed the horse's reins and pulled it along with them and galloped off leaving him out there.

(d) *Destruction.* Something belonging to the hero is damaged or destroyed.

Gang of saboteurs on a vital defense industry. They had effectively destroyed his machines and paralyzed the industry.

(4) *Cognizance.* Someone is curious about the hero and his doings; he is watched. Someone peers or probes into his affairs, asks questions.

Maybe it's some sort of spy or something like a secret event. He might be working on propaganda or something like that, and they have caught on to him, and they're entering his study here.

(5) *p Deference*
(a) *Compliance.* An individual or a group willingly follows the leadership or requests of the hero. A person is anxious to please him, to cooperate or obey. The obedience may be passive.

He looks like a very determined person and it looks as if the people are willing to follow what he dictates to them.

(b) *Respect.* The hero is admired by an individual, or a group. His talents or merits are appreciated; he is rewarded or publicly applauded.

He doesn't look like a very forceful character, but I think somebody will push him along so that he will gain the renown that he should for the wonderful discovery that he has made.

(6) *p Dominance.*
(a) *Coercion.* Someone tries to force the hero to do something. He is exposed to commands, orders, or strong arguments from a parent or authority.

He eventually goes back to his wife again and the marriage is resumed and it is simply because of the terrific pressure from the two families involved.

(b) *Restraint.* Someone tries to prevent the hero from doing something. He is exposed to checks, prohibitions, or restraints.

She comes to the point when the police come around, the secret police come around and they find that she is involved in the voluntary activity and they find the legal pamphlets on her and send her and send her to Siberia. She is sent to Siberia until the revolution.

(c) *Inducement.* Someone tries to get the hero to do something, or not to do something by pleading, or by gentle persuasion, encouragement, clever strategy, or seduction. (No threats of force are used.)

He is very disgusted. This afternoon he doesn't want to practice his violin. His mother had been coaxing him but without much success. This afternoon she is going to have to approach him in a little different way so she bargains with him that he can go out this afternoon on condition that he will practice his hour tomorrow without any trouble.

(7) *p Example.*

(a) *Good influence.* A person, group, or cause (social ideal, philosophy) influences the hero in a constructive way. A talented man serves as an exemplar.

We'll assume that this boy's been to a concert the night before and heard a good violinist, and is more inspired the next day.

(b) *Bad influence.* The hero is led into crime by his associates; or the level of his conduct or his ideals is lowered by following the suggestions or inducements of an untrustworthy or irresponsible person.

Son was brought up in Victorian idea, but in association with business friends got new ideas, has done something which is probably quite wrong.

(8) *p Exposition.* Someone tells, explains, interprets, or teaches the hero something.

Mr. Browdin is one of the best-speaking witnesses and we find him getting instructions from his lawyer.

(9) *p Nurturance.* Someone nourishes, encourages, protects, or cares for the hero. He receives sympathy, consolation, pity.

And this is some sort of a professional man that's taken him under his wing and been interested in his case and helped him toward his goal.

(10) *p Rejection.* A person rejects, scorns, loses respect for, repudiates, turns away from, or leaves the hero.

The young man has fallen in love with the daughter of the old man. The thing is that she is not particularly attracted to him and the young lady falls in love with a soldier.

(11) *p Retention.* A person retains something the hero wants; refuses to lend or give something to the hero; is stingy, miserly, or possessive.

He began to feel maybe there was something to this music after all. So he began to beg his mother to buy him a fiddle, and, oh, begged and begged, and his mother thought after thinking the whole thing over, since he had been so bad during the concert that there wasn't much use buying him a violin.

(12) *p Sex.* A heterosexual object is in love with the hero; or his affections are engaged by a seductress. The hero gets married.

This fellow met his girl at one of the public baths and had immediately been attracted to her and to be with her and so she likewise was attracted to him and they saw a great deal of each other and their friendship actually developed into quite a love affair although there was no marriage.

(13) *p Succorance.* Someone seeks aid, protection, or sympathy from the hero. There is a helpless, miserable, pitiful object to whom the hero reacts. Someone is rescued by the hero.

He found one family that needed someone to act as a father for a few days and he performed that duty well and then went on his way.

2. *Inanimate objects*

The inanimate objects in the hero's environment which affect his behavior should be noted. These should then be evaluated according to the suggestions indicated in the sections entitled, "Cathexes" (page 58), "Symbolism" (page 72), and "Needs" (page 50).

The boy is telling his mother that he is going to leave town to make money.

The boy saw the gun and couldn't resist shooting it.

He ran up to the window to see the plane go by.

3. *Social forces, pressures, and ideologies*

Frequently the hero's behavior is determined by social forces, pressures, and ideologies. These should be evaluated according to the suggestions indicated in the section entitled "Cathexes" (page 58). The hero's reactions to these social forces, pressures, and ideologies should be evaluated according to the suggestions indicated in the section entitled "Needs" (page 50).

She couldn't stand the old-fashioned attitude toward the girl's place in the home. So after she got her diploma she left for the big city.

He decided to go away and leave her because he was one of the "400" and she was not in the Social Register.

He came to tell his father that he was enlisting in the Army to fight against Fascism and to defend democracy.

An appreciation of the importance that various environmental stimuli may have for the individual case may be obtained from noting the intensity, frequency, and duration of the stimuli as described by the patient.

She was madly in love with him and wouldn't let him go.

Everyday his parents made him lie down to rest because he has a weak heart.

III. THE HERO'S BEHAVIOR

It is extremely important that the TAT analyst pay very careful attention to the hero's behavior and activities in the stories, since from these he will be able to infer and evaluate the patient's needs and drives. For the sake of simplicity, the hero's needs have been subdivided into three categories — activities which the hero initiates with regard to objects or situations, the activities which the hero initiates with regard to other people, and finally the hero's reactions to the activities initiated by others. This is an arbitrary division but it is believed that it will cover the majority of circumstances with which the examiner will be faced.

As an additional aid in analyzing the hero's activities, the needs (represented by the letter *n*) as defined by Sanford * are presented with examples. Although several of the needs rightfully belong under more than one of the subdivisions indicated above, each has been placed in the category which fits it best.

The beginner in TAT analysis will find it a valuable exercise to go through each story and identify all the needs that are to be found in it. Due to the pressure of work in a clinical situation, however, it may not always be possible to label all the needs in a series of TAT stories; however, such practice in a learning situation for the beginner will sensitize him to the significant data in a protocol. The relative importance of the various needs in the individual case frequently may be estimated on the basis of the frequency, intensity, and duration of each of the needs in the TAT stories.

1. *Activities initiated by the hero with regard to objects or situations.*

(1) *n Achievement.* To work at something important with energy and persistence. To strive to accomplish something creditable. Ambition manifested in action.

> So he goes through this school year after this incident, confident that he will do that sort of thing and never deviates from the course. He goes through the pre-med year college, then enters Medical School, goes through with flying colors, and after he gets his MD goes into internship.

(2) *n Acquisition.*

(a) *Social.* To work for money, possessions, property. To try to get some valuable object. To barter, trade, or gamble. Acquisitiveness, greed, or the desire for upward economic mobility manifested in action.

---

* *Ibid.*

He worked hard and saved his money so he could buy the house in the country.

(b) *Asocial.* To steal. To cheat, swindle, forge a check. (The aim may involve money, a valuable object, or even a person, as in kidnapping.)

Jimmy was a notorious little prankster around the neighborhood. . . . He was regarded as a general nuisance. He stole whenever possible and upset ashcans and was generally being chased by police for some prank. Jimmy and his gang pulled off some of the best bits of small-sized larceny . . . on this occasion they were engaged in breaking into a candy store.

(3) *n Change, travel, and adventure.* To be restless, ever-on-the-move. To crave new sights, new places. To seek adventure. To dream of visiting strange or distant lands. To travel, to go on an exploring expedition, to search for treasure.

Well, one of this group of explorers had heard about a land in the middle of South America on the, in the eastern part of Peru which had never been mapped; in fact, nobody had ever been there. So they resolved to form an expedition and go and they went to Peru.

(4) *n Cognizance.* To be curious. To gaze at something intently. To watch, peer, probe, ask questions of an inquisitive sort. To search for something; to investigate and explore; to act as a detective. Voyeurism.

She couldn't stay in her room by herself knowing that something might be going on in the other room. So she opened the door to see what was going on.

(5) *n Construction.* To order, organize, build, or create something.

Well, this is a students' room that has been rearranged in the form of a bar. Well, the bartender writes short stories and he and the girl are talking about Greenwich Village in New York and he's discussing with her the problem of constructing a story about a soldier, and ah, he's getting material.

(6) *n Counteraction.* To strive in order to regain (or maintain) self-respect. Injured or threatened pride prompting the hero to increase his efforts after failure or to try over and over again or go out of his way to overcome great obstacles; to overcome weakness, inferiority, inherited affliction, or timidity by doing the difficult, disliked, or dreaded thing; or to revenge an insult.

Or it could be that this fellow is very angry at how another fellow stole his girl. He's going to do something about it. He's telling this guy about it.

(7) *n Excitance, dissipation.* To seek emotional excitement in one way or another: travel, adventures with women, gambling, recklessly meeting danger.

There's some involved story about the three people and that's probably a picture in the paper of another woman. And well, probably both women are in love with this fellow and he has seen in the paper some event in her life that he should go to her. She's evidently a vamp but he likes that kind and he'll go to her.

(8) *n Nutriance.* To seek and enjoy food and drink; to feel hungry and thirsty. To take liquor or drugs. To do some work connected with foods or beverages.

Oh, we would call it, oh, a Twelfth Century, I suppose, and, and this magic cow is able to supply just enough milk so that everybody has his quart a day to drink.

(9) *n Passivity.* To enjoy quietude, relaxation, rest, sleep; to lie down. To feel apathetic, tired after little or no effort. To enjoy passive contemplation, reflection, or the absorption of sensuous impressions. To yield to others out of apathy and indifference.

They've been riding pretty fast and they're lying down for a little nap.

Looks like he's fallen asleep or kneeling down to pray, fallen asleep in the process.

(10) *n Playmirth.* To play games. To devote time to sheer amusement, to go on a party. To make jokes, laugh, wisecrack. To meet situations in a lighthearted, playful manner.

And I suppose in a little while his mother will come back and he'll start playing again, and wish that he could go out and play with the other fellows.

(11) *n Retention.* To hold on to an object, refuse to lend it, try to keep it from being stolen, conceal it from people. To hoard, collect, conserve objects. To be frugal or miserly.

There are two old misers on a desert island on the Pacific. They found treasure on the island and although a ship now, which now stopped at the island quite often, they were so fascinated by the money that they wouldn't go back, although they should have realized that the money was no good to them at all there because there was nothing to spend it on, they would stay there.

(12) *n Sentience.*

(a) *Epicurean.* To seek and enjoy comfort, luxury, ease, pleasant sensations, good food and drink.

The older woman is out basking in the sun there, leaning against the tree. It doesn't seem to me that she has too many thoughts. It's simply enjoying the sunshine there.

(b) *Aesthetic.* To be sensitive to the sensuous aspects of nature. To enjoy art, music, literature. To create, compose, write.

Isn't like a young fellow studying violin, contemplates about violin, probably pretty good artist, got interested in violin through some outstanding person, hero, who played the violin and the boy liked it; probably has a lot of talent, awfully intelligent, if taking such great interest when he is young; suppose not yet in creative stage; but the way he looks at it is significant, shows love for it.

(13) *n Understanding.* To strive for knowledge and wisdom. To study hard at school, to get an education, to read in order to learn something. To think, reflect, speculate in order to solve a problem. To travel or seek experience in order to attain wisdom.

All of her girl friends called her "bookworm" and "silly intellectual" and so on because she was ever fond of reading all the time, reading everything she could get hold of.

2. *Activities initiated by the hero with regard to other people.*

(1) *n Affiliation.*

(a) *Associative.* To establish or maintain friendly relations.

(1) *Focal.* To enjoy the company of a friend (or friends), to remain loyal. To work and play together. To feel strong affection (expressed or unexpressed) for some person.

He and his roommate got along very well. They stood by each other through thick and thin.

(2) *Diffuse.* To like all sorts of people. To be gregarious and sociable. To work or play with a group or gang.

Every Sunday during the summer he and a bunch of fellows from the neighborhood would go on a hike in the country.

(b) *Emotional.* To be bound to another individual by strong affection, sympathy, or respect. To fall in love, to marry, to remain
faithful.

> No, he's American, and, ah, at the hospital the, ah, the nurse who
> had, this French nurse who had formerly been a chorus girl in Paris,
> he had met her and he had fallen in love with her.

(2) *n Aggression.*

(a) *Emotional, verbal.* To get angry or to hate someone (even
though the feeling is not expressed in words). To engage in a verbal
quarrel. To curse, criticize, belittle, reprove, blame, ridicule. To excite
aggression against an individual or group by public criticism.

> He's gotten terribly mad at this Communist speaker, and he gets up
> and denounces him and he denounces the races, and he calls on the
> good Americans to defend their racial purity and their Christian her-
> itage against their racial idolaters, and he's right in the middle of his
> denunciation right here and he's shaking his fist and his hair is all
> disarranged.

(b) *Physical, social.* To fight or kill in self-defense, or in defense
of a loved one. To avenge an unprovoked (unjustified or criminal) insult or injury. To fight for one's own country, or for a friendly country,
in a war. To punish a misdemeanor.

> During the great advance toward Leningrad, when they thought that
> the whole city was to be besieged, he and his whole brigade instead
> of digging ditches, went out and grabbed shotguns and went out
> and fought in the front lines.

(c) *Physical, asocial.* Criminal assault. To hold up, attack, injure,
or kill a human being unlawfully. To initiate a fist fight without due
cause; or to avenge a felt injury with unusual severity or malignancy.
To fight against legally constituted authorities (parents, boss, government). To turn traitor, and fight against his own country. Sadism.

> He hated the other man so he decided he would go up and kill him,
> strangle him, and so he sneaked up on the second old man and this is
> the picture of the old man just coming around to kill, killing the
> other one that's lying on his belly.

(d) *Destruction.* To attack or kill an animal. To break, smash,
burn, or destroy a physical object.

> He was so disgusted with the tunes he played that he broke the
> violin.

(3) *n Dominance*. To try to influence the behavior, sentiments, or ideas of others. To work for an executive position. To lead, manage, govern. To discuss and argue in order to persuade others. To attack opposing views. To catch and imprison a criminal or enemy.

> Hypnotist had been practising for several years developing new skills that were unheard of. Here his patients are completely entranced, and under his control and his power of suggestion.

> This fellow is pretty idealistic first, leads his friends in strike, then gets some power himself. Is taking advantage of it.

(4) *n Exposition*. To inform, give news, explain, instruct, teach.

> He gets on the stand and pleads eloquently, ah, for some sort of rehabilitation for the group.

(5) *n Nurturance*. To express sympathy in action; to pity and console an individual. To be kind and considerate of the feelings of others.

> He took pity on the old man and told him not to worry. He then loaned him the money he needed.

(6) *n Recognition*. To seek applause, praise, prestige, renown, to enjoy approval, basking in the appreciation of others. To boast. To be conspicuous, attract attention, perform or speak in public, dramatize himself before others.

> He climbs up the rope and the whole audience in the circus arena applaud him when he reaches the top.

> He's amongst his friends and he's telling them of all the things he did overseas.

(7) *n Rejection*. To express scorn, contempt, or disdain in action. To turn away from things, people, occupations, or ideas that are alien to his interests.

> So he has — in spite of this way he has of dressing which simulates shabbiness itself, he himself is pretty much of a haughty individual and he happens to be walking along a rather dark street, and those to whom he has looked up to in the past are now causing his nose to be turned up.

(8) *n Sex*. To seek and enjoy the company of the opposite sex. To have sexual relations.

> This man is an artist. He finds a new model for his paintings and this new model is very much better looking than his wife, very much better looking than his wife and he has fallen in love with her and when he's fallen in love with this woman and he wants to

keep the affair more or less on the quiet, and while he is in his art studio, he paints her some of the time and, ah, he's finally gotten to the point where he has made her his mistress.

(9) *n Succorance.* To seek aid or sympathy. To ask for assistance; to depend on someone else for encouragement, support, protection, care; to enjoy receiving sympathy, nourishment, or helpful gifts. To feel lonely in solitude, homesick when separated from devoted individuals, helpless in a crisis. To seek consolation in liquor and drugs.

Or it could be a young fellow and another person that the young fellow looks up to more or less as a guide, father. He is asking the old man to take care of him till he can adjust himself.

3. *The hero's reactions to the activities initiated by others.*
(1) *n Abasement.*
(a) *Submission.* To comply unwillingly to another (perhaps alien) object, in order to retain or regain the goodwill of a cathected individual, or to avoid blame and punishment, or to avoid pain or death. To submit to insult, injury, blame, punishment, or defeat without much opposition. To confess, apologize, promise to do better, atone, reform. To acquiesce and resign himself passively to Fate, to endure terrific ordeals without counteractive efforts. Masochism.

His parents want him to work hard in business so he'll be rich. He'd rather study art. But after many arguments he gives in to their wishes.

(2) *n Autonomy.*
(a) *Freedom.* To escape or avoid regions of restraint or coercion. To escape from some confining space, to break out of prison. To run away from home, quit school, leave his job, or desert from the Army because of restrictions, obligations, duties. To leave or break off with someone in order to escape the obligations of relationship. The determination to remain independent, to avoid all entangling alliances or limiting prohibitions. To go off and do something that is legal and yet contrary to parents' wishes.

The mother looks mad. They probably had a pretty big argument. The way things look the fellow and the girl are going off anyway or maybe they have already run off.

(b) *Resistance.* To resist coercion. The hero refuses to do or simply does not do what is demanded of him. To argue against the judgment of a superior. To be contrary-minded, negativistic, argumentative, unyielding, resistant to authority.

He was an exceptionally proud youngster and he didn't like to obey orders. His mother spoiled him and, oh, he couldn't see any reason for obeying his father's wishes.

(c) *Asocial.* To do something that is not allowed, severely criticizable, or punishable, to a serious extent. To misbehave, to be disorderly or unruly. To run counter to moral or social standards: lying, cheating, gambling, drinking, whoring. To commit crimes, other than stealing.

The whole seems conflict between older and younger generation. He is trying to get away from their idea of his new and easy life, has something wrong with it. His mother is feeling very desolate, he is sorry that he hurt her. To make things concrete: he has had a love affair without marrying.

(3) *n Blamavoidance.* To fear reproach, blame, or punishment, and so refrain from wrongdoing; to inhibit temptations to do something unconventional or criticizable. To confess, apologize, atone, repent, in order to avoid more blame. To reform and become a good man.

He shakes his fist at the one in the class who did it. It's a little bit different from his ordinary behavior, and he realizes — Well, he's going to realize the effect on the class, so the next thing will be he'll come down and act in the extreme opposite, simply to make the class forget as soon as possible his rash action.

(4) *n Deference*

(a) *Compliance.* To fall in with the wishes, suggestions, exhortations of an allied individual. To be anxious to please; quick to agree, cooperate, obey. To follow the leadership of an admired individual willingly.

He didn't believe it could be done. And the other guy said, "All right, you just try to settle anything with me. Just don't fight anything. Just lie there, be drowsy." So he did, lie there, every time the fellow said something trying to soothe him why, he just said over in his mind echoing, "I feel drowsy," and pretty soon he's in the hypnotic state.

(b) *Respect.* To express admiration and respect in action. Hero worship. To acknowledge merit or talent, praise a good performance.

The old doctor was his idol and he stood in awe of him as he witnessed the operation.

(5) *n Harmavoidance.* To show fear, anxiety, apprehension, physical timidity; to avoid fights or physical dangers. To fear injury, illness, or

death; to worry. To run away when pursued by an animal, enemy (fearing injury), or policeman (fearing imprisonment or corporal punishment).

> He has attempted a suicide here, and the mental anguish at even the thought of his own death which before he had said would be greater, would be the solution to all his own problems, he found the thought of death itself even worse, and overwhelmed him to such an extent that he forgot his other troubles.

IV. CATHEXES

Vital data concerning a patient's needs may be gleaned from a study of the objects, activities, people, or ideas (sentiments and ideologies) that attract or repel the hero. Those objects, activities, people, or ideas that evoke a feeling of liking in the hero, and therefore attract him, are said to be positively cathected. Those that evoke a feeling of disliking in the hero and therefore repel him are said to be negatively cathected.

A. OBJECTS

Positive: He saw the violin in the window of the music shop and felt that he had to buy it.

Negative: The sight of the gun made him cringe. He had to turn away because he could stand it no longer.

B. ACTIVITIES

Positive: He looked out the window and saw the gang playing football. How he wanted to get out there and play.

Negative: The sight of the operation was so disturbing to him that he decided against becoming a doctor.

C. PEOPLE

Positive: The counselor looked like a kindly old soul so he felt that he could come to him with his problems.

Negative: She was so domineering that he promised never to see her again.

D. IDEAS (sentiments, ideologies)

Positive: He joined up to fight for Democracy.

Negative: He left the meeting hall when he heard the chairman speak about the advantages of Fascism.

V. INNER STATES

For clinical purposes it is necessary to study not only the patient's overt behavior but also his inner states — the feelings and emotions which may or may not be manifest in overt behavior. These data are reflected in the inner states experienced by the heroes in the various TAT stories. The circumstances arousing these states and the manner in which they are resolved should be studied. Several specific states usually mentioned by patients are: joy, elation, happiness, excitation, conflict, suspicion, dejection, pessimism, sorrow, grief, etc.

Happiness: The violin was the first gift he ever received. He longed to play it. Finally, he took some lessons and every time he put his bow to it he felt all good inside. He could count on his violin to pull him out of a slump at all times.

Conflict: I think that this is just a representation of an idea of a man who wants to do something and who is held back and inhibited by certain mores.

Pessimism: He left home to find a job but nobody wanted to hire. Now after walking up and down the streets for weeks he has given up hope of ever getting any work.

VI. THE MANNER IN WHICH THE BEHAVIOR IS EXPRESSED

When the hero has been or is stimulated by environmental forces, the clinician should examine the avenues of expression through which the hero responds. Specifically, the examiner should attend to the intensity of the expression and to the level at which the behavior is expressed. A careful study of the level at which the hero's behavior is expressed will frequently yield important clues as to which of the factors in the patient's personality as found in the TAT are on an overt level and which factors are on a covert level.* The levels of expression are roughly subdivided below.

A. FANTASY

The hero does not express himself overtly but imagines, wishes, or daydreams about how he would like to express himself.

They told him to practice his lessons and left the room. He stared at the violin and began to daydream how he was going to win the game on Saturday.

B. PRE-MOTOR LEVEL

The hero plans, considers, or thinks of various plans of action but he either discards them or decides not to execute them when the opportune moment arises.

---

* Additional suggestions concerning level analysis can be obtained from Tomkins, S. S., *The Thematic Apperception Test.* New York: Grune & Stratton, Inc., 1947.

After having seen his counselor, he went home and decided to map out a plan for the next year. He found the courses he wanted and the instructors he liked but when registration time rolled around he decided not to go down and register.

C. INHIBITED BEHAVIOR

The hero wants to do something but restrains himself because he is concerned about the consequences.

When they refused to hire him for the job because of his physical disability, he felt like " blowing his top." He caught himself in time and didn't say anything.

D. MOTOR LEVEL

The hero executes his plans and his reactions to others are on an overt level. For a careful analysis the following factors should be observed:

1. *Gestures:* When his boss saw the terrible work he was doing, he bawled him out. He just listened to his boss and when he was asked what he could say in his defense, he just shrugged his shoulders.

2. *Active reaction:* He sat in the room and decided what he would say. He got up, made a mad dash for the door and ran for her room. When he got to her room, he told her what he thought before she could tell him to sit down.

3. *Passive reaction:* The big boss called all the men in and told them that he didn't like the way things were going on around the office. He told them the way things should be done. John sat there and listened and was afraid to say anything. Even though he knew the boss was wrong he felt he had to comply with his wishes.

4. *Energies directed externally:* He knew that the group's purposes were the same as his own so he joined up with them and fought for their ideas.

5. *Energies directed internally:* When he failed in the course, he berated himself and became so self-critical that he couldn't live with himself.

VII. OUTCOMES

The conclusions of the stories must be studied and it should be noted whether they are happy or unhappy, successful or unsuccessful, whether the hero's problems are resolved, his needs fulfilled, or whether a state of conflict still persists. In addition to the outcome itself, attention should be paid to the conditions that precede the outcome.

Happy ending: Here is a fellow who has had it hard all his life. His folks died when a kid and never had any home. He is leaning against a lamppost wondering how nice it would be to have a home to go to, to have people to love you. Deep inside him he knows it all a dream. It never could happen. Later on he meets a girl, falls in love with her and gets things he missed most of his life — love and a home.

Indefinite ending: Here is a fellow just back from the service. He probably has a wife and kids. He's finding it difficult to get along, probably sat next to the window all night thinking what he should and shouldn't do. Before he realized it the dawn came, and he's still in the same boat as before, will probably do the same thing over and over again. Don't know if that gets him any place.

Unhappy ending: The man turned his head to the now still figure lying on the cot. He placed his arm across his eyes as if to blot out the memory of his evil act. He had choked to death his wife, who now laid there a victim of his own uncontrollable jealousy. She has at last found peace, but to him peace will never come. The torments of his conscience will afford him no rest. He will die a thousand deaths. Jealousy, the worst of evils, has claimed for his own two more victims.

CHAPTER 4

ADDITIONAL FACTORS TO BE STUDIED

In addition to the items discussed in the previous chapter, those primarily concerned with content material, there are other factors that should be studied and which frequently reveal critical data. These are:

    I. Patient's Behavior during the Test
       A. Overt behavioral manifestations
       B. Patient's reaction to the examiner
       C. The patient's reaction to the test situation as a whole and to each of the cards
    II. Relationship between the Instructions and the Sequence of Events in the Story
    III. Use of the Objective Characteristics of the Picture
       A. Omissions
       B. Additions
       C. Distortions
       D. Attention to particular details
    IV. Sequence of Reference to the Stimuli in the Picture
    V. Language
    VI. Symbolism

I. Patient's Behavior during Test

The patient's behavior during the test is a valuable aid in determining the significant material. Frequently this behavior is a direct result of the feelings, sentiments, anxieties, etc., which are evoked by the objective stimuli, the pictures, and the chain of associations that develop while the patient tells his stories.

A. *Overt behavioral manifestations*

The following are several of the behavioral and physiological manifestations that should be noted:

    (a) Pauses
    (b) Clearing the throat
    (c) Restlessness
    (d) Rubbing of bodily parts
    (e) Sweating
    (f) Smoking
    (g) Hesitation
    (h) Interrupting test to leave for bathroom
    (i) Tics

The behavioral and physiological manifestations indicated above may either precede or follow the critical data, and are usually a result of data that have been expressed very frankly, distorted, or suppressed.

B. *Patient's reaction to the examiner*

The patient's attitude toward the examiner frequently reflects the feelings, anxieties, tensions, etc., that have been stimulated either by the pictures themselves or by the stories he has told to them. In the midst of a test the patient may become inwardly disturbed and project his hostility on the psychologist. Such sudden changes in attitude, comments on the competency of the examiner, critical remarks about the value of the test, and the like, should all be noted immediately.

C. *Patient's reaction to the test situation as a whole and to each of the cards*

A good many important data are often obtained from the patient's reaction when he is first faced with the test. In this regard it is valuable to compare the fluency of his speech and the conjunctivity of his ideas in both the interview situation and the test situation. The patient who speaks freely and coherently during the interview and then during the test speaks haltingly, insists that he is a poor storyteller, etc., often is threatened by the test because of very definite psychological factors.

Specific cards may also elicit reactions from the patient which betray significant data. These are manifested by:

(a) Exceptionally long stories to any of the cards

(b) Exceptionally short stories to any of the cards

(c) Rejection of any of the cards

(d) Favorable or unfavorable comments about the scenes that are depicted in the pictures

(e) Comments in which the patient indicates that any particular picture is either relevant or irrelevant to his own case and the associations that usually follow.

II. Relationship between Instructions and Sequence of Events in Story

The instructions demand that the patient include the three periods of time — past, present, and future — in his stories. On the basis of the manner in which and how well the patient complies with the instructions, the psychologist may make certain judgments concerning:

(a) The patient's attitude toward the past, present, and future

(b) The period in time about which the patient is most anxious

(c) The patient's time perspective

Experience has shown that the following have proved to be valuable clues to the significant material:

1. The technique the patient adopts to deal with the problem of time.
   (a) Strict adherence to the instructions may at times reflect the patient's rigidity, e.g., the patient says to each story:

   > In the past the hero was . . .
   > Now in the present he is . . .
   > In the future he will be . . .

   (b) Smooth, free-flowing style which rarely refers to the order of the time sequence but follows it implicitly frequently reflects the patient's creativity, his organizational ability, or his control over his emotions.
   (c) Lack of any reference to a time sequence as manifested in a concrete and descriptive approach usually is indicative of one or a combination of the following factors: narrow time perspective, anxiety, low intelligence level, poor organizational ability.

2. The amount of the story devoted to each period of time may indicate the period in time which the patient considers important in his own life.

3. The significance of the events in the story that occur in each period of time indicates the periods of the patient's life which are significant.

4. The past, present, or future may be avoided by the patient because the associations and memories that the patient has of these periods may stimulate too much anxiety in him.

5. The hero's feelings and attitudes towards the past, present, and future in the stories themselves frequently reflect the patient's own attitudes to these periods of time.

> He dreads thinking about the past.
> He is looking forward to the future.

6. Changes or consistencies in the hero's behavior pattern as the story is developed from the past to the future should be noted. This may reflect changes or consistencies in the patient's pattern of adjustment.

> When he was a small boy he had a lot of friends, now he works by himself.
> He was always one to stand up for his rights.

III. PATIENT'S USE OF THE OBJECTIVE CHARACTERISTICS OF THE PICTURES

Much valuable material can frequently be obtained from a study of the patient's use of the objective characteristics of the pictures. Clinical experience has indicated that the patient's use and interpretation of the elements in the pictures are determined by any one or a combination of the following factors: intelligence level, degree of contact with reality, and the strength of various needs.

Several of the factors which are worthy of careful study are:

A. *Omissions*

Frequently parts of the picture which are particularly disturbing to the patient may be omitted from his story. In the extreme case, this results in the rejection of the picture and in the refusal to give any story whatsoever. For example, difficulties in the family are sometimes indicated by rejecting the man or the older woman in Picture #2. The revolver in Picture #3 and the rifle in Picture #8 may be omitted by patients with strong aggressive tendencies. Patients with sexual problems may avoid the picture on the wall in Picture #4 or refuse to discuss the nude female in Picture #13.

B. *Additions*

The figures and situations depicted in the picture are frequently insufficient for the development of a well-rounded and complete story. Therefore, the patient must supplement the elements available in the picture with data of his own choosing. These data are frequently significant.

PICTURE #17 There was a fire and this fellow tossed out a rope and climbed to safety. He had left his wife up there because she was always mean to him and didn't treat him right. When he got halfway down he began to think whether he should leave her up there to burn to death or go up to her. After a few moments of thinking he goes up and gets her down, and they try to make a go of it.

C. *Distortions*

The objective characteristics of the pictures may be distorted to suit the patient's individual needs. Since the facial expressions of many of the characters in the pictures are "neutral," any description on the part of the patient may be conceived of as a distortion which reflects how he considers himself or those in his environment. At times the complete picture may be so distorted that there is little similarity between the patient's story and the objective characteristics of the picture.

PICTURE #5 Although the room was dimly lit, he could make out her hooked nose and she looked like the witch in the old fairy tales.

PICTURE #11 Must have been a landslide. All I can see is a lot of rocks piled up. Dust in the air accumulated. One big stone gave way and the whole mountainside came down. Can't see any people at the time of the landslide.

PICTURE #19   This is a picture that a man has one night as he is completely alone and he can't understand it. It seems that he himself is exclamating pain and he stood up in the middle of the night. He sees forms and a horrible shape. He considers it the crystallization of fear and he wonders where this thing can come from because it isn't a part of reality and it isn't a part of experience and yet it is a part of his life more real it seems than any part of living reality. In the middle of the night this vision comes to him and becomes tortured by it and he decides to fight it. The only way he knows is by looking at it and the more he looks at it the more ridiculous and easy it becomes for him to overcome it. But so far it remains in his mind and it is harmless and shapeless. It looks much more difficult and much more piercing than it actually is.

There are other interpretations of the neutral figures which are considered distortions because they deviate from the usual perceptions.

The figure in Picture #3 and the young man in Picture #12 may be seen as females by male patients with strong feminine components.

D. *Attention to particular details*

A patient may be attracted to a single detail of the picture or spend a great deal of time describing some aspect of the stimulus material with which he is engrossed. Such behavior may reflect either strong needs or compulsive and obsessional trends.

PICTURE #4   His eyes looked as if they would be staring right through you.

PICTURE #11   I can see little faces in the rocks. This one looks as if it's smiling. This one looks as if it's sad.

PICTURE #17   Here's a gymnast who has kept himself in good shape. He can still climb a rope without using his legs at the age of 52. He has a strong, an outstanding physique. You can see his muscles bulge and he is sweating so you can see them glisten.

IV. SEQUENCE OF REFERENCE TO THE STIMULI IN THE PICTURE *

The psychologist should note the sequence in which the patient refers to the whole picture and to each of its details. He should observe whether the patient deals with the details in the picture in an orderly fashion so that the final production is well organized or whether the pa-

---

* This is roughly equivalent to the *Erfassungstypus* and sequence analysis in the Rorschach.

tient shifts from one item to another in a rather haphazard fashion so that the final production is disorganized and confused. If it is the latter, then the psychologist should attempt to determine whether the lack of organization is a function of a pressing need, anxiety, or the desire to account for all the available details. On the basis of such data, the examiner can usually characterize the quality of the patient's thought processes and also determine the conditions under which the patient's thought processes are apt to function most adequately or become most disturbed. Furthermore, if it is apparent that the patient is completely unable to or has extreme difficulty in developing coherent and well-organized stories, then the psychologist should attempt to determine whether or not this is a function of a more severe pathological disorder.

An obsessive patient who felt that he had to account for all the details in a picture told the following story to Picture #4:

> Well, I see here a man and his wife. He is not wearing a tie and looks sloppy. He has a far off look on his face as though he is dissatisfied with present conditions. She, on the other hand, is dressed in a white dress and looks neat. She's attempting to plead with him or attempting to gather from him just what his intentions are. I see a picture on the wall, which I don't think has any particular place in the home of a married couple. Strikes me as being somewhat of a pin-up picture. I don't see any reason for that type of picture in a home. The way the man appears to me at the present time I don't think that the woman, whom I believe to be his wife, is going to be very successful in dissuading him although she is a rather attractive woman.

A schizophrenic in remission who was still experiencing difficulty in situations that involved his wife, his mother, or both, told the following stories to Pictures #2 and #4. These stories were relatively more disorganized than those told to pictures in which no female figures appeared.

> PICTURE #2 In this picture here it seems that the field is being turned over for the plantation of certain crops. Seems like the mother might be there looking to the distance and looks like either his sister or his lady friend holding a couple of books ready perhaps to go home again. Well, it seems like the man is looking to the distance and sees somebody coming or looking at the, at the landscape. And the lady on the right here seems to think of perhaps some day she'll look into the distance. That girl there I don't know. I don't know. I don't know what she's thinking about. Perhaps of a future with the young man. The outcome would be something independent to the work that they're doing, that they will be doing and this farmer here.

PICTURE #4   This picture seems to relate to a couple about to be separated for some time, for what reason, maybe that he's going off to war or has troubles on his mind, maybe he has folks, would like to do things for his folks and do things for his lady friend, if it's a lady friend, it seems that way. And, well, the outcome of this, well, it's in the balance. Well, it's in the balance in another way if it's war waiting if he'll be back or not or if it's lonely to be away from her or not. He has a job to do and he wants to go ahead and do it.

V. LANGUAGE

The psychologist can usually obtain valuable clues regarding the patient's personality, intellectual level, and the quality of his thought processes from a study of his vocabulary and use of language. The more intelligent patients use adjectives, adverbs, polysyllabic words, and compound and complex sentences more frequently than do the less intelligent ones. Active verbs are frequently used by spirited, energetic, and counteractive individuals, while passive verbs are found in the stories of patients who tend to be inert, inactive, and submissive. Adjectives, and the nouns they modify, indicate the objects, activities, or sentiments which are positively or negatively cathected by the patient. Excessive use of adjectives may also indicate the patient's feelings of insecurity, his indecisiveness, or his propensity for rationalization. Similarly, excessive use of such adverbs as " perhaps " and " maybe " frequently highlight obsessive doubt.

Careful study of the patient's sentence structure and use of words reveals how well he can communicate his ideas to others. When the patient experiences difficulty in this regard, the psychologist should attempt to determine the nature of the factors that may be involved. Poor communication may be due to low intelligence level, anxiety stimulated by a single picture or the test situation as a whole, or it may be indicative of a severe pathological disorder. Neologisms should be noted very carefully, since they are indicative of autistic thought processes. The stories presented below illustrate the range of behavior that is found. All these stories were told to the same TAT picture (Picture #17). The people who told the stories, in the order in which they appear below, were: a successful professional man, a student with obsessive thoughts, a compulsive patient, a schizophrenic patient before insulin shock and psychotherapy and then the story that the same patient told to the same picture after therapy, and finally the story of a deteriorated organic. For our purposes here it is not necessary to analyze the content of the material but to attend only to the language and thought process. Note the level of integration in the first story; how the second patient becomes involved with his thoughts; the details referred to by the third; the autistic behavior of the schizophrenic in the fourth and his behavior after therapy; and finally the concrete unintegrated approach of the organic.

Subject #1

Michael McGillicuddy's legs weren't worth a damn but all his life he prided himself on the strength of his brawny arms. When he was 22 he went to work for the Herlihan Contracting Company and learned to operate a jack-hammer. Twelve hours a day he danced with that jack-hammer and the jolt and the jerk and the vibration, which would have shattered the nerves of a lesser man, gently massaged McGillicuddy's shoulders and provided an accompaniment to the tumultuous music singing in McGillicuddy's brain. Ten long years did McGillicuddy work for Herlihan, ten long years of working twelve hours a day on railroads and highways and rock tunnels and embankments, dancing to the tune of the air hammer. Ten long years did Bridget fill the dinner pail and for ten long years did Michael bring home the meager pay that Herlihan distributed to his rambunctious crew. Then it was that McGillicuddy met Paddy Mc-Gurk as kept the Killarney Athletic Club and as ran a stable of broken-down boxers and wrestlers. Among the things that Paddy provided for the regalement and entertainment of the denizens of his establishment was the rope hanging from the rafters of the gymnasium. Up and down the rope his worn-out fighters hauled their weary bodies, and up the rope went Paddy the McGillicuddy. And 'twas up the rope and down the rope and up the rope and down the rope that did the McGillicuddy from then on. For there was a joy in vertical locomotion for the McGillicuddy with his strong arms — three times as strong as the normal man's. It was child's play to pull himself hand over hand, with his legs hanging free, and a joy to come sliding down so as to be able to climb up again. And so for thirty years the McGillicuddy stopped at Paddy's place on his way home from work for a few quick runs up and down the rope. And 'tis there you see him now, 62 years of age, with a few gray hairs among the black, still in the joy of his youth as far as climbing up and down the rope is concerned.

Subject #2

It was in midday, during the middle of the summer, and Jerry was on shipboard. There was nothing much going on. A lot had gone on, they had been through a lot of harrowing experiences, but after all, they were now pretty much at ease . . . and all they wanted now was to get back and to be back home. And they thought of not too much else. And in the middle of the day they were at anchor in a harbor and thought it would be perfectly well for them all to go swimming. All they had to do was climb overboard, go down some sort of a rope or ladder, swim as long as they wanted, and then climb back up. Jerry liked to swim, it was one of his favorite sports, and as he climbed over the side, a good many of the men were already in the water, swimming around, having a good time, laughing, playing as a bunch of kids would. And as he climbed down, he stopped suddenly and looked off into the horizon, and admired what he couldn't have admired somewhere else besides going down the rope. Somehow it was better than usual. There were mountains in the distance, very blue, almost purple in places, and they had a figuration, an outline, which an artist would draw if he were almost, when he was getting a little more beautiful than nature, if that can be done, or thinks he's getting more beautiful than nature. But it wasn't just the mountains, it was the sea, which was a slightly different color, and this all went up into the clouds in the sky. They weren't threatening clouds of black or grey or anything, they were blue and white with different shades. They were billowing and streaming, and Jerry wondered if there could be anything more beautiful, and wondered if everyone would notice the beauty of what was already around them, and not wait for the joys which they thought were in the future, but rather admire what was there at the time, not worry about the bad things in life unless it was necessary, and so in worrying forget about all the good things. But they should look at the good things and make sure that they saw what was going on around them that was good. They should think of the wonders which Nature provides, and not only Nature — as he was thinking this over he also thought of the glory . . . the heroism, the more than heroism of the day-to-day contacts of his buddies, of their good and bad qualities, and how when you figured it up, in most of them the good qualities so overshadowed the bad ones that there was no worry left. And with that, he went swimming.

SUBJECT #3

Evidently someone in a gym, don't see any trunks, hardly be in a gym class. Climbing a rope with just his hands. Evidently now reached the top, slack beneath his hands more than if he would be climbing down. Climbing down, looking to see if timing is good. Outcome just reach the bottom. No strain on the man's face, no anxiety about it.

SUBJECT #4A

This man I see is going up a rope
His right hand is above the left
His left knee is above the right

His soles are even and they are both flat
Except the left which is flatter yet.

And on his crown —
(turns card upside down)
                    — he knows he's down
And turned upside down
For then he is going down to the ground.

But the face he has is not mine
For I own my own
And my own is all
Is all the one I know.
The other within me is the one I've loved
From the time I have seen her in her black cloak
But she is brown, and there she is
Down to the ground — round —
The earth is round, that's why I live on the brown.

The rope is hanging from above
And he goes head first, rather: soul first
Down to the ground
Where it is brown.

SUBJECT #4b (Post-therapy)

I see a muscular fellow letting himself down by a rope in a corner outside of a building. Letting himself down from the roof. It's kind of unusual, he's barefooted. Maybe it's a rope in a gym. He feels he can climb down easily because it's easier going down than going up and he has already reached the top and is going down. He is smiling triumphantly.

SUBJECT #5

Steeple-deck, steeple-deck
He paints a sign — steeple-deck — paint
Paint, paint, paint, paint
Cable, 10 foot apart
Painter — copper, steeplejack.

A patient's vocabulary and the manner in which he uses language may at times reveal the façade that the patient has erected in an attempt to hide certain feelings.

The following story was told to Picture #10. The patient's picturesque language, while not always inappropriate, revealed his desire to be considered an intelligent and knowledgeable individual. Combining the data from this picture with the material obtained from the complete protocol, it was evident that the patient was compensating for inferority feelings by adopting affected mannerisms.

> PICTURE #10.   In this grief-stricken picture, two parents are mourning the death of one of their relatives.   In unspoken words and silent consolement, nothing can be said to alleviate the remorse both of them feel deeply.   And therefore do not attempt to solve one of life's unanswered questions, the unexpected discontinuation of a dear friend.

VI. SYMBOLISM IN STORIES

There are many stories in which symbolism plays an important role. The psychologist would do well, therefore, to acquaint himself with the psychoanalytic literature on this topic.   A knowledge of the interpretive significance of the various symbols will aid the psychologist in unearthing important data.

Experience has shown that the following stories, when interpreted symbolically, yield valid data.   It should be noted, however, that the material presented below is to serve only as examples of symbolic interpretation.   The reader should be cautioned against the undisciplined application of the suggestions that appear below.   Before any interpretation of symbolic material is accepted, the psychologist should be certain that there are sufficient data to support his hypothesis.

Stories to Picture #1 in which the boy is seen as worried because he broke a string of his violin while playing with it are frequently told by patients who have experienced guilt over masturbation or who have castration anxiety.   Preoccupation with masturbation may also be inferred from stories to Picture #17 (but in this case guilt may or may not be an associated phenomenon) where the hero is seen " going up and down " the rope.

Stories to Picture #1 where the hero is deliberating over the inner mechanism and workings of the violin are found in patients who are preoccupied with or curious about sexual matters.   Specifically, their preoccupation may be determined by castration anxiety, curiosity regarding the difference between male and female sex organs, a desire for more information concerning the physiology of the reproductive organs.

Picture #8 may evoke stories in which the person on the table loses a limb in an operation.   These stories frequently reflect a patient's castration anxieties.   In Picture #11 stories involving difficulty controlling the animal, or those in which the hero is being pursued by the animals, frequently reflect the patient's inability to control, or difficulty in adjusting to, his instinctual and sexual drives.   Stories to Picture #12 in which the young man on the couch has given himself up to be hypnotized by the older man or in which the older man has forcibly hypnotized the young man and stories to Picture #18 in which the hero has been attacked from the rear or pulled to the rear, frequently reflect the patient's latent homosexual tendencies or overt homosexual experiences. In Picture #19 preoccupation with "eyes" (windows of the cabin) reflects the patient's guilt feelings.

The following stories were told by a patient who had difficulty in effecting an adequate heterosexual adjustment. On the basis of an interpretation of the symbolic material, it was determined that latent homosexual tendencies and fears of castration were two of the major problems that militated against a mature heterosexual adjustment.

> PICTURE #8 Here is a boy who has just set out to have his appendix taken out, and he dreams of being cut and is none too happy about the prospect. However, after it is all over he finds it's not too bad as he had made it out to be.

> PICTURE #12 This dates back to the days before the institution of anesthesia and this boy is about to have his leg amputated but not having any anesthesia they resort to hypnotism and he is being hypnotized by the only man in the picture. When the hypnotism is complete the leg will be amputated without pain but it is pitiful nevertheless that such a young man should lose his leg.

> PICTURE #13 This is a picture of a man who has just spent the night with a prostitute. She is exhausted from a night of excesses, but he is very remorseful now that the evening is over. He is a soldier who will return to his barracks in a short time, where he'll take many precautions to avoid winding up with a dose.

> PICTURE #14 This is a man who has spent a different evening than the one before. He has attended some highly stimulating musicale or he's heard some wonderful music and he's more or less in an exalted mood as he looks out at the skies and dreams about infinity.

> PICTURE #18 This is a picture of a man to be mugged. Pain and fear registered on his face, and the result of this is that he loses his pocketbook and almost his life but money is not so important anyway and he is lucky to come out alive.

In addition to the symbolism that is so frequently found in TAT stories, there are many instances in which other psychoanalytic mechanisms (displacement, condensation, etc.) operate and the clinician would do well to be aware of these in order to get the most from his data.

CHAPTER 5

TECHNIQUE OF INTERPRETATION

To separate the technique of interpretation from the technique of analysis is somewhat artificial and arbitrary. It is obvious that both the data selected as significant (analysis) and the meanings attributed to them (interpretation) are determined by the theoretical formulations which the psychologist has adopted.* Nevertheless it is necessary that interpretation be considered separately from analysis so that the psychologist may follow each of the steps involved in abstracting from the TAT protocol all that it contains.

A syndrome or cluster analysis is the first step in developing a complete and meaningful picture of the personality on the basis of the material obtained by following the procedure outlined in the previous chapters.

Syndrome or Cluster Analysis

By syndrome or cluster analysis is meant the analysis of TAT protocols to determine what factors in the patient's personality are interrelated and how they affect each other. Specifically, when a need, a press, a cathected object, etc., is indicated in any story, the psychologist should investigate that single story for the following:

(a) the conditions which precede the need, the press, the cathected object, etc.

(b) the intensity with which these factors are expressed

(c) the results or consequences which follow them

When this procedure is carried out for the first story in which any significant factor is noted, the psychologist should be on the alert to note all stories in which that same factor recurs. For each of the subsequent stories the same analysis should be made. The new data that are obtained should be compared and contrasted with the material gained from the first story in which the factor appeared. Thus, by constantly checking and rechecking, the psychologist is better prepared to accept or reject any hypotheses that he might have developed in the course of his analysis and interpretation. In general, it should be stated that no hypothesis should be accepted unless it is confirmed by data obtained from at least two stories. This is not a rigid rule and the following are several exceptions with which the reader should acquaint himself.

---

* The author has found the theoretical formulations described in *Explorations in Personality,* Henry A. Murray *et al.,* New York, Oxford University Press, 1938, most valuable in this regard.

(a) A patient may be sufficiently aware of his problems or sufficiently suspicious of the examiner's motives as to make conscious attempts to avoid revealing himself or his problem. However, over the course of the twenty pictures the patient may be unable to sustain this defense mechanism and the material which he has tried so hard to suppress does come to the fore. Therefore, it is possible to attach significance to material from a single story if one can defend the hypothesis that the patient is attempting to suppress or repress the material which is revealed.

(b) Analysis of several stories may indicate a significant syndrome in the patient's personality. This syndrome may highlight the importance of the data that appear in only one story, provided we accept certain formulations or hypotheses of one or another of the various theories regarding the psychology of personality.

The following examples will illustrate how cluster analyses are made. The first example indicates how we may select specific individuals in the patient's stories and study how the patient regards and reacts to them. In this case we are concerned with the patient's parents and only the material which is pertinent to them is quoted from the stories.

PICTURE #1 A child who is looking a little tiredly and disgustedly at violin. Parent probably forced him to take these violin lessons from looking at it. . . . If it was his mother who made him play, as it probably would be, he's probably trying to see how he could get his father to counteract it . . . chances are he went to his dad and asked about it. He probably tried to console him and persuade him it isn't a waste of time. He also said he'd speak to his mother but in any event, chances are, he probably was spoken to by both his parents, mother too. May have offered him some inducement — punishment if he didn't continue his lesson. This is probably not the first time he has rebelled against these lessons and probably won't be the last. But in the end he will always have to go back to doing them.

PICTURE #2 We have before us a scene of disagreement from the expression on the people's faces. Man has obviously denied some request that both of the women have made of him. Possibly woman is his mother and the girl is one that she wants him to marry. He seems to be more interested in farming and his freedom . . .

PICTURE #3 Young adolescent who seems to be crying bitterly about something. He may have wanted to go somewhere and was refused by his parents. He felt so strongly about the matter that for a while he was contemplating suicide.

PICTURE #6 We have a man and his mother standing quietly in a room. Man is probably her son. He evidently has done something that displeases his mother a great deal. Evidently he's got to overcome . . . His explanations and apologies have not been accepted as yet. He's down in the mouth trying to find a new formula that will satisfy his mother. After a while if he keeps trying, the mother will in the end give in on the condition that he never do it again.

PICTURE #7 Two men who are faced with a very important problem. The younger of the two is the one who seems to be the one who can't get the answer. They've probably been thinking for a while and they seem to be very helpful. He keeps staring at the younger one. The problem is not solved because there was not enough contribution made by the older man.

From the above material it is apparent that the patient regards his mother as an authoritarian and uncompromising person (Pictures #1, #2, #3, and #6), who insists upon dominating her son even to the point of wanting to run his life for him (Pictures #1, #2, and #6). His father, on the other hand, is the person to whom he turns when he is in difficulty (Picture #1). But even the father-son relationship is marred because the father is not the strong and wise person that the son desires (Pictures #1 and #7). Contrary to the son's desires, the father is succorant but weak and not so very wise (Pictures #1 and #7).

The next group of stories is cited to illustrate how data which are obtained from several stories and which reinforce each other tend to highlight the material obtained from a single story.

PICTURE #4 Looks as though a little argument here. Either sweetheart or wife. It dawned upon her that she's losing her grip and she's trying to find out what it is all about. He doesn't seem to want to face the problem there. Trying to be evasive by turning away to avoid it. It winds up in a terrific argument here. Probably he would strike her, push her away and get it over with. She has a pleading look on her face and doesn't seem to care.

PICTURE #10 Husband and wife. Looks as if something shattered their happiness. Could be that he's going to depart — no anger attached here, remorse on both sides.

PICTURE #13 Oh this picture ——. I don't know, this fellow here has had a terrible quarrel with his wife. Done something to her. Not necessarily his wife. He attacked her. That doesn't sound well. He was out of his head for a minute. Evidently something happened in his room because he has no hat or coat on. She's unclothed. He must have been the guilty person. Must have murdered her. Very unhappy ending that.

PICTURE #15 Very sad picture somebody being mourned here very much, probably his wife.

From the above stories, which are replete with plots of strife between husband and wife or aggression directed against the wife, it was evident that one of this patient's primary problems was that of marital discord. However, new light was cast upon his problem from the story to Picture #6.

> PICTURE #6 Looks like husband and son. I mean mother and son. Got a sad story to tell. Could be they had an argument. He decided to leave home. His mother is terribly upset about the thing. She looks like a sensible woman. She figures the less she has to say the better. He looks as though he is sorry for getting into the argument. Trying to dig up enough courage to face his mother and say that he is going. Could possibly have a happy ending. They could when they face one another forget about their argument and be happy. (Will he leave or stay?) He could stay. Looks as though he is not too angry and could be won back. It is a question of pride. . . . He will stay.

The story to Picture #6 was the only one in which a female figure was mentioned and in which there was a happy ending. Note that in this story the figure is the mother and the patient's first remark is to call her " husband," possibly indicating the " masculine " or superior role that the mother actually does play with regard to the patient. In view of the hero's submissive attitude to the mother in the picture, and the hero's desire to satisfy her needs, it was pointed out to the psychiatrist treating the case that it would be valuable to investigate the role of the patient's mother in effecting the patient's marital adjustment.

Combining Syndromes in the Final Report

Just as one's theoretical bias affects that which he will select for analysis and interpretation, so it plays an important role in integrating the material obtained from the TAT. The theory one adopts will often determine whether the TAT analyst will give a central position to a specific need, whether he will regard certain relationships as more important than others, and whether he emphasizes the ego, the self, etc. In view of the differences regarding theoretical approaches to personality, I have decided not to have an extended discussion of this problem but simply to indicate my bias here and there and to suggest that the reader rely on his own theoretical predilections as he approaches the problem of integration and communication.

At this point it might be well to note that two additional factors will affect the final report. Theoretical points of view aside, the audience with whom one communicates will affect the manner in which the report is given. It is obvious that a report written for one's own professional colleagues with whom one has come to agree as to terms will be different from the report which one writes for another who is not so well acquainted with one's own technical jargon. The reader will no doubt correctly infer in the cases that follow that each of them was undertaken because of a specific interest. The final reports on these cases differed in terms of the language that would best communicate the material to the others who were also concerned with the cases. For purposes of this manual an attempt was made to maintain some consistency.

Another factor that may well affect the final report is the purpose for which the report was written. For example, is a " complete " analysis of the personality desired, or is it to be focused upon a specific factor or group of factors, as may be the case in a research study?

In summary, then, theoretical approaches to personality, the audience with whom one has to communicate, and the purposes of the study will affect the manner in which the final report is written up. It is therefore suggested that the psychologist bear this in mind not only when he comes to the problem of integration but also when he is in the process of analyzing and interpreting the protocol.

CHAPTER 6

A PROFESSIONAL MAN

Starting with this chapter a series of TAT protocols is analyzed and interpreted. For didactic purposes the analyses and interpretations made of each of the stories in the protocols are presented as completely and as clearly as possible so that the reader may follow all the steps involved in arriving at the final analysis and interpretation. Each story has been analyzed according to the criteria presented in Chapter 3 and Chapter 4. The stories as told by the patient appear on the left half of the page. On the right half of the page are the analyses and interpretations plus additional comments which the reader may find applicable to a variety of cases. Therefore, at first glance, the material on the right half of the page may appear completely out of proportion to the patient's statements.

The cases have been so arranged that the more integrated individuals appear first and then the less well-integrated ones. These are followed by two cases whose protocols were obtained before and after psychotherapy. (A case before and after insulin shock therapy is included with the previous group.) It is hoped that in presenting the cases in this manner the reader may become aware of the integrative as well as of the disintegrative aspects of personality and that he may also consider the usefulness of the TAT in studying the outcome of therapy.

The Case of C. B.*

This man is 35 years old, married, and the father of two children. He is employed professionally. He is the youngest of five children — four boys and a girl. His parents are still alive. His TAT protocol was obtained when he served as a subject in an experiment. The protocol was handwritten by the experimenter obtaining the record. The stories were not timed.

TAT Protocol   Analysis and Interpretation

Picture #1

That is a picture of a small   The subject here has given us something
boy whose parents are musi-   of the background and setting for the

---

* It should be indicated at this point that my final report on this case, and other cases in this manual where I was directly involved, was not based solely on the TAT. Several other clinical instruments, including the Wechsler-Bellevue, Rorschach, and Sentence Completion Test, were part of the test battery with which the individuals were examined. The data presented in this manual, however, were obtained only from the TAT.

cians and he's just finished practicing on his violin, story. This approach is consistent with the "set" given him by the psychologist's instructions. Note that reference to the past is not stated directly as "in the past" but is implied in his characterization of the boy's parents and in the tense employed in describing the boy's activity. Such behavior, if it is consistent throughout the protocol, would make for smooth and well-organized stories and would reflect a high level of intellectual capacity and personality integration. The subject would have demonstrated his capacity to utilize his own resources in integrating instructions, stimulus (i.e., the picture), and the fantasy, needs, etc. that the picture evokes. It would therefore be a manifestation of good ego-strength or control. At this point in the analysis, the suggestion regarding the subject's capacity to effect integration is a hypothesis. It is necessary to determine whether or not he is able to maintain this level with regard to the present and future in this story and whether his approach will be consistent in the stories that follow.

Referring now to the content of the story, we find that the hero had been engaged in an activity which is the profession of his parents. He seems to enjoy this activity and there is no mention of coercion or pressure being put upon the hero. Since the picture contains the violin, the subject's reference to "musicians" may have been suggested to him by the stimulus material and it need not necessarily reflect either the subject's or his parents' interest in music or their profession. (Material obtained from the other stories may indicate that they were musicians or that the subject is interested in music but such an interpretation at this point would be based on very minimal data and, as experience has shown, it is likely to be in error.) Consequently, it is best that we attend to the underlying structure of the theme thus far, namely, that the hero has models or ego-ideals that he is trying to emulate. Whether or not these ego-ideals are within the family, as one might infer from the content of the story, or whether they exist outside the family, is a question which will probably be answered on the basis of the data that are to follow. At this point, however, it may be suggested that since there is no direct interaction between the parents and the boy, reference to them in the story may be related to the standards that they wanted their son to achieve, or the models may be outside the home.

It should also be noted that the source for the behavior in the story is the boy. Thus the subject is regarded as being internally or self-motivated and not dependent on constant direct sources of stimulation.

and he's daydreaming about his future when he'll be a great violinist like some of the old masters.

The dominant need in this story is achievement. The need not only stimulates fantasy behavior as indicated by the passage on the left, but also work behavior as indicated above in the boy's " practicing." Thus, to achieve, the subject has to work. This suggests that the subject may be realistic and not so dominated by his needs that he expects to reap his reward without any output or effort on his part.

The goal he is after is a high one. He desires to be like one of the " old masters." But he also feels that he has a long way to go. This statement is made on the basis of the discrepancy between the " small boy " and the " old masters."

While it is not uncommon for subjects to see the figure in the picture as a *small* boy, it is particularly significant in this story because of the contrast between the boy and the parents and old masters. Since the parents and the old masters are musicians and since the boy is practicing and fantasying about becoming a musician, it is suggested at this point that the " smallness " referred to above is not a pervasive feeling of inferiority but might well be limited to his feelings about himself in his professional activity. In other words, he does not feel at the present time that he is as good as the accomplished persons in his field and therefore may feel inferior to them. This may be a realistic appraisal of himself, as it would be of any young professional person when he compares himself with older persons who have attained major achievements. This might be regarded as a serious problem if such feelings hampered his efforts or stood in the way of his work. But note that this does not occur, for the hero does practice and the goals serve as a " pull."

Probably the outcome is that he is a child prodigy and will become more famous as he gets older.

It was suggested above that we need to attend to the organization of the story. Here, when the subject refers to the future, two things happen. First, the subject has to qualify that which is to follow by saying " Probably." Secondly, he refers specifically to " the outcome," interrupting the smooth flow of the story. The combination of both these details suggests that the subject has some doubt with regard to that which follows — the fame he will achieve. Nevertheless, since the hero does achieve fame in the future, it is probably more accurate to suggest that although the subject may have some doubt as to his future, he is hopeful. One should also note the use of the term " child prodigy " and that it relates to the present, inasmuch as the subject says the boy *is* a child prodigy. This may be regarded as being at variance with the interpretation given above as to the " small boy." The relative significance of both these characterizations can better be determined from additional material. However, at this point it may be hypothesized that the feeling of " smallness " may occur when the self is compared with others, and the feelings associated with " child prodigy " may be a reflection of his evaluation of himself as self — thus he regards himself as a man of talent who will make more use of his abilities in the future. If the interpretation regarding his feelings when he compares himself with the old masters in his field is correct then it suggests that he may be inhibited in their presence.

Summary Picture #1: The subject approaches the task in an organized fashion. He has a strong need for achievement and models or ego-ideals that he desires to emulate. He puts forth effort in order to attain the goals he desires. He regards himself as quite capable but feels somewhat inferior when he compares himself with those who have already achieved. This may result in inhibited behavior in their presence. Although he has some doubt as to what the future holds, he is hopeful.

TAT PROTOCOL	ANALYSIS AND INTERPRETATION
PICTURE #2	
This is a picture of a family — probably in the old country. The parents are of peasant stock with little or no education,	Casting the setting of this picture " in the old country," while not rare, is somewhat unusual. From the contents of the picture it is not impossible that this could be the old country. But because of the relatively infrequent nature of this description it is necessary to answer the question of why the subject selected

it. One possibility is that the subject is attempting to increase the psychological distance between himself and the picture and thus not become too involved with it. Another possibility is that the subject's parents may well have come from the " old country " or be for him representatives of a culture different from his own. Still a third possibility is that in describing the setting of his family background he may be telling us the kind of conditions he had to live with in his early life. In any case it is also necessary to be aware of the discrepancy between the parents in the story to Picture #1 and the parents in this story. In the first story the parents were musicians and figures whom he emulated; in this story, however, they are peasants. Thus, not knowing, prior to the analysis of these stories, the real characteristics of his parents, we are not in a good position to make a judgment now, for we have conflicting data. A probable inference is that these stories reflect alternative models that the subject sees before him and his reaction to each of them.

but the daughter of the family has decided she will go to school to get some education.

The motive force for education is internal. It is self-directed. The question may be raised whether education as a goal is desired by the subject, since books do appear in the picture. This question may be answered in the affirmative because data are available from the first story in which a professional activity was positively cathected by the subject, his reverence of the " old masters " and the intensity with which he pursues this goal.

But at the moment of the picture, the mother has been arguing with the daughter

Note that the storytelling manner has changed here in that the subject makes a direct reference to the " moment of the about wasting her time in school.

picture." This alerts us to the fact that that which follows may have been the stimulus for the alteration. Analyzing the material, we find that it has to do with conflict in a social situation. Consequently, it is suggested that such situations may well interfere with the subject's capacity to behave in the best integrative manner.

The "parents" are mentioned previously; however, only the mother is selected here for the conflict with the daughter. This suggests that the mother may have had a more dominant role *vis à vis* the subject than the father.

But the daughter is going ahead anyway.

The heroine does not give in to the mother's arguments but pursues her goals. This suggests the lack of submissiveness to the parents and the strong cathexis for the goal.

The outcome is that she does get a rather good education and does raise her station in life by a successful marriage to someone more her equal in education.

One of the effects of education is that it permits one to rise above one's station in life. Thus education and a successful marriage facilitate upward social mobility. The theme in this story is a Horatio Alger theme consistent with the subject's need achievement.

Summary Picture #2: The subject's need achievement and upward social mobility through education is manifested here. He is self-motivated and the goals he desires may be at a higher or different level than that set in his own home environment. He is steadfast in his desire to achieve his goals and overcome obstacles that are put in his way. His mother rather than his father may have been the dominant parental figure. Interpersonal conflict situations are somewhat difficult, but not impossible, situations for him to deal with.

TAT PROTOCOL

ANALYSIS AND INTERPRETATION

PICTURE #3

That is a boy who has just been outside in very active play

Two comments are in order here. The first is a brief one concerning the section of the story in the left-hand column and the other is a more general one that refers to the total story. This segment of the story reflects the subject's energy level — in this case it appears to be high. The second comment is more complex. Note that the story starts with an activity, the activity is interrupted, the story then shifts to an inner state, and finally it concludes with another activity. To some extent the structure of the story here is similar to the first story. In the story to the first picture the subject made reference to an activity and then shifted to an inner state. Both of these stories differ from the second in that no shift to " inner activity " occurs in the second story. One possibility for this lack of shift may be that of the three pictures considered thus far only the second has contained more than one person. Thus it is hypothesized that when left to himself the subject is apt to engage in ruminative or fantasy activity but in social situations under stimulation from the outside he is apt to be more active.

and during the course of the play his bicycle was smashed

The smashing of the bicycle is an aggressive act. But it is interesting that the aggression occurs without any aggressor having been mentioned. There is no mention of other individuals or of other objects. There are two possibilities: either the subject anticipates or sees hostility in the external world, or he himself has aggressive tendencies. If the latter is the case then it is interesting that the aggression is disembodied, i.e., not attached to either persons or objects and therefore may be regarded as an aspect of the self that is not accepted by the individual. It may be that he has attempted to dissociate aggressive tendencies or feelings from his personality. Aggression may be ego-alien or repressed. The statement that aggression or hostility may be a difficult state for the subject to deal with may be supported to some extent by the datum that the subject has not incorporated or made mention of the gun in the picture in his story and also from the data in Picture #2 where the manner of telling the story changes as the subject deals with a conflict situation with the mother.

It is obvious that no bicycle appears in the picture. Why was it chosen? Here one hypothesis may stem from analyzing the activity of bicycle riding. In bicycle riding the rider makes it go because he applies force to the vehicle. It is a self-directed activity. This is consistent with the self-directedness pointed out in the previous stories. Utilizing this interpretation of the bicycle, and considering it in conjunction with the statement that it has been smashed, suggests that a self-directed activity has been interfered with. In this sense the theme here is similar to that which was found in the second story, where a goal decided upon by the heroine was interfered with by the mother. The point that is being suggested here is that the subject has either experienced or anticipates that his independent strivings may be interfered with in some way — possibly by some aggressive act.

and he felt very sad about this so he went inside to his room and sat on the floor and thought about it.

The response to aggression and the interference with his independence is withdrawal into himself. Although the hero " thought about it " there is unfortunately no reference as to the nature or content of his thought.

To make the story end happily

Note the attempt " to make the story end happily." He has " to make " it come out this way. This suggests the intensity of the sad feeling that was associated with the material described above and also the conscious effort that the subject may have to exert to achieve the happiness that he does not experience now.

the bike was not beyond repair so it was repaired and he again had a bicycle.

Just as there was no reference to who or what did the smashing of the bicycle, so there is no mention of who did the repairing. It is as if things simply happen or get done. Does he believe that there are forces outside operating on people or things? Is this avoidance of people? We will have to check these possibilities against data that will appear later. At the moment it may be said that on the basis of the stories analyzed thus far the subject has avoided any mention of people, other than the hero in this story; in the first picture they do not enter into the story but serve as models, while in the second picture the one interaction with a person mentioned thus far is not a satisfactory one. It is therefore suggested that the subject may be a "lone wolf." One of the reasons for such behavior is suggested by this story, in that his independence may be interfered with.

One might also ask whether the fact that the subject has not mentioned that the boy repaired the bicycle himself may not reflect upon his capacity to deal adequately with frustrating situations. This too will have to depend on additional data.

Summary Picture #3: The subject may be the sort of person who anticipates frustration either from others or factors in the environment which may impede the progress he desires to make toward his goals. He has not accepted his aggressive tendencies or feelings and has difficulty in dealing with them. His reaction to the manifestations of aggression appears to be withdrawal into himself. Finally, he appears to be a "lone wolf" who does not find it easy to engage in social interaction, possibly due to his concern that others may interfere with his independence.

TAT PROTOCOL	ANALYSIS AND INTERPRETATION
PICTURE #4	
Oh, this is a story about a man and woman in love,	The subject is able to speak of and deal with a heterosexual situation. In so doing he may be able to accept positive affect.
but at the start of the picture the man was going to attempt something very dangerous.	This subject does not seem to manifest any fear of danger. Indeed, he seems to strive to master dangerous situations.
Let's say he was a circus parachute jumper.	Both aspects of this occupation are interesting. First, parachute jumping is a very masculine sort of activity, and secondly, performing in a circus is a kind of exhibitionistic activity from which one might gain the approval of others. Thus it is suggested that the subject has a desire to fulfill and be approved of for performing well in a masculine role.
His girl friend — it isn't his wife yet — doesn't want him to attempt the dangerous feat so she's trying to persuade him not to go.	Again (cf. Story 2) a woman stands in the way of his doing something. It seems as if the subject is trying to prove himself before he feels that he can marry the girl. He has already told us that they are in love and she does not want him to go. By speaking of the dangerous nature of the feat it is obvious that he thereby adds to his own prowess.
But he goes anyway and performs the dangerous and difficult feat of the parachute jump and then retires from circus life	As in the story of Picture #2 the subject follows through on his initial intention.
with the money he's made, and buys a farm, marries the girl, and lives happily ever after.	Performing the difficult feat in addition to that indicated above is also an instrumental act to retiring. It is therefore suggested that the subject's orientation with regard to his work may not be such as to obtain satisfaction from what is inherent in the activity but that it is a subgoal to a more distal goal. Focusing

on the retirement also suggests that a good deal of tension may be involved in attempting to achieve his goals and that he may look forward to a more passive situation where he does not have to strive so much.

It is also important to indicate that the subject is capable of establishing a heterosexual relationship, and that his goals, in addition to the achievement themes mentioned previously, include happiness and retirement.

Summary Picture #4: The subject is capable of establishing a heterosexual relationship. He seems to feel that he has to prove himself. He has a desire for approval from others but this apparently has to be attained on the basis of his performance. His goals in addition to achievement themes spoken of earlier include happiness and eventual retirement.

TAT PROTOCOL	ANALYSIS AND INTERPRETATION

PICTURE #5

This is a picture of a very well-kept house. The woman of the house is an exceptional house cleaner. Her house is always immaculate, but her husband is more the easygoing type.

The woman is not a "mother" nor is she like mother-figures in other stories. Orderliness and cleanliness are consistent with the subject's personality characteristics inferred thus far. He may have learned these characteristics from his mother but they are part of his personality now. Therefore it is suggested that he has identified with the woman.

At the moment of the picture the woman has just discovered the husband lying on the divan sound asleep in his old dirty clothes that he works in the garden with.

A conflict situation is described regarding the manner of cleanliness.

The outcome of the experience causes her to get very angry and afterwards she thinks about this

When the heroine's plans or mode of behavior is interfered with it results in feelings of hostility. These feelings are not expressed openly but are "thought through." Thus it may be said that the subject tries to understand himself and that he has difficulty with hostile feelings. The latter hypothesis is consistent with the data of Story 3.

and realizes that the house is a place to live and not a show place	This is important, for it indicates the importance of having kept the place clean and orderly — it was for others and not for one's self. This is consistent with the subject's behavior in the previous story where he performed the dangerous feat as a stepping stone to a more distant goal. And so here the cleanliness is not an end in itself but has as its significance the fact that it makes the house into a show place — something for others to admire. It therefore suggests that he is concerned about how others may evaluate his behavior.
and she gradually changes her ways and makes a much better wife because of the change.	The subject may be amenable to change and the change may be more in the direction of easing up, relaxation, and not being too concerned about the evaluations of others.

Summary Picture #5: The subject cathects orderliness and cleanliness. He is concerned about what others may think of him but there is evidence to suggest that this is not a satisfactory mode of adjustment to the subject and that he may desire change in the direction of more relaxation and not being too concerned about the evaluations of others.

TAT PROTOCOL	ANALYSIS AND INTERPRETATION
PICTURE #6	
This is a picture about a son who's just told his mother — oh, let's have him enlist in the Air Force — he's going to enlist in the Air Force.	The hero initiates the activity.
She's very sad about this because she feels that it's too dangerous.	Note the similarity between the theme in this story and that encountered in the fourth story. In both stories the theme is similar, with the exception that the mother is substituted here for the girl. In view of this similarity, one might well raise the hypothesis whether the subject has not used the same techniques with women who are possible sex

But he goes ahead, learns to fly, downs 10 German planes, gets his decorations, and comes home safe and sound.

objects for himself as he has in his relationship with his mother in the past.

Again the subject embarks upon a dangerous mission, performs an amazing task, and is triumphant. The quality of this story is adolescent and its content reflects his intense desire to prove himself, his need for recognition, and his sublimated aggression. Note that this is the first story in which the subject expresses hostility directly — but it is expressed in a socialized manner.

Summary Picture #6: The subject sees himself as not fearing danger, and conquering it. The subject's fantasy appears adolescent. It is also suggested that the subject may have utilized similar techniques in winning a wife as he has in proving himself to his mother. Strong need for recognition and sublimated aggression were also indicated.

TAT PROTOCOL

ANALYSIS AND INTERPRETATION

PICTURE #7

This is a story about two men — the older man is president of a rather large corporation.

In the stories thus far the subject has spoken about solitary hero figures and told stories to pictures involving the hero and women. In this story it should be possible to learn something of his relationship with men.

It is interesting to note that in the light of his strong achievement need, the subject speaks of older men as having arrived already — he is " president of a rather large corporation."

The young man hasn't proved himself yet, rather well,

Here the subject makes a direct statement consistent with a hypothesis that has been suggested previously — the subject's desire to prove himself.

and at the moment of the picture, there has been a business meeting with the officers of another corporation.

The young man and the older are in alliance. This story reflects his need for affiliation with people of high status — an additional datum that supports the hypothesis regarding upward social mobility in Picture #2.

The young man has just finished making a very brilliant offer to take over the other corporation, and the older man is looking on with great respect.

Note how the young man is characterized here — " brilliant." This may well be consistent with the manner in which he thinks of himself or would like to think of himself — as a superior person. The fact that the subject is in an executive position suggests his need dominance, and his " offer to take over the corporation " his need acquisition. Finally, the " looking on with great respect " reflects his need recognition.

Now he knows that the young man that he's picked for his successor will successfully fill the job.

The story ends successfully, for the young man does rise. It is interesting to note that the subject here and in the previous story has to *do* something before he feels that he has arrived. In other words, he wants the judgment of him to be made on an objective basis.

At the beginning of the analysis of this story it was suggested that we could probably learn something new here — the subject's relationship with men — while previously we had had information regarding his relationship with women or his solitary situations. From this story we have learned that the subject desires to ally himself with older, established men and that he feels he can do as well as they. In contrast to this, in his relationship with women he proves himself by indulging in an activity in which they cannot or do not usually indulge. Underlying both of these is the desire to be a superior individual and the need to prove himself.

The reader may have observed that the subject's stories reflect a very strong desire to achieve and to be superior. Such intensity and the fact that the need is manifest in diverse situations raise the question whether these motivating forces are manifest in the subject's overt behavior — that he is a driving, pushing individual — or whether his ambition is more controlled and less manifest to others. At this point it is suggested that the latter is more tenable for two reasons. First, there is a Walter Mitty-like quality about the story — the need to prove himself which may be an indication that his behavior is compensatory for feelings of inferiority. Secondly, he is unable to deal adequately with feelings of hostility. If he were to push in order to get ahead this would bring him into direct conflict with others and this is what he tries to avoid.

Summary Picture #7: The subject's need to prove himself is supported in this story, as is his drive for upward mobility. The subject fantasies of himself as a brilliant person. Need dominance, need acquisition, and need recognition were indicated in this story. It was also hypothesized that the subject is not likely to manifest his ambition overtly with the same intensity as is reflected in the stories.

TAT Protocol

Analysis and Interpretation

Picture #8

This is a picture concerning a boy and his father. They were out hunting and the father met with a hunting accident. He dropped his gun and shot himself in the abdomen.

This segment deals with an aggressive theme. Note that the aggressive act occurs accidentally and unintentionally, suggesting once again the subject's difficulty in dealing with this need. Furthermore, since it is the father who is shot it is likely that the subject has aggressive feelings toward the father or superior adult males.

The picture is the boy's memory of the hunting accident, of how the doctor came to the little farmhouse where he had taken his father and how the doctor immediately operated on his father to remove the bullet with the farmer's help. Because of

The significant aspect of this segment is that the subject was capable of rising to the occasion and doing something constructive about the accident. The aggression does not disrupt the story. It should also be noted that once again, as in the first story, he has a model which effects his professional career.

this work by the doctor, the
boy decides to become a physician and he does.

Summary Picture #8: The subject's difficulty in dealing with aggression
is again indicated. But here it is not so intense as to disrupt his behavior.
There is additional evidence of the importance of models or ego-ideals
for the shaping of his future.

TAT PROTOCOL	ANALYSIS AND INTERPRETATION

PICTURE #9:

This is a story about four brothers who . . .

The cast of characters here is somewhat unusual in that it consists of brothers. Most often the picture is seen simply as a group of men. Consequently, it is likely that the story may well refer to sibling relationships.

are, say, sinking an oil well. They're oil-field workers. They're sinking this oil well on their own property. The three older brothers always regarded the younger one as somewhat of a youngster

The relationship between the older brothers and the younger one is de-scribed — they did not regard him as one of them. Indeed, he was regarded as inferior to them — " a youngster." The fact that the activity takes place " on their own property " — something that they hold in common — suggests that the activity described may well refer to re-lationships within the family.

Why are they oil-field workers? One hy-pothesis is that he may have specific in-terests in this. Another is that in view of the implicit significance of money in his achievement themes oil may have been selected instead because of its finan-cial value. Finally, it may be suggested that the nature of the activity, digging for oil, is a symbolic representation of important needs in the subject's person-ality. This will be elaborated on later.

and the three older ones had just given up their efforts to bring in the oil well in disgust and were resting and wondering where they should go to get a job,

Others give up in their efforts,

but the young one had gone ahead by himself and drilled just a little bit farther and brought in a well.

whereas the younger brother persists in his efforts and outdoes them. Thus, adding this datum to the information that was available previously, the subject not only strives to outshine women and older male figures but also older sibling figures. In addition, the hero puts forth more effort than the others and therefore achieves his goal.

At the moment of the picture he is just approaching to wake up his brothers and tell them that they have an oil well.

The hero in the story has achieved his goal. He has found the oil well. But he does not use it for himself. He goes to his brothers to tell them that *they* have an oil well. In other words, the subject does not work merely for his own pleasure or for any material reward but rather the work here appears to be an instrumental act through which emotional gratification or some satisfaction that may come from an interpersonal situation can be obtained. This may well reflect the significance of the subject's job for him. His interpersonal relationships may well depend upon how successful he is on the job.

As a consequence the older brothers looked with new respect on the youngest.

Having accomplished what they could not do, he gains their respect. This is the second story (the first was in Story 7) where the hero indulges in an activity to gain respect from older males.

Earlier in the analysis of this story it was suggested that the activity in the story may be symbolic of some intense need in the subject's personality. It is suggested that the activity (the digging into the earth for oil) is symbolic of his desire to prove himself as a man to his brothers. To be sure, the same interpretation is apparent without involving the symbolic character of the activity.

Summary Picture #9: The subject is a persistent individual who apparently seeks to outdo others who might be superior to himself initially, through realistic accomplishments, in order to gain their respect. Underlying this may be the subject's desire to prove that he is as masculine as other men are. It is also suggested that his interpersonal relationships may be affected by how well he does on his job.

TAT PROTOCOL

ANALYSIS AND INTERPRETATION

PICTURE #10

This is the story of a weak-willed housemaid in the employ of a high government official.

This story is rather unusual in two respects. First, its theme deviates from the usual theme in that it does not involve some kind of close emotional relationship between the two individuals in the picture. This suggests that the subject may have difficulty in manifesting warmth in heterosexual situations. At first sight this statement may appear to contradict one of the data in Picture #4 where he spoke of the man and woman in love. In interpreting the fourth story it was suggested that the subject may be able to accept positive affect. If this hypothesis were valid then in a situation such as that manifested in Picture #10 which so frequently elicits warm relationships, one would anticipate that the theme of his story here would deal with a positive relationship between the two figures in the picture. The fact that it does not suggests that warmth may not be a consistent characteristic of his love relationship. This is supported to some extent by the data in the other stories — his need achievement is so dominant that much of his energy goes in this direction; consequently he may have little energy left over for warmth. Furthermore, previous data also suggested that in order to attain positive social relationships, the subject had to achieve. Thus these relationships were not sought or maintained for their own sake but were dependent on how well he thought of himself as a result of his achievement. Since he still has the need to prove himself, it is suggested that he may also feel insecure in his heterosexual relationships and this too would diminish the warmth.

The man in the story is at the moment trying to persuade the housemaid to steal some important documents for him. He's an agent for a foreign power.

This is the second unusual aspect of this story. It is quite inconsistent with the themes of the other stories, in which the hero realizes his ambition through persistent effort and honest work. Nevertheless, it may be regarded as consistent with the personality of an intensely ambitious person who may entertain some underhanded means of achieving his goal.

In view of the above, it becomes a problem to determine whether the subject might indulge in practices that he attributes to the "agent." It is hypothesized that he will not, although it is not unlikely that such ideas may have occurred to him. There are two factors which suggest this hypothesis. First, experience has shown that a theme which is on the face of it so inconsistent with the other themes as this one is, and in this case is such an unusual story to this picture, usually reflects a repressed need. The same interpretation, however, could be made on the basis of data which are more consistent with the subject's verbalization. The male is an agent for a *foreign* power. This suggests that what this man represents is ego-alien, or foreign to the subject. One other datum should be highlighted here. In view of the data regarding repression in this story, in view of the manner in which the subject deals with aggression, and in view of his intense ambition, it is suggested that the subject may well appear as a controlled individual. To be sure, this control is reflected in the manner in which the subject has rather frequently interrupted the smooth flow of his stories by saying, " At the moment of the picture," or a similar phrase.

Despite the hypothesis just suggested, the reader may well wonder with whom the subject has identified in this picture. It is suggested that the subject has more strongly identified with the woman. This is based on the fact that she gains in status by being in the employ of " a high government official " and this would be consistent with the subject's previous stories, which are related to status striving. Secondly, the woman in this story is in a position very analogous to the heroes in the previous stories — she is yet to be proven.

The fact that the female has been described as " weak-willed " previously suggests that the subject may too be weak and that the strivings manifest in the previous stories may be compensations for the weakness.

However, although the housekeeper

Twice before in this story the subject has referred to the female in the picture as a housemaid; here, he " slips " into calling her a housekeeper. The second occupation represents a rise in status. It is interesting that this " rise in status " occurs at a turning point in the story where the female is going to confess. Thus it appears that when the plot is at its lowest level ethically the female has low status but when it is about to change to a higher plane then her status changes also.

Since we know that the subject is inclined to be upward mobile it is suggested once again that the behavior adopted by the female is more apt to be characteristic of his own behavior in real life.

is greatly tempted because of the persuasion of the man, she immediately goes to her employer and confesses all,

The conscience of the heroine wins out over the persuasion and temptation.

and the enemy agent was captured by her confession although it broke her heart to do so.

Just as in the other stories, the "weaker" person becomes the hero by the time the story is completed. But there is another significant item here. Note that the female did the "right" thing although it broke her heart to do so. From this it is hypothesized that feelings for the subject are not given very high priority. This is again consistent with the data mentioned previously that concerned the subject's manner of perceiving this picture, and the previous reference to Picture #4.

Summary Picture #10: The subject's intense drive and ambition may have led him to entertain ideas in which he would go to extremes in order to achieve his goals. But these ideas are ego-alien and it is likely that in his behavior he adopts and follows a path that is more consistent with socially acceptable behavior. The subject tries not to permit feelings to play the determining role in what he has to do. It is also suggested that he may appear as a controlled individual.

TAT PROTOCOL

ANALYSIS AND INTERPRETATION

PICTURE #11

Hm . . . that's a weird one. Is this supposed to be a man?
(It can be anything you like.) *

This is the first time that the subject has made such a comment to a picture. Since this picture is the first of the more unstructured series, it is likely that the patient's comment is his reaction to this lack of structure, a desire for clarity which is consistent with his need for control. It is interesting, however, that he was quite able to recover and develop a coherent story.

The setting is back toward the beginning of the earth, not the beginning of the

The hero is experiencing difficulty in providing adequately for his family and thus despite the high-energy level and

---

* Comments in the parentheses are those made by the psychologist administering the test.

earth, but prehistoric times. The man, the little figure here is a man, has been out hunting food for the family. He is having a hard time of it.

His family is starving so he gets up in this path

drive spoken of earlier, it may now be suggested that the subject himself is experiencing some difficulty in keeping his family supplied as he sees fit.

Why is the family starving? The choices available to the subject are legion. It is suggested that fantasying the family in dire circumstances is a reflection of his hostility toward it. But since he is also engaged in getting food for it, his attitude toward the family is more adequately characterized as ambivalent. Seeing the family as starving also emphasizes the role he has to play.

and is suddenly attacked by this reptile coming out of the hole in the cliff

Press aggression.

and is partly afraid

The fear is not a total one — thus reflecting the subject's courage.

and knows he has to survive or his family doesn't.

The security of the family depends on the subject.

So the outcome is in ensuing battle between reptile and self. He conquers the reptile and at the same time the reptile furnishes food for his family and everybody is happy.

Again the subject conquers the odds and gains his end. Two additional factors appear here. First, the activity mentioned here is eating — this is an oral incorporative activity and is consistent with the ambitious strivings and acquisitiveness that have been manifest in the previous stories. The second factor to be pointed out is that it is unusual for the reptile to be eaten in the stories told to this picture. Usually it is sufficient for the reptile merely to be slain. It may be of some value here to attempt a symbolic interpretation of this material.

The story starts with the hero in search of food. This may be regarded as a reflection of his need for security. While seeking satisfaction for his needs he encounters the reptile — a male or penis

symbol — which represents a press masculine aggression and which threatens
to interfere with the satisfaction of his
needs. In this subject's case, it may
well be either his father or brothers or
both, as inferred from the previous stories. The subject does not fear the reptile completely; the need for security
(" to survive ") is strong and he solves
his problem by killing it and incorporat-
ing the penis orally. Thus he becomes
in his own right a male and has at the
same time the security he desires. Such
oral incorporative behavior is a childish
fantasy that seeks to become like that
which is incorporated, in this case the
male, and thus indicates that the subject felt weakness in his masculine
role. Combining this datum with the
previous material regarding his masculine exploits, it may be said that these
exploits are in the nature of a masculine protest. (Usually, " masculine protest " is used in referring to certain behavior patterns of women, but in its initial meaning it referred to males.)

It is interesting to note that the story
was cast in prehistoric times. In doing
so, the subject increases the distance between himself and the psychological significance of the material revealed.

The analysis of the symbolism in this
story was presented in order to account
for the unusual behavior in the story.
It should be pointed out that the dynamics obtained by such an analysis are consistent with the material obtained from
the nonsymbolic analysis of the other
stories. The reader who does not feel
adept in using such interpretation consequently would not have lost too much
material in this case.

Summary Picture #11: The subject finds it somewhat difficult to provide adequately for his family. There is a suggestion of repressed hostility toward the family, yet he sees himself as being the individual who is solely responsible for satisfying their wants. Feelings of inadequacy regarding his masculinity were also indicated, as was his attempt to make himself feel more secure.

TAT PROTOCOL	ANALYSIS AND INTERPRETATION

PICTURE #12

This is a story about a young man who falls in with bad companions and he is introduced to the older man in the picture who is a hypnotist and at the same time a thief, criminal.

This is the second story in which the hero almost strays from the straight and narrow. In this and in Story 10 the heroes are weak-willed and the asocial act is instigated by someone else (in this story the companions introduce the hero to the hypnotist). The projection of the asocial act onto others, it is suggested, is a function of his own repressed tendencies. Furthermore, it is also interesting to note that wherever the hero starts out passively, he almost gets himself into trouble. Consequently, it is suggested that keeping busy, for this subject, or striving to attain his ambition, may be motivated in part as a means of avoiding the indulgence of what he may regard as asocial and therefore ego-alien impulses.

At the moment of the picture the young man is being hypnotized by the older man. The older man has as his aim to send the younger man out on a job of robbery, or murder, let's make it murder,

The older man is dominant here and the asocial impulses are reflected in what the older man has in mind.

but the young boy being of strong will, this is against his will and he fails to carry out the assignment given him when he was hypnotized

The hypnotic suggestion does not take; consequently it is suggested that the subject has built up resistance or has strong defenses against asocial impulses. Yet he seems to have some guilt about these

but immediately goes to the police and confesses all.

impulses for he goes and confesses to the police, who might well be regarded as super-ego figures.

And that winds up the story and he's free to go on to a better life.

Not having given in to the impulses and having confessed them, he is able to go on to a better life.

Summary Picture #12: The subject experiences pressures from asocial impulses against which he has erected defenses. Experiencing these impulses does not leave him without guilt. However, the guilt does not become intolerable for him. Finally, it is also suggested that these asocial impulses come to the fore when he assumes a passive role. Consequently, it is conjectured that he strives to maintain a dominant position in order to check the inner tendencies.

TAT PROTOCOL

ANALYSIS AND INTERPRETATION

PICTURE #13

Hm — we'll make this a story about a young soldier who . . .

Note the change in storytelling manner here. The subject starts by saying, " Hm — we'll . . ." This is the first time he has reacted in this manner and it suggests that being directly confronted with a sexual stimulus may result in some difficulty for him.

during the course of the leave — furlough, goes to the big city and during the course of doing the rounds of the night spots

Need excitance.

is picked up by a girl. She, of course, takes him to her room; he spends the night there,

Note that need sex is dealt with in a passive manner by the subject. The girl takes the initiative in picking him up. If we consider this story in conjunction with the previous ones the theme here is not consistent with the others. In a good number of the previous stories the hero engages in some very masculine activities (shooting down 10 German planes, parachute jumping, etc.) but here in a frank heterosexual situation he is rather passive. This datum, it is suggested, corroborates the earlier suggestions regarding his feeling of weakness in a masculine role.

but in the cold light of dawn, he realizes what he has done the night before and gets out of the place as fast as he can. This makes him a real good kid. The memory of this night weighs heavily on his conscience; he knows that he can never become an upstanding citizen, so during the course of a battle, he exposes himself to battle and ends his life.

Satisfying his sexual needs in the type of situation described leads to guilt. Leaving the situation tends to diminish guilt for a while but his conscience is so strong that his behavior continues to weigh " heavily on his conscience." His act is an ineradicable blemish and results in suicide.

Note that in Stories 10 and 12, when the subject almost engaged in an asocial act, he was able to get out of it by confessing, but here when he indulged in an act which is not acceptable to him the guilt is too strong and leads to punishment. Two other hypotheses may be drawn from the comparison of these three stories. First, because he succumbs to need sex in this story and he did not succumb in the other stories suggests that his need sex may be strong and because it may get him into trouble has to be guarded against. Secondly, the subject, because of his conscience and the asocial tendencies which are striving for expression, may well have to devote energy to keep these impulses under control and thus is again described as a vigilant or tense person.

Boy! Be a lot of dead soldiers if they all did that.

Upon concluding the story and having gained some distance from it, the subject realizes the discrepancies between his own behavior or code and that of other males.

Summary Picture #13: Sex is a problem for this subject. When the subject assumes a passive role he is drawn into committing an act which is not consistent with the standards he wants to maintain. In this instance it is the sexual act when it is performed outside of a marital relationship.

He has a strong conscience and therefore intense guilt and need for punishment are aroused.

TAT PROTOCOL	ANALYSIS AND INTERPRETATION

PICTURE #14

This is a — make this a picture of a young astronomer who has been working very hard and is on the verge of a great discovery and immediately before this picture he has spent the night at the telescope and the great discovery is just a little bit beyond him. He can't come out with the answer. At the moment of the picture dawn is breaking, thus ending the night's work, gazing out toward new dawn and at the same time trying to figure out the new discovery, trying to perfect it. Outcome would be, to make it a happy ending, he does perfect the discovery and become famous.

The theme in the story is quite similar to those encountered previously. There is a strong desire for accomplishment which is achieved after strenuous application. Again the accomplishment occurs in the future and this plus the manner in which it is stated suggests that this is the subject's wish in this regard. Another item which is similar here with the other stories is the subject's tendency to overdramatize the difficulties that he encountered. The activity in the theme would be scored need cognizance.

Summary Picture #14: The subject is an energetic, hard worker with a strong need for achievement which he strives to fulfill. Need cognizance was also indicated.

TAT PROTOCOL	ANALYSIS AND INTERPRETATION

PICTURE #15

This is a picture of the surviving member of those last-man clubs. All of the members have died except this one man.

The hero has outdone all other men in this story just as he has in other stories. Only the content is different here. Underlying this is the competitive attitude once again, and his evaluation of the self.

At the moment of the picture he is standing in the cemetery surrounded by the

Loneliness and need affiliation are reflected in this story; even being better than the others is not completely satis-

graves of his friends and he is reliving some of his former life with his companions. All that he has left is his memories. He wants to join his friends and the outcome is in a few days he passes away in his sleep and joins his friends in the great beyond.

fying. It is rather interesting that the subject has not developed other stories in which he could satisfy his need affiliation with other people. The closest he came to it was in Story 9, but there it was more of a desire to attain respect from the siblings.

Summary Picture #15: The subject's competitive attitude and high evaluation of himself are reflected here. Data were also obtained regarding need affiliation and loneliness.

TAT PROTOCOL

ANALYSIS AND INTERPRETATION

PICTURE #16

Let's imagine a field of wheat waving in the breeze and there's a young farmer and his wife standing hand in hand looking over the field. This is the acme of their dreams in that they have waited and worked for quite a few years trying to produce a reasonably good crop and to pay off the mortgage on the farm. At the moment of the picture we have imagined, wheat has grown and is ready to be harvested and everything turns out fine. Wheat is excellent yield, pays off mortgage, and has enough to buy more land.

In contrast to previous achievement themes, this one is described as the " acme of their dreams " — and might be regarded as the final goal toward which the subject is striving, since the reader will recall that one of the primary motivating factors for his achievement themes in the previous stories was the subject's desire to prove himself. The final goal appears to be marital bliss and economic security.

In this story the couple stands hand in hand, suggesting the capacity to accept warmth and tenderness, but once again it is associated with success and economic security.

It is also interesting to note that warmth and tenderness are expressed toward the wife but that sexuality is expressed in Picture #13 toward a woman who might have been a prostitute. This suggests that the subject may have difficulty in integrating adequately physical sexual desires and the tender feelings that are associated with sex.

Note also that up until the last sentence of the story one might have suspected that the subject and his wife had achieved complete happiness. But no. The last sentence indicates that he still continues to acquire additional land, suggesting the intensity of his acquisitive needs.

The question may be raised regarding the selection of the farm for this story. In view of the fact that nothing is suggested by this picture it may well be that he does have a strong interest in farming. The biographical excerpt preceding the presentation of this case indicated that this subject is a father. The setting in the story told to this picture would have been a "natural" one for including children. Yet they are omitted. Why? One possibility is that the needs manifest in this story are so intense as to cause him to overlook them. Or, he may desire the wife's affection all for himself, without the children as competitors. In any case, it is suggested that there is a problem in this area.

Summary Picture #16: The acme of the subject's desire is to attain happiness in marriage and economic security. It is hypothesized that he may have a specific interest in farming. Possible lack of adequate integration of physical sexual desires and the tender feelings associated with sex is also suggested. His incorporative and acquisitive desires are very strong.

TAT PROTOCOL | ANALYSIS AND INTERPRETATION

PICTURE #17

We ought to make this one a sailor back in the days of | The theme of this story is very similar to Story 7 and to some of the other stories

old sailing ships. In a battle between the two ships, part of the rigging is shot away and needs to be repaired immediately. Because of the danger involved, the captain calls for volunteers and our young man in the picture bravely steps forward; and at the moment of the picture he's going aloft to work on the rigging.

where the subject saves the day for others and himself.

There are two stories in this series where things are broken — in this story and in the story to Picture #2. But there is an interesting difference between the two. In the story to Picture #2 the hero was a boy and the bicycle was repaired but no one is mentioned as having done the repairs. In this story to Picture #17 the hero is older and does the repairs. If the smashing of the bicycle and the breaking of the rigging are interpreted as castration, or in more meaningful psychological terms as feeling inadequate as a male, then it may be suggested that only later in life has the subject felt capable of overcoming or counteracting these feelings of inadequacy.

And the outcome is his efforts to save the ship and he achieves his ambitions of becoming a midshipman.

Realistic accomplishment such as that described in the first segment of this story results in reward. But in light of the intense ambition manifested by the subject in previous stories, it is rather interesting that the subject settles for " becoming a midshipman "; certainly becoming a midshipman after being a sailor is more realistic than becoming a captain. Consequently it may well be that the subject is realistic about what he is able to achieve.

Summary Picture #17: Although the statements regarding the subject's ambition are again supported, here the new datum is that the subject may well be realistic regarding what he is able to achieve.

TAT PROTOCOL	ANALYSIS AND INTERPRETATION

PICTURE #18

We'll have this young man, who is — because of financial trouble, I guess,

Economic difficulty and therefore failure in view of the subject's high need achievement leads to

is about to jump off the Golden Gate bridge.

the contemplation of suicide and from it we may infer depression. (Such depression is not uncommon in individuals with strong oral-incorporative needs.) It is interesting to note that even when suicide is contemplated it is in a very heroic fashion — the Golden Gate is selected.

The significance of the failure is further reflected by the fact that suicide is a rather unusual theme to this picture.

At the moment of the picture a passer-by has seized him to prevent the suicide. And the outcome would be that the man who saved him is able to help him out of his difficulty.

This is the first time in the stories told thus far that the protagonist in a story has been directly helped by another person. Thus when he is in difficulty he can receive help.

Summary Picture #18: Economic failure may result in depressive moods and intrapunitive reactions.

TAT PROTOCOL	ANALYSIS AND INTERPRETATION

PICTURE #19

Hm. Can I imagine another one here? (Subject is referring to Picture #16.) We'll make this a snow-covered cabin in the north woods and two trappers are snowed in inside. They've been snowed in a long time

The theme here starts with two men who are in close contact with each other. This results in suspicion. The question is, what are they suspicious about? The answer to this question will come later, but for the moment it should be noted that he does not trust others.

and are becoming quite suspicious of each other.

But they're old-timers at this and know what will happen if something isn't done to relieve the tension.

This suggests that suspiciousness or tension in interpersonal situations are not experiences which are entirely new for the subject and that the techniques which follow for dealing with this situation may be techniques which the subject has tried in the past.

Let's see, what do we have them do? — So they mark the cabin exactly in half and each moves his belongings into his half, and they cook their own food and so forth and don't try to talk to each other; and in this way, they survive the blizzard and then when spring thaw comes, they're still all right.

Internal controls are not sufficient to deal with the tension. A consciously contrived situation has to be developed in order to deal with the problem. And the control developed is a thoroughgoing one; it stops all possible communication between the two trappers. It should be noted that this technique is used rather than one in which the two individuals discuss their feelings toward each other and cooperatively develop a method of dealing with their problem. The situation in which this occurs is one in which both characters are of equal status; consequently it suggests of the subject that when he is in a situation with someone who appears as an equal, tension develops and that the only way in which this can be dealt with is by imposing rigid controls. (As will be seen in the next section, this matter of equality has to be refined somewhat.)

(What suspicion do they have of each other?) The one feels that he's doing most of the housework and the other feels that he's doing the major share.

The suspicions arise from a consideration of who is the dominated and who is the dominating person or with regard to feelings of being taken advantage of. Accepting the subject's statement as to the reasons for his suspicions and considering it together with some of the material which has been presented previously, it may be suggested that the subject's approach to social relationships demands that individuals must be divided into superior and subordinate positions, and his desire to achieve the superior is so great that if he cannot achieve his desire then free communication is not possible. The reason for seeking to establish the status of people in social relationships has been touched upon previously — e.g., the desire to prove himself pushes him into his desire to achieve the superior position. On the other hand, it has been observed that when he is in the subordinate or passive position, he is pulled into situations where asocial or ego-alien impulses come to the fore and thus it is to be avoided. The subject's response to the examiner was interpreted above in terms of its structure but additional data may be obtained by interpreting the content. Note that the content refers to a feminine activity. Analysis of the previous stories indicated that the subject was concerned about his masculinity. Considering the content of " housework " in conjunction with his concern regarding masculinity, it is suggested that the subject is dealing in this story with his fear of his homosexual impulses. Note, however, that he was able to develop control over these impulses in this story.

Summary Picture #19: In relationships that involve possible equals, the subject does not manifest trust. He appears to be quite sensitive to the status that each person has in a social relationship. He is concerned about being taken advantage of. To avoid conflict, the subject requires strong controls.

TAT Protocol	Analysis and Interpretation
Picture #20	
This is a young man on Christmas Eve who is walking through the streets; and it's snowing, of course. He has no family and is on Christmas Eve, so he's quite	Here we have a picture of loneliness and despondence which stems from the lack of friends.

despondent not having no place to go and no friends.

The outcome is that during the course of the walk, he meets with a group and — with a group, let's make it Christmas carolers to do it up right. They invite him to join them in their rounds.

The others take the initiative in establishing social contact. It is rather interesting to compare this and other stories in which the other figures take the initiative with those in which the hero takes the initiative. The latter are characterized by actions that involve the attaining of goals or the proving of oneself. The former are characterized by need affiliation or social or asocial impulses. Thus it may be suggested that in the subject's need repertoire he is more capable and more adept at putting into action the achievement motive but he has more difficulty in accepting his asocial impulses and in being adept at establishing social relationships to satisfy his need for affiliation.

And so he does and makes a — and finds that they're friendly people, and so he at last has friends on Christmas Eve.

The need affiliation becomes satisfied as a result of the initiative that the others have taken.

Summary Picture #20: Lack of friends results in loneliness and despondency. The subject does not have the technique for implementing the satisfaction of his need for affiliation. Others have, and take the initiative to help him in this regard.

Final TAT Summary

This subject is an ambitious and striving individual with a high level of aspiration. To achieve his goals he is capable of applying and willing to apply himself energetically and conscientiously. In the face of obstacles he perseveres and applies himself diligently until he has achieved his goal. He is not one to expect that he can attain his aims without expending effort. The work which gratifies him most at the present time is that which has social prestige or status attached to it, for he is an upwardly mobile person. The work might well be professional in nature or executive-administrative, where he is in a dominant position. His immediate goal is to attain job security and his more distant goals are retirement and happiness with his family. His drive, however, is so strong that it will probably be quite some time before he decides that he has arrived. Associated with his need for achievement are his desires for recognition, approval, and dominance.

Underlying the need for achievement and the other factors indicated above is his feeling of inadequacy as specifically related to his masculinity. He compensates for this by a strong desire to prove himself, to prove that he is a man equal to if not better than other men. He is unaware of the dynamics of this situation and it is unlikely that he is conscious of any anxiety that he would relate to it, although its effects are no doubt apparent in his behavior. He is not an introspective person who would be inclined to seek the dynamic roots of his behavior. On the contrary, he is more inclined to be a doer, generally directing his energies externally rather than internally. When he does ruminate, and he is inclined to do so when he is frustrated and his autonomous actions are interfered with, he is more inclined to think about his lack of success or his hurt feelings rather than his motivation.

Although the ambition is intense, as indicated above, it is suggested that he is not likely to be a " pushing " or aggressive individual. He has difficulty in dealing adequately with social relationships, especially with the feelings of hostility that these situations might stimulate, and too close contact might reveal his inadequacy. These factors may well interfere with his capacity to be assertive and to be dominant. Thus while he desires positions of dominance he is frustrated in this regard.

Emotionally this man is a controlled individual. A good portion of his energies is directed to holding hostile feelings in check and to repressing sexual desires. He has the capacity to express the more tender and warm emotions but this is dependent on how secure he feels in his job and how well he thinks he is achieving his goals. To express warm feelings without the feeling of adequacy that comes from achievement would likely be regarded by him as a sign of weakness. One significant means for dealing with his tension is to utilize his job as an outlet for his energies. To be sure, this is not a completely satisfactory means of dealing with his repressed desires, for they are constantly pressing forward for expression.

This subject regards himself as a capable and talented person with a good deal of ability. At first sight this might appear to contradict a previous statement regarding feelings of inadequacy. However, this is not so, for his feeling of self-worth or his positive self-regard is apparent primarily in his field of work. That is, he regards himself as a " good man " in his chosen profession, while the feelings of inadequacy refer to interpersonal situations of a more informal variety, where he may have to form closer ties with others. In other words, his major source of ego-income is what he can accomplish on the job. It is also likely that only later in life did he come to regard himself as possessing the means of attaining ego-satisfaction, while earlier in life feelings of inadequacy may have been more intense.

The subject approaches problem-solving situations in an orderly and systematic fashion. He is not inclined to get sidetracked by minute details but rather concentrates on appropriate and relevant issues. His habits in this regard are such as to emphasize neatness and cleanliness. Such behavior requires almost conscious effort on his part and there is some evidence to suggest that he would much prefer to relax these standards. Relaxation of these standards, however, might also result in the relaxation of the controls which are imposed over instinctual desires. Since these might stimulate too much anxiety, it is unlikely that he will be able to achieve the relaxed manner he desires without outside aid. Another aspect of his problem-solving behavior is that he is inclined to communicate his results in a concise and laconic fashion.

The subject does not find it easy to establish social relationships. He tends to be suspicious of other people and is concerned that they may interfere with his desire for autonomous behavior. He also sees social relationships in terms of status and a dominance-submission hierarchy and is concerned that he may be placed in a submissive role which he tries to avoid; he tends to be a " lone wolf." This results in feelings of isolation, loneliness, and depression. At such times, if others take the initiative and invite him into or include him in their group he welcomes their action. Thus while he can initiate action with regard to work and achievement, he is not as effective in social situations.

Older male figures who have achieved success in their fields serve as models for him. He seeks to emulate their success and his self-confidence described above stands him in good stead in this regard. He seeks to prove to them through realistic achievements what he has to offer and thus gains not only prospects for advancement but also recognition. A probable source for this behavior may well be in his early relationship with his father and male siblings — a source also for his desire to prove himself as a male. Because of the role that older male figures have in his framework and because of his strong need achievement and the dynamics underlying and associated with it as described above, it is likely that he is apt to see peers in his own field as competitors.

Female figures serve as a source of love and affection for him. He gains this also only through accomplishment. The source here may also lie in his early relationship with his mother, in which he may have attempted to prove to her that he was as good as his father and brothers. Although both in this instance and in the situation described previously the source of his behavior may stem from early childhood relationships, the subject is not completely dependent on family ties for gratification. He is not dependent on his family of origin but has been able to find other persons more appropriate with his present station for the development of object-relationships. In the area of heterosexual relationships he tends to dissociate need sex from love and affection. He may well have some conflict in integrating the picture of the idealized female and the female as a sex object.

Insofar as his family is concerned, he sees himself as the provider. Consequently economic security is an important factor to him. Children do not appear in his stories and fantasies and this may be an area of tension. One gets the impression that he feels that after having achieved success he and his wife alone can attain happiness.

The subject is not fixated in the past. The present for him is a time for channelizing his effort to achieve success in the future. With regard to the future he is somewhat concerned but nevertheless on the hopeful and optimistic side.

Notes from C. B.'s Case Folder *

C. B. was born 35 years ago on a farm on the East coast. Both parents are still alive and neither had more than an elementary school education. During the depression his father gave up the farm and went into business. The subject would like to return to the farm on which he was born but feels that there is no opportunity for someone with his training there.

The family is described as being in the " lower, lower . . . great big middle class." The family owned its own home, never had anything extra, and was accepted by the other members of the community. Since the children have grown up and have become moderately successful the parents have gained in status in the community.

The father is described as a good worker who ran the household. The mother was a churchwoman. The relationship between the parents is described as harmonious and neither is regarded by C. B. as a favorite, although he was more respectful of his father. Religious atmosphere in the home was rather strict; the children were not permitted to smoke or drink, but " none of these took."

C. B. says he had relatively little contact with all except his next oldest sibling, a brother. All siblings, including the subject, have graduate degrees and with the exception of the subject, who is presently employed as a research scientist in an industrial organization, they are now engaged in a cooperative business venture.

The subject has had conflicts with two siblings. One of them a good deal older than our subject " always got away with things " and even at the present the subject does not approve of this brother's marital and extramarital behavior. With the next older brother C. B. had a good number of fights in childhood. His parents would let the two of them

---

* The material presented above is a condensation of C. B.'s remarks during an autobiographical interview with him. No interpretation of these remarks is made.

"fight it out" until they saw that C. B. was getting too much punishment and then they would interfere — for which interference C. B. was thankful. He and his brother, however, would gang up against the other kids in the neighborhood. During adolescence the competitiveness still continued. They would compete for the same women and it was as a result of this competition that he had his first experience in intercourse during adolescence. The two would vie with each other to see "who can get the mostest."

Aside from his brother, his social contacts during childhood were generally limited to one boy companion, although he did have other acquaintances. During this period he also had as an ideal a fictitious character who lived by himself and who was not bothered by such people as his brother. In general, the subject describes himself as self-confident at home but shy away from home.

The subject does not recall much of his early childhood experiences. He had the usual childhood diseases — his brother would get them first and pass them on to him. He does remember being breast fed, being weaned at an early age, probably "played with my feces because I know my children do." He also recalls that his mother regarded him as the best baby she ever had but cannot elaborate on this.

C. B. has a professional degree. During grade school and high school his grades were very good. His grades in the first graduate school he attended were low because of his interest in the co-eds. He therefore transferred to another institution where there would be less temptation. But his training here was interrupted by his enlistment in the armed services.

He supported himself during college. He engaged in athletics but never had major achievements in this area because he was too short.

During the time he served in the armed services he saw a lot of action. He was never afraid because things were going too fast. If anything, he always had "a feeling of exhilaration" after the battle was over. He says he had no difficulty in adjusting to civilian life, and returned to complete his education.

Since he had already been married by the time he left the service, he returned to school with more serious intentions. His grades improved and he took a prominent role in extracurricular activities that were more in keeping with his professional interests. Despite his role in such activities he does not regard himself as a leader but a follower, and says that if it were not a small clique he belonged to he would have taken a much less prominent part. The others selected him, however, because he was the oldest in the group.

He does not describe his wife in terms of personality characteristics but in terms of her attractive appearance. The two discuss his work and are of one mind in training their children. He would like them all to be good citizens, and possibly to have one of them follow in his footsteps.

He had a difficult time with his first child, whom he would discipline by beating. He has since learned to control his temper.

C. B. says he was always interested in science. In childhood he was influenced by the biographies of famous persons; in adolescence an older friend permitted him to experiment in his laboratory, and in graduate school a major professor always had an eye on him because C. B. was so situated that he could always be seen by the professor while the latter was outside.

In referring to the satisfaction he got from his work he says, ". . . partially (it was) actually showing them (his findings) off to somebody else, showing I could do something, and also discovering new things." At the present time he has the further satisfactions that his work " is an exacting, clean-cut thing and when it happens it's right here. You don't have to dilly-dally around there. And, oh, probably I get some satisfaction out of . . . people in my profession are rare." He has the greatest faith in the ability of people in his field and believes that the future of society is in their hands.

His ideal superior is one who would tell him how he is doing and when he is doing well would leave him alone. He does not like his subordinates to be dependent on him but to carry out what he prescribes for them to do. His present position is a good one, for he has freedom — he is a " free agent."

One of his shortcomings he regards as lack of poise and self-confidence in social relationships and he admires individuals who have them. He believes he is well liked by others but has no interest in "small talk." His colleagues and superiors limit their contact with him to the job. He does not socialize with them outside of work.

As to his future, he anticipates competition and indifference on the negative side and recognition, goodwill, and respect on the positive side. As to society in the future, he hopes that through the effort of the people things will gradually straighten themselves out so that " we can enjoy life, enjoy companionship." In such a world he would like to be " just one of the people " and " perhaps " make a contribution to knowledge.

CHAPTER 7

A WOMAN COMES FOR THERAPY

The Case of Mrs. Oak

Mrs. Oak is a woman in her late thirties who is married and the mother of two children.

TAT PROTOCOL	ANALYSIS AND INTERPRETATION

PICTURE #1 *

10″ Well, you can't really tell

After a slight pause and some hesitancy, the client uses the second person pronoun "you." Interpreting this quite literally, she might be saying that the examiner can't really tell what is going on in the picture. And, if this is so, then she might use the implicit freedom in this statement to do what she wants to or she might retreat from this freedom. On the other hand, the "you" in her statement may stand for "I" but why does she not say so? Perhaps to say so would be a more assertive act, a sign of independence, and because it is a self-referent it also leaves her as the locus of responsibility. If this hypothesis is valid, then underlying it may be an inadequate self-concept or poor ego-integration. Furthermore, the fact that it is not "I" but "you" also suggests that one of the client's defense mechanisms against her own felt inadequacy is projection — she sees in others what are her own shortcomings. To evaluate this tendency to project, one must bear in mind that the test situation has just begun, and it may be that only under the initial stress of the test situation does

---

* The protocol presented above was electrically recorded and then transcribed by the research staff of the Counseling Center of the University of Chicago. The author wishes to thank Dr. Carl Rogers for permission to present this case here.

this projection occur. Consequently, it will be necessary to check on other such circumstances in the remainder of the protocol. It may well be that as we continue to analyze the stories that follow, the subject may either revert to herself and give more expression to her own feelings of inadequacy and her tendency to project will increase, or if the anxiety diminishes or if we have overestimated it, that her approach will become more objective.

The " can't really tell " suggests her uncertainty and this continues in the second segment that follows. Her awareness of the unstructured nature of the picture suggests that she might have preferred more structure in the environment; this would give her something to lean on and would balance the indefiniteness she feels inside. It is here one may see how the relatively weak personality structure affects the perception of the external world.

whether the boy is unhappy or, or just pensive,

This tells us what she is indecisive about in the picture. Note that she uses feeling and thinking terms — both of these refer to two aspects of personality. The use of these two words in such close connection suggests that the client herself may well be in conflict regarding these two aspects in her own personality. Thus it may be that neither the feeling approach to life nor the thinking or rational one has resulted in adequate satisfaction. She can trust neither as a means of attaining the goals or the satisfactions she desires, for they may well be in conflict with each other; what her feelings tell her is not consistent with how she analyzes or thinks about a situation. The use of the word " pensive " also deserves comment. The fact that she does use this word appropriately suggests that the client may well be fairly well educated and that her intellectual level is high. Furthermore, it is also possible, and this hypothesis we can only check with the data that follow, that the use of this word, rather than saying " thinking," may reflect her intellectual aspirations and that she sees herself, in part at least, as an intellectual individual.

but, uh, it would seem to me that he is — isn't particularly happy,

The subject decides that the hero is not happy and this, it is suggested, is a reflection of her own unhappiness. The fact that the feeling aspect of the dichotomy is selected may well indicate that this is predominant in her personality.

that, uh, probably there's a, a drive for achievement that would be too much for a child that age.

Here we have one of the reasons for the subject's unhappiness: her level of aspiration may be out of keeping with her ability to attain it. The stated drive may also be cited as evidence for the previous suggestions regarding her desired role as an intellectual — that she may wish to attain a role for which she is presently not prepared.

One should also observe the level on which this story takes place. The subject does not describe or discuss any of the hero's actions or activities. She refers primarily to his inner state and motivation. This suggests that the subject is not an outgoing person but rather someone who is concerned with these two areas in her own life — inner states and motivations.

I wouldn't know whether it could be from his parents or someone he's known that he's trying to live up to.

One of the differences between the beginning of the story and the part that follows is the fact that the subject, with increasing frequency, utilizes the personal pronoun " I," thereby indicating that the psychological distance between the self and the test or testing situation is decreased. In so doing she reveals the extent to which she is involved with herself. If this predominates it might well be suggested that the subject is self-centered. It also suggests that the projection referred to above may be reaction to stress but after she calms down she gets closer to herself.

The client says, " I wouldn't know . . . ," yet she continues with the story to suggest she does know. The not knowing, it is hypothesized, suggests her attempt at denial but the fact that the material does come out indicates that it is rather strong.

The segment of the story in the left-hand column indicates the source for the achievement drive. It is an outside source and not internalized. This may well be the conflict in herself — the external pressures require behavior that does not conform with her own needs. In any case, the subject expresses a need to live up to external standards. (Note the difference between this case and the case of C. B. In both cases there were models to live up to. C. B. internalized them, while Mrs. Oak feels it as an external force, and this suggests the presence of a conflict in this regard. To see the contrast between someone who is relatively more outgoing and action-oriented, the reader is again referred to the first case.)

Uh . . . I rather hope that he'll just sort of put this behind him and go out and have some fun.

On a wishful level, the subject desires for the hero (herself) that he would not have this drive and not live up to the models that are set before him. It should also be noted that the desire for fun occurs in a comment about the hero by the subject. It is as if it might be too much for the subject to see this desire in the hero for it may, therefore, be too much evidence for possible conflict between the hero and the characters in the story. It is as if the subject were afraid to permit herself the expression of this conflict even in the storytelling situation. It also suggests that living up to the outside models is a strain — " no fun," and that she would like to be more relaxed.

And as for the outcome of it, uh, I just don't know . . . I'm just . . . he probably won't. He'll probably try to please. That's about all, I think.
1′ 40″

When the subject gets to the outcome, she is rather hesitant and disjunctive. Her conclusion is a submissive one; she gives in to the external forces. She does not satisfy her own needs. The fact that she objected to these external forces previously and then submits suggests that hostility should be aroused. Since it is not mentioned, it is hypothesized that it may be repressed. The disjunctivity may well be a manifestation of the conflict she herself experienced, and indicates that under stress her thought process may be disjunctive.

Summary Picture #1: The client appears to have a relatively weak ego-structure or inadequate self-concept. She may be inclined to lean on external sources of support. She feels she has standards to live up to and this causes quite a strain for her. Although she would like to get out of this situation and relax, she submits to the external pressure. This may well result in feelings of hostility but they now appear repressed. The client is engrossed in her feelings and thoughts, and of the two the first predominates. Under stress her thought process is apt to become disjunctive and she is apt to project her own feelings onto others. As the stress diminishes and she calms down her tendency to project diminishes and she becomes more engrossed in herself. Denial as a defense mechanism is also indicated.

TAT PROTOCOL   ANALYSIS AND INTERPRETATION

PICTURE #2

13″ Well, I th— I think of rather hardy pioneer stock (words lost) uh, good values and certainly not, not any tension.

In this segment there is an instance of one of the problems involved in the recording of TAT stories — words are lost. As in this protocol, whenever this happens it should be indicated. Fortunately, there is still sufficient material available for interpretation.

The figures are described as hardy stock. This may well reflect her own ability to work hard. The fact that she refers to them as " pioneer " suggests that this is her first family or family of origin from whom she may have learned the value of working hard.

The client denies the existence of tension in the picture. However, it is likely that she would not be aware of this if she herself were not under tension. Talking about the tension in the negative suggests that she may try to deny it or it may indicate once again her desire to get away from this tension and relax.

Note further that good values and tension do not go together for her. Building on the assumption that she is tense, it is further suggested that one of the reasons for her tension may be that she believes her values are wrong. In the light of the first story, one of the values that may result in tension is the submissiveness she spoke about earlier.

The, the, uh, girl seems to, uh, want to learn things,

This is need cognizance. The desire to learn things is consistent with the previous suggestions regarding her positive cathexis for an intellectual role. In view of the fact that a book does appear in the picture, this interpretation should not be weighted unless it is supported by other data.

but I don't think that, uh, what she learns is going to confuse her. She's going to use it well.

The statement here is an odd one. Although there is a desire for knowledge, it is possible, so the subject thinks, that too much knowledge may be confusing or, in the light of the last sentence, that the knowledge that a person has may be used erroneously. The reasons for this are probably manifold, but we may sug-

gest a few possibilities. Lots of knowledge for a person who, like the subject,
is submissive, may result in problems because she never utilizes the knowledge
and yet she may feel the pressure to utilize it. It may also be that new knowledge may open up vistas for the subject
which are contrary to her background
and present situation and she may then
experience conflict in seeking to decide
in which area to cast her lot. These are
only two hypotheses which we need
check in the material which follows.
Her positive statement that the girl is
going to use her knowledge well may be
regarded as a positive intention which
may not be manifest in action because
she does not yet appear to be an active
person. Finally, it is suggested that the
data here with regard to " learning " refer to her anticipation of therapy and
her feelings about it.

And, uh, I don't see a — any
connection between the man
and the girl.   Probably
should be, but there isn't
any . . . far as I can see.

The possibility of a relationship between the man and the girl is denied by
the subject. This sentence construction
is rather interesting for it implies either
that the subject may have thought of
the possibility that such a relationship
could exist or she may desire such a relationship and then she denies it. The
content of the sentence also suggests
problems in the area of heterosexual relationships.

Another hypothesis based on this story
is that the subject may have felt rather
acutely involved in seeking to attract
her father's attention or in effecting a
relationship with him in competition
with her mother. The reason for this
suggestion is that frequently the woman
against the tree and the man are seen as
parents or husband and wife. (The latter in this case would have been plausi-

ble, since the woman is seen as pregnant.) Since the subject speaks of a possible relationship between the man and the young girl, it is suggested that she may have sought to take the mother's role (either in reality or fantasy). The father is the preferred one of the parents. This hypothesis, on the face of it, may appear rather tenuous, and it can only be checked against the data that follow.

And the woman at the tree . . . probably pregnant . . . but, uh, it's a good bit a feeling of, of, uh, being at ease, per— at, at, at ease in the world.

The fact that the subject perceives the woman against the tree as being pregnant, and this is followed by the comment that she is at ease, suggests the hypothesis that sexual gratification or motherhood are states that are satisfying to the subject and that not having them may result in tension. Again ease appears as a positively cathected state — one that the client does not have for herself.

(Pause) I, I would say that, that, uh, by and large the, the, the outcome looks pretty healthy. I feel like a, a healthy kind of a sense to this one. Sort of a, a relaxed goodness to the thing.

There is no interaction among the characters in this story. The only tentative one that was suggested was between the man and the young girl but this was mentioned and dropped. Despite the lack of interaction which reflects her difficulties in interpersonal relationships as well as her difficulty in heterosexual situations, the client turns to the outcome. She appears to be using the instructions as a means of getting out of her predicament.

In dealing with an outcome she comments on the picture in terms of the feeling she gets from it, thus reinforcing the hypothesis that she is involved with feelings to a large extent. Just why she should get this positive feeling it is hard to say unless the relaxed state she referred to in describing the woman in the picture is the state she desires for herself.

And I'm not the least bit concerned for these people. They'll be all right.
1′ 27″

And, if so, it is a hopeful note with regard to therapy.

Here in the last sentence, it is apparent that the distance between the subject and the card is further increased. Her statement says that people who are healthy she need not care about. This suggests that she may be concerned about people who are not healthy and dynamically this may be related to the fact that she does not regard herself as healthy. Thus the basis of her relationship with them is identification. Furthermore, her comment also suggests that "unhealthy" or tense people need care and since she falls in this group, this is what she needs.

Summary Picture #2: The client has difficulties in interpersonal relationships and specifically in heterosexual ones. This may well be based on her relationships with her parents, in which she was attracted to her father but her needs were not satisfied. She is a tense person and this tension may be related to her feeling that she has the wrong values. She is concerned that what she may learn in therapy may confuse her but she intends to use it well. She associates sexual participation or motherhood with a good state of being. She reacts to situations in terms of her feelings and may well identify with the underdog. She feels she needs help.

TAT PROTOCOL

ANALYSIS AND INTERPRETATION

PICTURE #3

4½″ Well, life can just be too much sometimes. I wouldn't know what she's so despondent about but, uh, think it's kind of a complete dejection, frustration of a kind and I . . . and there's just no help, no, uh, uh, things are just too much . . .

Life can be quite stressful for our subject. The client feels despondent, dejected, and frustrated. There is also a helpless feeling here with respect to the possibility of getting help for her difficulties.

Oh, uh, probably what brought this on was the loss of someone who is a kind of prop to the . . .

One possible source of the depressive tendencies is given us by the subject — the loss of someone who served as prop. This sentence also reflects the strong dependent needs of the subject. It also suggests that the therapist may well need to be aware of these feelings, for the client may be inclined to use him as a prop too.

I, I wouldn't know whether it, it would be a man or . . . I don't think so.

Again the subject denies, and thereby emphasizes for us, the fact that a man has served in a critical role as a prop for her.

Uh, the outcome, well, she'll go on but I, I rather doubt whether she'll be straightened out. I see a . . . it's . . . I just have the feeling that she isn't going to find her way.
2′

The dejection is rather intense here, as is her doubt as to the future.

Note the difference between the reactions to Picture #2 and this picture. In the former she was more optimistic than in the latter. This suggests her ambivalence with regard to the future and the fact that she may well be subject to mood swings. Also note that in Picture #2 the heroine was going to learn things and here she was left to her own devices and therefore the pessimism is intensified.

Summary to Picture #3: The subject tends to be despondent, frustrated, and dejected. These feelings are associated with having lost someone who can serve as support for her dependent needs. It is also suggested that at this point she may be ambivalent as to the outcome of therapy.

TAT PROTOCOL

ANALYSIS AND INTERPRETATION

PICTURE #4
7″ I think this is a happy kind of thing. Uh, two young people, uh, who aren't going to be bogged down by life.

Just as in Picture #3, life appears to be a stress and strain for our subject. She appears to have the feeling that life can be full of happiness but there is always the possibility of becoming bogged down.

They're not going to try to, uh, to maintain a, well, a

In the analysis of the first story, it was suggested that one of the sources of the

kind of keeping up with the Joneses, and they're going to have an awful lot of fun.

subject's difficulties may be her submissiveness to others' standards. This hypothesis is substantiated in this story. In this story the additional datum that is obtained refers to her class consciousness and social status needs. " Keeping up with the Joneses," however, puts a strain on her. Another similarity between this story and the first should be noted. In both of them there is the choice between living up to models that others set and those that she can set for herself. In those that she sets for herself, she emphasizes " fun." This may reflect her desire to escape the pressures that have developed and to discharge the tension that has accumulated.

Uh, oh, I suppose they met recently or not too long, uh, ago. I don't know whether they're married or not . . . it just doesn't seem very important.

For our client a positive attitude toward life need not necessarily come from a marital relationship but in a relationship with a male. In view of what was said previously in the above analysis and because the couple in this story need not necessarily be married, this suggests that her own marital relationship may not be satisfying. Because of her previous attempts at denial it is suggested that marriage is important to her but if the dependent needs pointed out above are intense, then she may not be able to establish a mature relationship.

But, they, I, I have the feeling, they're, they're, they aren't going to have much trouble, they're going to have fun.

She appears to fear the possibility that she will encounter trouble. It is almost as if she may anticipate it and therefore find it.

Uh, she's a very vivacious kind of, of, uh, person, and, uh, he seems rather, uh, serious and he has a lot of awfully good stuff in him, I think. And then as I said, the whole thing is, is, is, is

Here the client gives us the elements that are necessary for the positive relationship she desires, a feminine, girlish woman and a mature male. It is likely from her description of the girl in Picture #3 that she is far from being like the heroine in this picture and thus she may

a, uh, a cheerful pleasant kind of thing. In fact it's a very nice picture and I like it.   1' 52"

feel far from being able to attain the ideal romantic relationship she describes in this picture.

It is further interesting to note that the stories usually told to this picture involve a conflict between the two individuals. In marked contrast to these, our subject tells a very positively toned story. In view of this discrepancy and because she reacts so much in terms of feelings, it is hypothesized that the client may desire the kind of heterosexual relationship discussed here but it is on the level of wish and not one that is as yet available to the client.

Summary Picture #4: The client believes that happiness can be secured but there is always the possibility of difficulties. Her frustration tolerance with regard to these difficulties is rather low and one gains the impression that she anticipates these difficulties and therefore finds them. Happiness for her would mean a relationship in which she can play the feminine girlish role with a mature male. While marriage may be important for her it is unlikely that she can have a mature relationship with this attitude. Marital difficulties are also indicated.

TAT PROTOCOL

ANALYSIS AND INTERPRETATION

PICTURE #5

8" This is a woman who is, uh, rather filled with apprehension.

The client sees apprehension in the woman in the picture and this is regarded as a reflection of her own state.

What kind I don't know and she probably doesn't know.

It seems that the apprehension is generalized and nothing specific; therefore she does not believe she knows what it is. It may also be that the apprehension is so intense that she may not wish to probe this matter.

Note that the subject differentiates " I " and " she." It is as if one had expected the woman in the picture to be a living being. This suggests the possible looseness of ego-boundaries as a result of the intense emotion.

They, uh — Just what was in the background to make her feel like that, uh, well, that's hard to say too. She's certainly very unhappy and, uh, well, lonely. Well, I feel sorry for her and the, the outcome I just, uh, it's difficult. I don't know. 1′ 59″

The client starts speaking of "they" and then drops it. This suggests that she may know that her difficulty lies in an interpersonal situation but will not speak of it at this time.

Loneliness and unhappiness are again revealed here. The client feels sorry for the heroine and this, it is suggested, is based on her identification with her as pointed out above. And once again the outcome is "difficult."

It should be noted that in Stories 2 and 4 the outcomes are positive but in Stories 3 and 5 they are on the negative side. An important difference between these two sets of pictures is that the former portray social situations including males, and the latter portray only a single female. This suggests that her optimistic feelings are effected by the stimulation she receives from social interaction (in terms related to the behavior hypothesized above) and her dependence on them, for when she is left alone she becomes depressed.

Summary Picture #5: The client is an apprehensive person who does not wish to focus on the source of her anxiety and therefore she may experience it as diffuse anxiety. Being alone results in feelings of unhappiness and loneliness. Her dependence on social interactions rather than herself as a source of strength was also hypothesized.

TAT PROTOCOL

ANALYSIS AND INTERPRETATION

PICTURE #6
4″ This one I like too, but, uh, makes me feel like some, some very stimulating conversation going on.

The communication with the external environment is perceived as occurring through feelings. The statement "makes me feel" may be contrasted with the approach of saying "there is a very stimulating conversation going on." But rather than objectifying the situation the client personalizes it.

The, the uh, the uh, it's probably at a party and the girl is young and, uh, terribly pleased because she can, uh, impressing so worldly a man.

The satisfaction with the self comes when the subject is able to impress others and, more specifically in this situation, a " worldly man."

And, uh, and he is apparently intrigued with her.

This attitude is reciprocated by the man.

Uh, nothing much will come of this, but it, it's, uh, on the whole very pleasant.

The relationship between the two can go " just so far." It is interesting that even on a fantasy level of telling stories the subject cannot permit herself a more thoroughgoing and satisfying relationship. In view of the material obtained previously it is likely that the subject does not permit herself to develop this relationship further because she anticipates failure, and this failure may be dynamically related to her tendency to prefer a dependent relationship.

And he looks as though he knows a great deal, I mean a great many things and, uh, he's an acceptant kind of person.

Here are characteristics of a male whom she can cathect positively. He has to know a great deal and be accepting.

And she is, uh, is, well, she isn't at all sure of herself, but awfully cute and, uh, quite pleased.

Here there is a contrast between her emphasis on internal and external factors. She is not sure of herself but feels more certain of her physical attributes. It is likely that her not being sure of herself is an obstacle to achieving a more stable relationship with men she cathects.

The outcome of this is, it will probably be nothing except a pleasant kind of experience for both of them. 2′ 24″

The present is enjoyed for what it is worth and the relationship does not go too far.

Summary Picture #6: The type of male the client cathects is one who is worldly wise and acceptant of her. In this situation she is unable to carry it through to a complete relationship because she is uncertain of herself and uncertain that she will achieve the kind of acceptance she desires.

TAT Protocol	Analysis and Interpretation

PICTURE #7

14″ Well, this picture I don't particularly like. I, I, it seems to me an artificial kind of a thing.

In contrast to the situation described above, which involved a positive heterosexual relationship, here we find that a situation involving mother and child is described as an artificial situation and in general terms it may be regarded as a negative situation.

Well, uh, the child, I feel, is being a good child because, well, it's expected of her,

The " good " behavior arises not because the child believes that it is rewarded as an end in itself but rather because good behavior is expected by others. In other words, behavior is not determined because of internal factors but because of external ones — or the expectations of others. This may be the factor that inhibits the client. It is what she believes to be the expectations of others that stifles her own spontaneity.

and the, uh, mother is being a good mother in quotes. She's doing the things that she thinks is, is going to make the child a presentable kind of person.

Like the child, the mother's emphasis is on making the child " presentable." This again reflects the importance of others. But the client's dissatisfaction with this attitude is apparent, in that she speaks of a " good mother in quotes." Thus her previous statement of artificiality becomes more clear. It is that the externals are there — the good behavior of the child, and the mother's motivation to keep the child presentable — but the basis or the foundation for the relationship may be unsatisfactory.

I don't get any feeling of, of genuine warmth there. I don't think that she, she's able to give the child what

The inadequacy of the relationship stems from the fact that it is lacking in warmth. A critical aspect of this is that the adult woman is incapable of mani-

the child actually needs for its growth.

festing warmth. Thus it may be suggested that the client finds dissatisfaction in her own relationship with her child or children because she is unable to establish a warm relationship. Whether she herself experiences or experienced lack of warmth in her own relationship with her mother is a hypothesis that has not been suggested previously but it is certainly one that should be considered here. If the woman in Picture #2 was her mother, then it is very likely that the client herself did not experience warmth with her mother.

And the outcome will be just like so many of these things. (words lost) uh, girl will grow up without too much, uh, sensitivity and she'll proceed to raise her children in the same way. And she'll proceed to raise her children in the same way. And the mother will have done a good job, and that's all. 1' 57"

This segment may well reinforce the last sentence, for she sees the pattern continued through a generation. It may also reflect her belief that her own children will repeat her behavior with them, with their children. They will be insensitive to their children's needs. Furthermore, the fact that there is no change in the behavior even though she is aware of what is wrong with the relationship is a reflection of poor ego-strength.

Note that the mother is said to have done " a good job." This is exactly the opposite of what she has done and may be an attempt to rationalize her own behavior and also her inability to express hostility with regard to the poor job that was done.

Combining the material from the previous stories with the datum regarding the lack of warmth toward her own children here, it may be suggested that her own dependent and " girlish " (or infantile) needs are so strong that she herself wants what her children ask her to give. It is apparent that she will have difficulties in this regard.

Summary Picture #7: The client finds mother-child relationships unsatisfactory because they are lacking in warmth. There is an emphasis on what others may think of one's behavior and therefore spontaneity is inhibited. The client is aware of what is missing in her relationship, but is unable to do anything about it. It is hypothesized that the client may have experienced cold relationships with her own mother, and also that her inability to give to her children may be related to her own intense desires in this regard.

TAT PROTOCOL	ANALYSIS AND INTERPRETATION

PICTURE #8

5″ Oh, this is a girl who, who's, uh, who's finally doing whatever it is she wanted to do. Now just what it is I don't know, but I have a feeling that it's something absolutely removed from her, uh, previous background.

The client has grown dissatisfied with her previous behavior. She does not have a completely formulated plan in mind but, whatever it is, it is going to be very different from the past. The desire to change is a positive sign. The intensity of the reversal may well refer to her intense dissatisfaction with her present state.

Uh, maybe she's going to paint, maybe she's going to sculpt, but it's something removed, that she, she, uh, never even allowed herself to dream of, and it wouldn't be possible for her to do. And, uh, she's terribly pleased with the whole thing.

Creative urges are being stimulated within her. It is important to note that her desires are for solitary creative activities; this does not mean to underestimate their significance, but it is interesting to note that she does not speak of creative interpersonal relationships. It may well be that she requires the experience of creating by herself before she ventures off into interpersonal situations. Finally, it should also be noted that she regards the creative activities she speaks of as far removed from what she has been doing, and therefore it might be regarded as a manifestation of how dull she regards her present environment. Note also how constricted she feels because she " never even allowed herself to dream of " these things because she did not think it possible that she would do them.

Uh, she's a, a girl who is, has always gone along doing

The reason for her " lack of creativity " or capacity to manifest her own individ-

what, what other people thought she should, should do, and trying to do the right thing.

And, uh, finally as I said she's going to do what she wants to do, and she isn't going to let anything stop her.

And while she isn't going to be hilarious about it, she's going to be terribly pleased and terribly satisfied. And on the whole, uh, quite contented. I don't think she's going to do any kind of great work or any kind of terribly important work, but she's going to please herself. And in pleasing herself, she's, uh, she's certainly going to be a, a much nicer person than she has been. (No time recorded)

uality, if we want to speak of it that way, is that she is living her life in terms of what others expected of her. And in her own terms the "right thing" is that which others expect of her.

This is the goal that she desires to achieve — freedom for herself.

The word "hilarious" suggests that the client is almost carried away with the idea. But this subsides and the client brings her goals within reach. It is obvious that she has been emphasizing the need for pleasing herself and that this might well be a reaction against the kind of role she has been playing heretofore — pleasing others. Note that as a result of pleasing herself she becomes a "nicer person." This suggests that she is not only dissatisfied with the submissive role she has played but her own self-evaluation has been low.

Note that this is the first positive story told to a picture in which a solitary figure appears, and this may be a more hopeful note for therapy.

Summary Picture #8: The client has a strong need to please herself, to give expression to her "creative urges," to manifest her individuality, and to give up her role of pleasing others. The prognosis for therapy in terms of this story is positive.

TAT PROTOCOL

ANALYSIS AND INTERPRETATION

PICTURE #9

10″ Well, the, the, uh, girl in the, uh, background is, is, uh, seems quite distressed by something. Uh, I would say that these two girls are, are, uh, either sisters or have

Once again a relationship between two women is a stressful one. The relationship is a close one but betrayal has occurred.

been very close to each other, and it seems to me the,
the, uh, uh, girl who seems
so distressed has betrayed
some kind of a trust.

I don't seem to feel any men
involved in this thing.

If no men are involved why does she
speak of them? Men may well be regarded as important in that women will
get into difficulty over them.

It's probably, she's just, uh,
obsessed with the things that
she's been thinking about,
about this girl in the foreground.

Thoughts that she has about other people bother her. A good deal seems to
be going on intrapsychically — intense
feelings as described above and the ob-
sessiveness indicated here. Note that
even in a picture such as this one in
which there is action, the client still stays
on a feeling or thinking level, thus high-
lighting her constriction.

And the girl in the, uh,
front, by the tree knows exactly what's going on in her
mind, and, uh, I — I think
she's glad it, it's sort of her
way of solving this whole
thing. She's probably really a cruel kind of person and
she's glad to see that this
girl is so completely upset
and distressed. Uh, the outcome of it, uh, well, will be
that the friendship or relationship whichever it is will
be completely broken off.
And, uh, there'll always be
a very unpleasant taste
about the whole thing. But
the girl who seems so distressed will be the, the one
who will really be hurt by
the thing.   2' 31"

In this story it is rather difficult to determine with which of the two figures
the client is identifying. On the one
hand, since the roles are about equal, it
may be suggested that these two figures
represent two aspects of the self. On
the other hand, because she says at the
end of the story that the girl who is distressed is the one who is really hurt and
because her personality structure is such
that she may be expected to identify
with the person who is hurt, it is suggested that the first person spoken of in
this story is one with whom she has identified for purposes of this analysis.

Taking the first hypothesis, it may be
suggested that the two aspects of herself
that are significant are the distressed as-

pect and masochistic tendency reflected in the cruelty of the second of the figures in the story. In the story it may have been possible for her to cast these hostile feelings on a person with whom she does not identify, for she cannot accept these feelings for herself. These feelings may not be in keeping with the nice person she would like to be.

Considering the second hypothesis as the more appropriate one, it may be suggested that she sees herself as the distressed person and that she perceives other female figures in her environment as being hostile toward her.

As additional data are gathered it is hoped that it will be possible to differentiate as to which of these two hypotheses is the more significant.

It should also be noted that the relationship between the two figures is broken — thus suggesting that she feels that no rapprochement with women can occur or that her two separate tendencies can be more positively integrated. In view of the fact that the distressed one is " hurt " at the end, it suggests that power and strength may win out.

Summary Picture #9: Relationships with other females are stressful. It is possible that she either sees other females as being hostile toward her and herself as distressed, or it is also possible that one part of the self is seen as distressed and obsessed and the other part is punishing.

TAT PROTOCOL	ANALYSIS AND INTERPRETATION

PICTURE #10

7″ Well — this is in a warm kind of thing. I seem to think of a, a young girl with just sort of, oh, bubbling over with a, a what up to now has been a frustrated

Two feelings, affection and sex drive, have overlapped in such a fashion that the client is confused about them and therefore is probably unable to discriminate between them.

feeling of warmth and affection that's all mixed up with with, uh, sexual drive that confused her and worried her,

This statement also suggests that sex has been difficult for her to handle.

It should also be pointed out that in contrast to situations involving women, which are negatively toned for the client, situations involving men are more positive.

Note her awareness that it was the mixed-up nature of her feelings and sex drive that confused her.

and, uh, she was misunderstood by many young men, hurt,

The juxtaposition of her own confusion and the statement of being "misunderstood" suggests that the young men may have assumed that her desire for close contact, a manifestation of her desire for warmth and affection, was a desire for sex and thus they "hurt" her. Furthermore, it should also be noted that this man is described here as a "young" man and that in the picture the figure is an older person. Since she more positively cathects the older person, it may be assumed that she does so because she expects that he can discriminate between the desire for warmth and affection, and sex.

and this is, is a, seems to me a kind of coming home, a finding of a place where, that she could feel free and to just bubble forth with what she feels.

The client speaks of a "coming home." Then later in this segment she defines it as a place where she can feel free to express what she desires. Considering this datum with the material obtained previously, it suggests that this is the kind of thing she was not permitted to do in her own home.

But there is more to this. First, her statement just prior to this "coming home" involved a discussion of her sexual relationships which were dissatisfying and then she retreated from them to home where she can "bubble forth." This retreat and the bubbling forth appear to be little girl-like in behavior. In other words, it may be regarded as an immature way of dealing with her problem. It is also interesting to note that the "home" she desires is personified in an adult male and this may well be a manifestation of her desire for a comforting father-figure. Finally, it should also be pointed out that here one finds data that can be useful in the therapy. That is, the client may well establish a quick positive transference or enjoy the acceptance and warm aspects of her therapy and not do anything about solving her problems. In other words, she may find the little girl-father relationship too satisfying to deal with males at her own level.

And, uh, yet, uh, because she feels this freedom and a kind of warm acceptance is, is bound to be good for her, it'll strengthen her. He, he's a very nice person. But it's a warm feeling to the whole thing. It's almost perfect.
2' 25"

The client anticipates that warmth and acceptance will strengthen her and in a sense she has prescribed her own remedy. The emphasis on strength here suggests that she may not stop with the dependent relationship but utilize the accepting nature of therapy for constructive efforts. The question is, strengthen her for what? Previous material suggests that she wants strength for freedom for her personality. She has not in the stories broken down the specific aspects of the freedom she desires. On the basis of the material collected thus far it is apparent that one aspect of this freedom involves not doing what others expect of her. But she is not inclined to face deeper material such as integrating her sexual drive and effecting a mature heterosexual relationship. This too can result in freedom. The client is aware of her desires with respect to the first point just mentioned, and it is likely that in the course of therapy she will have an easier time effecting this than the second, of which she is not aware.

It should also be noted that in this whole story the needs of the woman are paramount. There is no interaction and the needs of the man are not discussed. Consequently, it may be suggested that she cannot see the others because of the intensity of her own problem. This suggests strong egocentricity.

Summary Picture #10: The client sees relationships with adult men as more positive than with younger men. This may be related to her desire for a father-figure. One reason for this is that she believes they can differentiate between her desire for warmth and affection, and sex. She herself is confused about this combination of needs and is aware of this confusion. She has stronger needs for the former than the latter. She retreats from relationships that involve sex. The client, at this point, appears to be egocentric. She is more of a taking than a giving person, and it has been pointed out that she may be able rather quickly to establish a relationship in therapy. She may be able to utilize the accepting nature of therapy for more constructive steps forward.

TAT PROTOCOL	ANALYSIS AND INTERPRETATION

PICTURE #11

19″ I, uh, get the feeling that this is a very remote spot, probably, uh, Scotland, and probably it's something that happened long, long ago.

The client in this picture has placed the locale of her story in a distant place and in the historical past. Such material may refer either to an event that has occurred in the past or a psychological datum that the client has repressed or is presently suppressing. In this case it would be of interest to know why " Scotland " was selected. Its significance for this client cannot be determined from the available material.

There's a feeling of a small group of people trying to escape from a very unpleasant kind of weird situation that they've been in, and the,

The client is responding almost completely in terms of feeling, and the direction of action is an avoidance one.

uh, the whole atmosphere is, uh, kind of weird, lurid kind of thing.

Uh, and there's a some kind of animal off to the side, something from the under-world, just a weird kind of thing.

In an effort to determine what the client is trying to escape we do not get much direct aid from her remarks, other than that it is from the "underworld." This, it is suggested, may refer to instinctual drives. Specifically, it is suggested that the animal in the picture may well be interpreted symbolically as reflecting male sexuality and that she is trying to escape this. Evidence from previous pictures supports this hypothesis.

But the outcome, well, they'll probably escape in this story, will go down as a kind of one of the happen-ings. But the whole thing is bleak and weird and just unreal to me.
2′ 28″

The people get away but no material is presented as to how they get away. There is no planful behavior or buildup in most of the stories. Actions just oc-cur. It should also be noted that the client says they "probably escape," sug-gesting her own doubt as to the effective-ness of her escape.

Summary Picture #11: The client tends to run away from her problems and in the face of them tends to react primarily in terms of the feelings that they stimulate in her. The feelings may be so intense that they blur the capacity to make differentiations. It is suggested that the spe-cific problem referred to here is her inadequate adjustment to a hetero-sexual situation and her tendency to repress sexual drives.

TAT PROTOCOL

ANALYSIS AND INTERPRETATION

PICTURE #12

17″ Well, this seems to me to be a situation wherein this younger girl has, uh, been the ward of this older person, and she's been raised by her and, uh, given all the educational advantages but to a certain purpose.

One of the problems in this story is to determine with which of the two figures in the picture the client has identified. We suggest that she has identified with the older woman, and the younger wom-an may be her daughter or daughters. This is based on the psychological sim-ilarity between the characteristics ascribed to the older woman in this story and the characteristics of the client as in-ferred from the previous stories. On the basis of Picture #8 it was inferred that the client would "like to do whatever she wants to do"; on the basis of Pictures #7 and #10 it was hypothesized that the client may pay more attention to her own needs than to the needs of others, and in Picture #7 it was assumed that her capacity to give warmth to younger females was inadequate. With the hypothesis that she has identified with the older woman in mind, let us now turn to the analysis of the story.

From the first segment of the story it is apparent that the relationship with the younger girl is not a close one — the girl is a "ward" of the older one. Furthermore, note that the older woman gave the ward "all the educational advantages" for certain purposes. This is like the "artificial" relationship in Picture #7; the younger woman is given educational advantages but not necessarily love. But why educational advantages? This, it is suggested, is again consistent with the client's own needs, for the previous evidence seems to suggest that her strivings are in this direction. Consequently, there may be a "living through" the children, as is found to be the case later in the story.

The older person is a very designing kind of person and is, uh, has plans for her which are, well, shall we say, not too good. She's just not considering what this girl wants but, uh, uh, she has, in other words she's going to accomplish something she wants. I'm not at all sure what it is, but it's, it's, uh, it's not going to be too good. She's a very designing kind

The older person is characterized as "designing," a "shrew," and someone who does not consider the other person's needs. Furthermore, she also seeks to pay off her "grudge against life" "through the girl." This grudge, it is suggested, has resulted from the client's own unhappiness in life.

of an old shrew, and, uh, probably has a grudge against life that she's going to pay off somehow through this girl,

The question may be raised as to how it is possible to assume that the client has identified with the older woman whom she characterizes so negatively in this story. First, on the basis of at least two previous stories it has been assumed that the client has some awareness, conscious or unconscious, that she is dissatisfied with her own values. In Picture #2 "good values" were not associated with tension, and in Picture #8 the client was to become a "nicer person." Secondly, the older woman in the picture is much older than the client; thus it is easier for her to project her negative feelings onto this woman. Consequently, it is suggested that the client has identified with the older woman in the sense that in talking about her she has revealed herself but not necessarily in the sense that she has necessarily completely accepted this aspect of herself. It may well be, however, that awareness of her own negative characteristics is coming closer to consciousness and that this is one of the factors which has generated the tension that has motivated the client to seek therapy.

and the outcome of this thing, it's going to be pretty unpleasant, I think. The, uh, girl herself which she, uh, she's apparently lacking in certain sensitivities, is, uh, is going to be the one who ultimately is certainly going to get hurt. And that's, uh, about all that I

The outcome is an unhappy one for the girl.

Note that the girl is described as "lacking in certain sensitivities," but is this not also similar to the older woman's behavior, since she too was insensitive to the needs of the girl?

can imagine on this one.
3' 01"

Throughout the above analysis it has been assumed that the client has identified with the older woman. To be sure, it might also have been possible to assume that in this story the client has been talking about her relationship with her own mother and describing her own conformity to the standards imposed upon her by a " cold " mother and the fact that she has been hurt as a result of it. If one assumes this alone then it would not account for the conflict the client may be experiencing with regard to some of her own values. In the above presentation it is assumed that the mother may have been similar to the older person but that the client had internalized some of her behavior patterns and is now growing more unhappy about them.

Summary Picture #12: Part of the conflict that may have motivated the client to seek therapy is her growing awareness of negative aspects of her own personality. These refer to her being a " shrew " and a " designing " person who has very likely lived through her children as a means of " paying off a grudge against life." Her relationships with her children are characterized as " cold " and it was also suggested that her own behavior pattern may have resulted from internalizing the behavior patterns of her mother.

TAT PROTOCOL   ANALYSIS AND INTERPRETATION

PICTURE #13G *

19" It rather strikes me as if being — some of these pictures seem to bring a kind of feeling of moving back into history. Just why I don't know.

The material here suggests that the client may well be recalling a previous historical event. The manner in which she puts her comments suggests that ego-boundaries are weak and this is manifest in the " feeling " of moving back into history and not knowing why.

---

* For some reason, probably due to an oversight, Picture #13G instead of #13F was presented to the client.

This one is giving me the sense of a young girl,

The figure of the girl is obvious in the picture, yet the client does not say, " This is a young girl . . ." or utilize a construction in which the figure is pointed out with any kind of definiteness — the client " senses " a young girl. This is consistent with her emphasis on " feeling " throughout; she is more responsive to inner states than outer stimuli, but it may also be suggested that the client's anxiety level may be so high that she is unable to be definite about that which exists in her environment.

of a royal blood in the inside of an old castle. The, uh, I guess the feeling that, uh, probably because, because of the background she's been pretty much all alone, and the, uh, climbing stairs indicates to me, her feeling of being, not necessarily unhappy, but just sort of lonely, on her own. The, uh, blankness I see at the top of the picture makes me feel that the climb is to a happier place.

The material is interesting, for here one may observe how fantasy must have played a significant role for the client. Thus, life in reality was unpleasant so she constructs the fantasy of being in a castle and being of royal blood. It is a means of utilizing fantasy in order to compensate for an impoverished reality situation.

Uh, probably she, she's up, going up to simply play in a room where she'll find a few cheerful companions. They, uh, uh, maybe she's just going up there to lose herself in, in books or thoughts. I'm sure that she would be, she would certainly be doing a lot of daydreaming.

She starts with companions but then ends in solitary activity. Mentioning companions may be a reflection of her desire for companionship but, since this is replaced by a solitary activity, it suggests that early interpersonal relationships were dissatisfying for her.

The outcome, uh, well, I think she's just going to go on being the kind of person she is, with a medium for escape up the staircases, and

Trying situations were escaped from by turning to fantasy and books and this pattern is continued later in life.

having her brief moments
of, well, the kind of pleasure that she happens to find
there. 3′ 28″

Summary Picture #13G: The client retreats from difficult situations into
a world of fantasy in which she compensates for her lack in realistic situations. The material suggests that this pattern of escaping from trying
situations may be one of long standing.

TAT Protocol	Analysis and Interpretation

PICTURE #14

23″ Well, this is the story
of a young man who, uh, has
some, some very serious
thoughts, and has gone
away by himself. He's probably made some breaks with
his family and his friends
and he's gone off to think.
Just to think things out.
Uh, he, he's probably concerned with state of the
world and he has gone to
someplace where he can be
a-alone and a, a clearer view.
The, the, uh, this is probably the result of a long period of frustration and conflict within himself. And so
now he, he's, he's come to
the point where he's just beginning to see things. He's
just beginning to get certain
realizations of what, what it
is he wants, a sort of finding
himself. Uh, I get a certain
relaxed feeling in, and a, uh,
feeling of, of him being comfortable and the outcome is
it's bound to be pretty good.

This story is in some respects similar to
and in certain other respects different
from the previous story. It is similar in
that once again the hero goes off by himself to solve his problem. It is different
in that in this story there appears to be
a more direct way of dealing with the
problem, while in the previous story
there was an escape. These differences,
especially where one story is obtained to
a younger figure and the other to an
older figure, often reflect change in the
person's behavior as a function of age.
Thus in Story 13 the client " escaped "
from her difficulty by retreating into
fantasy; in this story she leaves others
and retreats to an inner world, but here
the inner world is not of fantasy but of
thinking, and the purpose of the thinking is to get a clearer view. Since the
client came for therapy it is suggested,
in view of the above material, that the
prognosis is good. The fact that the
hero is " just beginning to get certain
realizations of what it is he wants " suggests that the client may have taken the
initial steps to making progress. This is
not regarded completely as a wish, since
the situation occurs in the present, although the wishful aspect is strong
since there is still progress to be made.
Furthermore, it should be noted that the
client is optimistic. Finally, it should

be pointed out that one of the conditions for getting a clearer view of things seems to be the need to break off old relationships with both family and friends.

I think he's going to find that, uh, he's really been taking himself a little bit too seriously, that, well, that after all there's so much that he *can* do and, he'll probably settle down into a, rather relaxed way of life.

The client here provides her own diagnosis for her difficulty. The lay language " taking himself a little bit too seriously," may be regarded as similar to the discussion of the material presented above, that the client is too deeply immersed in her own feelings, is not reacting to external stimuli realistically, and may be exaggerating her present condition. It should be noted that the client is aware even prior to therapy that there is " so much that he (she) *can* do," in order to attain release from her tension and subsequent relaxation.

Uh, I'm apparently being again much too practical, but there's nothing, I mean if it comes out it's just, uh, I'm sorry. 3' 05"

This apparently is a comment to the test administrator. It is interesting that as soon as the reality of the interpersonal situation intrudes, she becomes apologetic and intrapunitive, and when she says that she is being " too practical " it suggests that she has doubts as to what she can realistically attain. This bit of realistic interpersonal data tends to support some of the interpretations made above.

Summary Picture #14: The client has come to seek therapy after a good deal of inner stress and frustration. The client has thought a good deal about her problems and feels that there is something she can do about them. One of the conditions for the solution of problems is breaking with social relationships that she has established heretofore. She has some awareness that she has been " taking herself too seriously." The prognosis on the basis of this story is good.

TAT PROTOCOL

ANALYSIS AND INTERPRETATION

PICTURE #15

14" I have a feeling that I've seen this picture before. Uh, I'm sure I have.

The client may have seen this picture before but this need not necessarily detract from the significance of the material, provided the client can make up a story about it.

Uh, this is a man who has lost someone who is very, very close to him. And, uh, it happened a long, long time ago. And, uh, again this feeling of, uh, of weird kind of evilness. It's a, uh, sense of, the only, way I can describe it is, is evilness in quotes, everything you can't say. Uh, he, he himself is not a cruel person, a, he's just lacking in, in many things, a kind of spiritual lack. And yet he finds himself out here with all of these, uh, symbols of, uh, spirituality and he's trying to bring about a better kind of feeling within himself. Now of course he just isn't going to succeed because there's nothing there — he, he lacks this thing. The, uh, person he lost had a certain influence on him, but this could never reach him really. Uh, I feel that he, he was responsible for her death. I say her. It . . . it turns out to be her, I see. And, uh, but not through murder or anything, because he doesn't have that kind of a drive. I mean it's, he simply killed her because he lacks. He just doesn't have whatever it is that, that means the will to live. The outcome is, is, well, he, he's just a lost soul. 3′ 42″

In the previous stories where men were involved it was indicated that the client has a positive cathexis for mature and accepting men. In this story, another type of male is described, one who lacks spiritual values (just what these are specifically is not clear). Because he lacks these values, a woman who tries to be close to him does not succeed in forming a relationship with him and he " kills " her.

Since the client says that the story refers to a situation that occurred " a long, long time ago," it is suggested that this refers to her relationship with her father. She wanted to have a closer relationship with him than she had but this was not forthcoming because of his " lack." (This ties in with the comment she made to Picture #2 where she says, " I don't see any connection between the man and the girl. Probably should be but there isn't any . . . far as I can see.") Her influence on him did not reach him. Because of this experience it may well be that she has sought out the men described in Stories 4 and 6, with whom she wants a relationship but one that will not necessarily involve sexuality. The fact that she probably has not found men who can satisfactorily meet her needs is apparent from the previous data, which suggest that she feels bogged down in life. Consequently, it is suggested that her relationship with her husband may also be unsatisfactory, for he too may lack the " will to live."

Note also in this story how the client rationalizes the man's cruelty and does not express hostility to him directly for what he has done. It should also be noted that she regarded much of her relationship as " evil " but this refers to " everything you can't say "; consequently it may be difficult for her to speak of her feelings and experiences in this regard.

Summary Picture #15: The client was unable to establish a close relationship with her father because, as she sees him, he lacked "spiritual" qualities. The lack of warmth in this relationship may be involved in her seeking heterosexual situations in which she can satisfy her dependent needs. It was also suggested that her marital situation may not be satisfying and that she has difficulty in dealing with her hostile feelings.

TAT PROTOCOL

ANALYSIS AND INTERPRETATION

PICTURE #16

9″ Mm-hm. Well, uh, this is a picture of, of, uh, lots of people being very busy. There's, there's a job to be done and, I get the feeling of a kind of group thing, a project that, a, a group of people, oh, probably they've had some kind of, of disturbance within the community and they've decided that they're just going to get together in the evening, solve the whole thing. They, uh, had their, uh, problems with, with, uh, certain people within the group who feel that maybe it's just a waste of time, but there's a good feeling of business and, wanting to get the job done. The, uh, outcome is, is going to be successful, I'm sure and, uh, perhaps what

The theme of this story is a constructive one. There is some difficulty, the group gets together in order to solve it, and despite some dissension in the group, it solves its problem. This again is a hopeful prognostic sign for the patient's future in therapy — something is being done, energy is being expended in the solution of a problem. The fact that a group has to be involved in the solution suggests that she feels she cannot solve her problem by herself. And the fact that it is a " community " problem suggests that she sees her problem as involving more than herself.

Finally, her last statement suggests that not only does she want help but " more important " is that " the people will get to know each other." Thus she is seeking acceptance and wants people to like her.

is even more important, the
people will get to know each
other and probably they'll
like each other. 1' 57"

Summary Picture #16: The client is seeking help because she feels incapable of dealing with her problems on her own. Furthermore, her
need for affiliation and acceptance have already been pointed out.

TAT PROTOCOL	ANALYSIS AND INTERPRETATION

PICTURE #17

Well, this is a story of a girl.
Uh, she lives in a, a, uh, port
town and she's very curious
about what goes on all over
the world and when the
ships are due she goes down
to the bridge and watches
and hopes to learn things
that way. In the back of
her mind someplace is the
idea that, that some day she
too is going to leave. Uh, I,
you get the feeling that it,
it, uh, she's going to leave,
uh, by fair means or foul
and, uh, she's an interesting
kind of person who isn't
just, just isn't going to be
tied down, uh, to where
she doesn't want to remain.
The, the, uh, she, she seems
to have very little connection with the, uh, the people who ship in, uh, the
stevedores. They only mean
a link to her between where
she is now and where she
hopes to go. The, uh, setting for the, of the general
feeling that I get is, is just
her, her obsession with, with
what she has planned. It's
a, it's a carefully planned-

As in so many other stories, so here the
client spends a good deal of time in talking, but refers to little action. She
spends a good deal of time in thinking
and planning and seems to have gotten
satisfaction from the fact that she has finally made up her mind to change her
present situation. She may look forward
to therapy as a means of gaining the
strength to act on her plan.

Her motivation for change is strong,
since she is " going to leave by fair
means or foul," and again she is going
to break her present ties (" just isn't going to be tied down "). Her self-concept
here is a positive one, for she regards
the woman as " an interesting kind of
person." Finally, it should be noted
that the men (stevedores) have no heterosexual significance to her but are only a means to an end.

out kind of thing that she is going to carry through some day, and she's quite satisfied to bide her time, knowing, well, if she has decided is going to come true. In the meantime she, uh, she really isn't very unhappy, uh, where she is. It, it's just, she has just set this goal and she certainly is going to maintain it. *3' 31"*

Summary Picture #17: The client desires to leave or change her present environment and she seems to have gained satisfaction from having arrived at a plan. She may be looking forward to therapy as a means of gaining the strength necessary to break her present ties and to gain some independence. Her self-concept in this story is a positive one.

TAT Protocol

Analysis and Interpretation

Picture #18

24" Well, this is a story of mother and her son. How, uh, he's, he's a good boy but always been a, a terrific problem and, uh, finally he, he has gotten himself into some very serious kind of, of, uh, trouble, and, uh, he, he's just helpless to do anything. And yet his, his mother, his mother knows that she, that she, she's going to have to send him away from the town where they live. Uh, oh, she, she's come to the point where she knows that she just can't help him, there just isn't anything that she can possibly do for him; he's sort of a lost cause now.

Men are good but problems. They get themselves into trouble and they are "a lost cause." Nothing can be done for them and they are rejected.

It is interesting to compare this story with the story to Picture #15. In Picture #15 the client described a situation where the male rejected the woman. Here, finally, the woman rejects the man. She does nothing to help him because nothing was done to help her and her needs probably remained unsatisfied.

In view of the dynamics discussed in the analysis of Picture #15, it appears that she feels her own husband is a lost cause and that the only situation she can develop is one where she rejects him.

The fact that the client sees the male as a son suggests that she regards him as more immature than herself.

And her understanding of it and her, her grief because she does know this thing is, is very apparent. Uh, it's a terribly unhappy kind of a, a story because she's going to be miserable, just miserable, he's, he is just a lost cause, there just isn't a darn thing that she can do.

The client feels badly about what she has to do but apparently can go through with it.

He's going to leave because he has to. He's going to go elsewhere and, uh, be lost, miserable, probably very much disliked by people, and uh, certainly come to some, some very unpleasant end.

(No time recorded)

It is not sufficient that she has rejected the male, but adds that he will be " miserable," " disliked," and come to a " very unpleasant end." This, it is suggested, reflects the intensity of the hostility that she feels toward the male.

Note that the earlier stories suggested that she has felt lost. Whether she sees the male as a " lost cause " primarily because this is the way she felt about herself or because he is realistically so it is impossible to tell from these stories, for we are dealing only with her attitudes. However, in view of the dynamics discussed previously regarding her relationships with men it is suggested that she may have selected as a mate a male who is realistically inadequate in terms of satisfying her needs and is therefore a lost cause insofar as she is concerned.

Summary Picture #18: The client feels the need to reject her husband because he is " a lost cause." She feels badly about this but she does not feel it is possible to help him. She expresses her intense hostile feelings toward him in an indirect manner here.

TAT Protocol

Analysis and Interpretation

Picture #19

31″ This, the first story that comes to my mind is,

This is a rather interesting comment by the client. She gives the house a per-

is the, probably ought to be titled, the story of a house that frightened itself.

sonality. It is a physiognomic perception and suggests once again the client's inadequate ego-structure.

Her statement that the house frightened itself suggests that the client regards herself as having frightened herself. This is consistent with her previous story to Picture #14, where the hero has been taking himself too seriously. In other words, it may well be a reflection of the client's realization of her own involvement in her problems.

It's, uh — and yet it's, it's kind of amusing too. There's a kind of whimsy here. Uh, let's say that's, uh, a house that was built by someone who, who had a rather perverted sense of humor. And, uh, probably thought it, it would be a good idea to have the kind of a, a house that would, well, wouldn't be too inviting to people to come to, and, uh, so that he in the end, that is on the outside and, so that he in, uh, turn could make the inside a complete surprise, a, a, just the kind of place that you would never expect. The, uh, by which I mean very comfortable and charming and warm. The outside is, is really intriguing. The, the whimsy to it and, and I guess the, the same kind of reaction as one might get like they say " boo " to a, a child, a kind of playful front. — It's, it's hard to cook

In this production the client emphasizes the differences between the external and internal parts of the house. This, it is suggested, is a reflection of the discrepancy that the client experiences in herself. Specifically, it is the discrepancy between that which is presented to others — the external part of the house — and that which is not manifest to others — her inner feelings. From previous stories it has been inferred that the client has felt dissatisfied with her behavior or present status and she is striving to achieve a more relaxed state. This is congruent with the analysis made of the story thus far. The client's statement toward the end of the story, that she does not get a " feeling of definite personality " reflects the ambiguous state that she finds herself in at the present time. In other words, she does not experience herself as a total, integrated personality. It may be said that she is one thing unto herself but she believes that she is different in social situations or is seen differently by others (i.e., " uninviting "), and that she has difficulty in integrating all her feelings.

up any kind of an outcome because I don't get a, a, uh, feeling of definite personality here. It's, it's, uh, and, uh, well, I probably have, have to go back to saying, it's very much like saying " boo " to a child. 3′ 49″

Her statement with regard to saying " boo " to a child is interpreted as being a continuation of her thought that the house frightened itself and, more specifically, is her means of diminishing the anxiety that may have been stimulated in her by the picture itself or the anxiety that may have developed in her during the course of telling the story. Furthermore, referring to a child here reflects her own immaturity.

Summary Picture #19: The client's inadequate or relatively weak ego-structure was pointed out here. She seems to have some awareness of how she is involved in her own problems. She frightens herself probably by dwelling on her own difficulties. She does not feel like an integrated personality and seems to be aware of the discrepancy between her inner self and the façade she presents to others.

TAT PROTOCOL

ANALYSIS AND INTERPRETATION

PICTURE #20

20″ Well, this is a story of a young girl who, uh, has an appointment and, uh, she's keeping this, a, appointment outside because it seems to me that, that it involves some kind of a situation that has to be settled.

The definiteness of the story thus far is somewhat out of keeping with the client's approach to the stories up to now. Up to this point the more consistent theme is one in which the protagonist is planning or getting ready for action. Here, however, there is something that " has to be settled." This is a positive prognostic sign, for it suggests that the client may be ready to settle up accounts.

The unique aspect of this story thus far is that the appointment has to be held " outside " because it involves a situation that has to be settled. What does the " outside " mean? Two hypotheses are offered here. Outside may mean that in order to settle her problems it has to be done away from home or through therapy, since it is known that the client has come for therapy. Another hypothesis stems from the use of the phrase " to meet one outside " in interactions which are toned with hostility and aggression and a score has to be settled. It is likely that both hypotheses are correct. That is, this story refers to the client's anticipation of therapy in which she is going to settle a problem that has to do with her feelings toward her husband.

Uh, she's going to meet a man, I'm sure, uh — she's a nice person and, uh, who is (words lost) but there's a problem there.

The client, having identified with the girl in the story, may be said to regard herself as nice. Thus she has built up some feeling of adequacy and therefore is more prepared to deal with the problem.

Uh, he's going to come and they're going to talk this whole thing out and I have a feeling it's going to be successful. No, uh, feeling of sadness really to this thing. — What the problem is I don't know. But anyway, it's going to work out okay, I'm sure. They're going to have words about things. Uh, certain unpleasantness first, but it's going to work out okay, I'm sure of that. And, uh . . . well, that's all.

Despite the anticipated unpleasantness of the situation, the client is still willing to face it and is optimistic as to its outcome.

I just haven't been very dramatic this morning. 3′ 03″

While in telling the story the client demonstrated some firmness, in the realistic situation with the tester she again becomes apologetic.

Summary Picture #20: The client appears to be ready to deal with her problems and while she is aware of the unpleasantness that may be involved, she is optimistic as to its outcome. It is suggested that one of the problems she is going to deal with is to settle the score with males.

Final TAT Summary

Mrs. Oak is a worried and troubled woman who feels that she has had as much as she can take. She wants to break with the ties and relationships that she finds so frustrating now and desires therapy in order to gain the strength to make such a break and to establish herself independently, to be free, and to satisfy her needs.

The client has a rather weak ego-structure. She tends to be ruled by her feelings and to become immersed in them to such an extent at times that she does not clearly differentiate between her inner feelings and external reality. Under such pressure her thought processes are apt to become disjunctive and it is difficult to follow her. However, she manages to recover rather well under less stressful conditions, and should be able to establish a good therapeutic relationship, for she has some awareness of the extent to which she can dwell on her feelings, thoughts, and motivations, and the fact that she does not understand them too well and thus becomes anxious about them. She does not herself feel too well integrated. On the one hand she tends to regard herself as a rather inadequate person, and on the other she feels that she is a nice person with potentialities. The latter seems to be a more recent development associated with her intent to seek therapy. She does not at the present time feel that she is a completely " nice " person, for she has become aware to some extent of her hostile feelings and domineering attitude, probably specifically related to her children, and she does not like this too well.

For a long time, Mrs. Oak seems to have accepted and given in to the standards set up by others. She has always felt the need to comply, to keep up with others, and to present a façade that will be acceptable to them. Thus she cathected education as an important virtue and was concerned about social status factors. This pattern, however, was very constricting; it obviously did not provide her with an opportunity to manifest her own individuality, and while she gave in to others she apparently did so by suppressing her own assertiveness and this resulted in tension. At the present time, she feels the need all the more strongly to be herself, to be independent, and, feeling that she cannot achieve this by herself, she looks for help.

Mrs. Oak is troubled by her sexual needs. Sex and her need for acceptance by a male and warmth from him seem to have been confused. Physical contact to satisfy her needs is to be avoided. Indeed, what she wants primarily are warmth and acceptance. Since in order to satisfy such needs she would have had to establish a close contact with a male it is obvious how her behavior might have been confusing to men and why she therefore feels hurt and misunderstood. She feels that older men would understand her better and therefore cathects them more positively than younger men. With the former she desires a role in which she can be the little girl who basks in the glory of being accepted by the older and more knowledgeable male. Closer sexual contact is not to be established. A married state might be desirable for some women, and even for herself, but she is not prepared emotionally to establish such a relationship on a mature basis. Her behavior with men seems to be related to her early relationship with her father. She wanted contact with him but did not seem to get it and thus she may be seeking to make up for it now. Men who do not give her what she wants she rejects as she herself once felt rejected.

Another aspect of her immaturity is her desire to take from relationships and not give. She is primarily concerned with her own needs and has relatively little regard for the needs of others. Thus she may be described as an egocentric person. One condition in which it may appear that she does not behave in this manner is when other people are in trouble. With these people she can sympathize and empathize, but here too it seems to be an outlet for her own frustrated feelings for having been in difficulties herself. She identifies with these others.

Her relationships with women are conflictful for her. She regards them as domineering and as competitors. She may well project the negative side of herself onto them and others. In general it may be said that she has found relatively little satisfaction in interpersonal relationships and to deal with this she retreats into a world of fantasy where she compensates for all she lacks and tries to make plans with regard to her future. She cannot retreat completely from social contact, for then she is beset with feelings of loneliness and dejection which she finds quite intolerable. Feeling accepted by a male who will not seek sexual contact can often bring her out of this depressed state. Thus she is dependent on external stimuli to help engender positive feelings and feels relatively little strength inside herself.

Mrs. Oak is quite unhappy with her husband and family. She seems to feel that her husband is a " lost cause." She does not believe that there is anything she can do to help him and the only thing seems to be to reject him. In part it may be that he cannot give her the sort of love she desires and she feels hostile toward him because of this. Her relationship with her children is likewise unhappy. She seems to have utilized them as a means of making up for her own unhappiness in life. She does not seem to have considered their needs and did not give them real warmth, just as her own needs may not have been considered by her own mother, who may have been a cold person. She is troubled by her relationships with her children and this too may have stimulated some guilt in her. Her behavior with her children is not consistent with the self-concept that she would like to develop for herself. Her family situation seems to have been so frustrating to her that she seems to feel that she must break these ties or the behavior patterns that have been developed in this relationship.

As pointed out above, Mrs. Oak feels that she wants to start a new path in life. Having made a decision to seek therapy she feels a little stronger and more optimistic about being able to achieve her goals. To be sure, she is somewhat ambivalent about therapy and concerned whether what she will be able to learn will confuse her more or whether she will be able to use it. Despite this concern she is hopeful. It should be pointed out that despite Mrs. Oak's strong desire for independence there is a strong need dependence — to use others as props — and this, coupled with her attitude toward older men — her desire for acceptance by them — may result in her becoming too dependent on the therapist, especially if the therapist is a male. In addition, one need also beware not to accept immediate improvement as a sign of any marked change, for this may be her reaction to the immediate feeling of acceptance. It should also be pointed out that she has a tendency to utilize denial as a defense mechanism. She is also more apt to speak of general feelings, as manifested in her sensitivity to situations, rather than concrete events. However, she seems to be ready for therapy; she has done a good deal of thinking about herself, she is quite dissatisfied with the present state of affairs, she feels that she can benefit from help, and therefore the prognosis is regarded as good.

Notes on Mrs. Oak

" The presenting situation was that Mrs. Oak was a housewife in her late thirties who was in a deeply discordant relationship with her husband, and also much disturbed in her relationship with her adolescent daughter, who had recently been through a serious illness which had been diagnosed as psychosomatic. Mrs. Oak felt she must be to blame for this illness. She herself was a sensitive person, eager to be honest with herself and to search out the causes of her problems. She was a person with little formal education, though intelligent and widely read.

" By the fifth interview any specific concentration on her problems had dropped out, and the major focus of therapy had shifted to an experiencing of herself and her emotional reactions. She felt at times that she *should* be ' working on my problems,' but that she felt drawn to this experiencing, that somehow she wanted to use the therapy hour for what she called her ' vaguenesses.' This was a good term, since she expressed herself in half-sentences, poetic analogies, and expressions which seemed more like fantasy. Her communications were often hard to follow or understand, but obviously involved much deep feeling experienced in the immediate present.

" She was unusually sensitive to the process she was experiencing in herself. To use some of her expressions, she was feeling the pieces of a jigsaw puzzle, she was singing a song without words, she was creating a poem, she was learning a new way of experiencing herself which was like learning to read Braille. Therapy was an experiencing of her self, in all its aspects, in a safe relationship. At first it was her guilt, and her concern over being responsible for the maladjustments of others. Then it was her hatred and bitterness toward life for having cheated and frustrated her in so many different areas, particularly the sexual, and then it was the experiencing of her own hurt, of the sorrow she felt for herself for having been so wounded. But along with these went the experiencing of self as having a capacity for wholeness, a self which was not possessively loving toward others, but was 'without hate,' a self that cared about others. This last followed what was for her one of the deepest experiences in therapy (between interviews #29 and #30), the realization that the therapist *cared* — that it really mattered to him how therapy turned out for her, that he really valued her. She experienced the soundness of her own basic directions. She gradually became aware of the fact that though she had searched in every corner of herself, there was nothing fundamentally bad, but rather that at heart she was positive and sound. She realized that the values she deeply held were such as would set her at variance with her culture, but she accepted this calmly . . .

"One of the outstanding characteristics of the interviews was the minimal consideration of her outside behavior. Once an issue was settled in her, the behavioral consequences were mentioned only by chance. After she had 'felt' her way through her relationship with her daughter, there was little mention of her behavior toward the daughter until much later when she casually mentioned that the relationship was much better. Likewise in regard to a job. She had never worked outside the home, and the prospect terrified her, yet she thought it highly important if she were to feel independent of her husband. She finally settled the issue in her feelings to the extent that she said she thought now that she could look for, or take, a job. She never mentioned it again. Only through a chance outside source did the therapist learn that, at about the end of therapy, she chose an establishment in which she wished to work, applied for a position, ignored the turndown which she received, and convinced the manager that he should give her a trial. She is still holding the position. It was the same in regard to her marriage. She decided that she could not continue in marriage, but that she did not wish to break up the marriage in a battle, or with resentment or hurt. Shortly after the conclusion of therapy she achieved this goal of a separation and divorce which was mutually agreed upon.

"When she left therapy it was with the feeling that a process was going on in her which would continue to operate. She felt that the relationship with the therapist had been very meaningful and in a psychological sense would never stop, even though she walked out of the office for good. She felt ready, she thought, to cope with her life, though she realized it would not be easy." *

* A discussion of the case of Mrs. Oak, from which the above material is quoted, is to be found in Rogers, C. R. and Dymond, R. F. (eds.), *Psychotherapy and Personality Change*. Chicago, Illinois: University of Chicago Press, 1954, p. 262.

CHAPTER 8

A MALE PATIENT STARTS THERAPY

The Case of F. A.

This patient is a 26-year-old unmarried male who is the fifth of seven children. He is employed as an apprentice carpenter. The patient came for psychiatric help because he was troubled by his " inability to concentrate and nervousness."

TAT PROTOCOL   ANALYSIS AND INTERPRETATION

PICTURE #1

* —— Well, first of all,

The manner in which the patient perceives the test situation will frequently influence the kinds of stories he produces. The psychologist should attempt therefore to determine as early as possible just what the patient's perception of the test situation is. The examiner is aided in this regard by clues that can frequently be obtained from observation of the patient's behavior during the test, his comments and asides, the language which he uses, and from stories in which there is interaction between a person who represents that patient and another who represents the examiner.

This patient takes some time before starting his story and his comments indicate that he is somewhat uncomfortable and uneasy when confronted with the test. His discomfort may stem from the fact that he regards the test situation as one in which his abilities will be evaluated, in which case he may feel that the test results will " prove " that he is or is not a very capable individual, or he may be more suspicious and regard the test as the psychologist's means of

---

* Since no stopwatch was available at the time this test was administered, only excessive pauses were indicated by the length of horizontal lines.

unearthing the content of problems and conflict areas which he has so carefully kept from public view up to now. His delay in response time may also indicate that he is a cautious and planful individual who desires to take his time in organizing the story in his own mind before verbalizing it. These are only some of the ways in which the patient might have perceived the test situation and some of the factors which might have been involved in the delayed reaction time which appears at the beginning of the story. At this point it is obviously difficult to interpret exactly how the patient perceives the test situation. Additional clues will be forthcoming from the stories that follow.

as far as I'm concerned ——

It is difficult to indicate the patient's voice quality when he makes certain remarks. The reader therefore loses valuable clues. Thus if this remark, " as far as I'm concerned," was spoken in a strong tone of voice then it might indicate the patient's assertiveness. However, it should be noted that the patient's voice quality in this instance was rather weak. He appears therefore to be a hesitant individual who wishes to set the limits in the examination even before he tells his stories. He wants the examiner to know that what he will say will be determined solely by his own experience and his remarks will reflect only his private opinion. This is a means of safeguarding himself against any criticism from the examiner. It is as if the patient were saying to the examiner, " This is my opinion. You may have yours. Since my remarks are only opinions, I feel free to change them when you present the facts. Then I shall be as right as you are."

He decided to take violin lessons.	In one brief sentence the patient attempts to satisfy the examiner's request to tell what happened in the past. Although he does not tell what made the boy decide to take violin lessons, it is significant that the hero makes the decision himself. Such decisiveness, if it is characteristic of the patient, is inconsistent with the interpretation of the patient's remarks that was made prior to the start of his story. Therefore either the first interpretation is incorrect or we may be dealing with material from two different levels of the personality. If we are dealing with data from two different layers of the personality, then some of the characteristics described above may occur in overt behavior, while others may appear only in fantasy life. Again we must await additional data before it is possible to state the level to which our data refer.
He began to take them and advanced to a stage	The use of the word " advanced " is interesting, especially since it appears so soon after the boy " began " to take violin lessons. It reflects the patient's desire for advancement or his need for achievement.
where I'd say he has run into a passage in music which he is finding difficult.	The path to the goal is not without obstacles.
He's very ejected at the present time,	The use of the word " ejected " is particularly significant. Obviously the patient meant to say " dejected." From observation of the patient's behavior, it was clear that he did not think he was using the wrong word. Evidently he has heard the word " dejected " before and he now relies upon auditory memory when he wants to use the right word. But what is the significance of the use of the wrong word " ejected," aside from the fact that it indicates that the pa-

tient's reaction to frustration is dejection and sadness? To explain the interpretation which we have given to this remark, it is necessary to digress for a moment and make several general comments.

In our culture a great deal of value is attached to the ability to use polysyllabic or "big" words. A person's vocabulary level is usually accepted as a means of estimating his intelligence. Furthermore, some people think that it is highly correlated with a person's knowledge and his accomplishment in academic life or in life outside of school. To use "big words" is also frequently regarded as a sign of being "cultured" and therefore of high intellectual and/or social status.

Thus we can expect some individuals, whose actual intellectual or social status is low but who nevertheless place a great deal of importance on status roles in social situations, to overcompensate for their inadequacies by using words which they identify with high status. These individuals are frequently intellectually ambitious and have high levels of aspiration. They wish to be accepted by others as bright or capable individuals. These persons betray themselves by using "big words" inappropriately. The fact that their use of words is incorrect reflects the discrepancy between their real capacities and their level of aspiration, or the discrepancy between their real and their desired roles in social situations.

Therefore, because of the manner in which the patient used the word "ejected" it is assumed that the patient has certain intellectual aspirations which are beyond his reach and that he is dissatisfied with the role he has played in life.

The second hypothesis, which is derived from his use of the word " ejected " and which follows from the assumptions indicated above, is that the patient has attempted to assume a definite role in the test situation itself. The test situation is a social situation.* Although the patient's primary objective in the test should be to tell stories, he realizes that the examiner is constantly evaluating these stories. Thus, as in other social situations where the patient knows his remarks serve as the basis on which other people evaluate him, he believes that the examiner's evaluation of his abilities will be determined by the content of his stories and the manner in which he tells them. Just as the patient has learned from past experience that he has been accepted or rejected on the basis of his productions, so he believes that the psychologist will utilize the same criteria in evaluating him. Fearing that the psychologist may reject him if he manifests any inadequacies, he tries to impress the examiner by using " big words " and at the same time he makes a very deliberate effort not to reveal to the examiner what, according to his own interpretation, are the negative aspects of his personality. However, it is highly improbable that he will be able to do this in all twenty of the stories. This is the first indication, therefore, that we should be on our guard in analyzing the stories. It is very likely that there will be several stories in which he will reveal his real problems and conflicts, and the way in

* Many of the factors discussed by Schachtel in his article entitled " Subjective Definitions of the Rorschach Test Situation and Their Effect on Test Performance," *Psychiatry*, Vol. 8, No. 4, November, 1945, pp. 419–448, apply equally well to the TAT test situation.

which he actually deals with them; and other stories which will reveal the manner in which he would *like* to deal with them and the way in which he would *like* to be regarded by others. It is likely, therefore, that many of those objects, activities, and sentiments which are very positively cathected in the stories, or which have a great deal of value attached to them in our culture, will be those which the patient would like to have or would like to assume. On the other hand, those objects, activities, or sentiments which appear to have negative values are more apt to be those which are the characteristics which the patient does possess and which he hopes to deny.

(Should the reader find himself in a situation where the patient has used the wrong word, he is cautioned not to ask the patient to repeat the word or to indicate by any means that the patient has made a mistake. To do so would suggest to the patient that the examiner has seen through the façade and that the examiner has pierced his first line of defense. Should the patient become aware of this, he may become completely inhibited and his stories might not be very revealing. If the examiner wishes to know if the patient does know the correct word, he should reserve his question until the end of the twenty stories.)

downhearted to think that he can't get it.

The patient is strongly motivated to be a success and he regards the presence of any frustration as a reflection upon his ability. When he encounters difficulty he is sad and, more important, his pride is hurt and his ego suffers a severe blow. Note also that the frustration does not lead to any aggression directed toward the outside world, but that all reactions to the frustration occur internally. It is therefore suggested that the patient is more intrapunitive than extrapunitive. This hypothesis should be checked with the data that will follow.

Looks to me like

See analysis that was made above of the patient's comments when he began this story.*

the type that in spite of hardships he's going through, that he'll come out in the end,

The dejection of the previous sentence is now supplanted by a more optimistic outlook — the hero is successful " in the end." It is doubtful whether this indicates real restriving or real counteraction in the patient himself. The patient tells us nothing about how the boy actually does overcome his obstacles but rather indicates by the use of the future tense that it is something that will happen. It has not happened in the past or in the present. Therefore, utilizing the hypothesis which was developed as to the role which the patient is playing in the test situation and the fact that the successful completion occurs in the future, it is suggested that he would like to be counteractive but that he probably is not.

as one who will be a stand-out in his profession.

Obviously the patient means " outstanding." The patient's remark reflects his high level of aspiration. This, plus the fact that he uses a word which he does not know very well, corroborates the previous hypothesis concerning the patient's desires for great achievements.

Summary Picture #1: The patient appears to have been uncomfortable and uneasy while taking the test. He has a level of aspiration beyond his capacities and it is suggested that he perceives the test as one in which he will have to prove his abilities. He attempts to erect a façade as a bright and capable individual and hopes that by assuming roles of

---

* Since the patient makes several such similar comments throughout the set of stories we shall not continue to highlight them.

high status value he will be accepted by others. He is easily discouraged when he encounters frustration and although he would like to be counteractive under such conditions, it is doubtful that he actually is so.

TAT Protocol	Analysis and Interpretation
Picture #2 I'd say he's a man who married young.	Three individuals appear in this picture — an older woman, a younger woman, and a man. In his story the patient speaks only of two — the farmer (the man) and the daughter (the younger woman). The third person, the older woman, is included in the story only by implication. It is assumed that the hero in the story is married to the older woman. This is a significant clue and its importance can be appreciated only if we compare it with the " clinical norm " for the stories told to this picture by young men. When young men tell stories to this picture and the man in the picture is married, his mate is the young woman. The older woman is usually seen as either the man's mother or the young woman's mother. The question therefore arises, why does this patient select a character which is usually seen as a mother-figure as the mate for his protagonist? The tentative hypothesis, at this point: that mother-son relationships at the present time appear to be quite significant in this case. This hypothesis is based on a very inadequate clue and it should be very carefully checked against the data which follow before it is accepted or rejected.
He was a hard worker and he is now at the point of seeing all his realizations coming true on the farm which he owns.	He is an energetic and ambitious individual who is desirous of achieving success by his independent efforts. Many individuals who have been exposed to and believe in the Horatio Alger myth reveal their philosophies of life in stories

similar to this. In these stories the hero, by dint of his own efforts, achieves great success. Clinical experience has also indicated that such patients may frequently become intrapunitive when they do not succeed in their plans. They believe that they do not succeed because they do not try hard enough and not because their plans are unrealistic.

He's a man that is happily married with a daughter going to school at the present time. He's a man of great foresight who will undoubtedly in the end achieve the goal which he has set out to accomplish.

The behavior of the hero indicates that the patient is purposeful, goal-directed, and persistent until he achieves his ends.

This is a very happy story and if it represented the actual status of our patient's life then he has no need to come to the clinic. If everything goes so well with him then he does not need aid. It is therefore suggested that this story does not represent the patient's true status but rather his desired status. Thus much of the data in this story is on a fantasy level.

It is also interesting to note that in the stories to both Picture #1 and Picture #2 there is little, if any, social interaction between the hero and any other individual or individuals. The inability to construct a story involving social relations suggests the possibility that the patient has found his own social relations quite unsatisfactory. Combining this hypothesis with the one suggested in the previous story, that the patient achieves his goals on a fantasy level, it is suggested that the patient tends to retreat from inadequate social relations to a world of fantasy in which he achieves all that he desires.

Summary Picture #2: The patient seems to be an energetic and ambitious individual with a high level of aspiration. He hopes to achieve his ambitions primarily by dint of his own independent efforts. There are two additional hypotheses suggested: mother-son relationships appear to have particular significance at the present time and the patient tends to retreat to a world of fantasy in which he achieves his goals because he finds his present social relationships quite unsatisfactory.

TAT PROTOCOL	ANALYSIS AND INTERPRETATION
PICTURE #3	
What could that be down there? (It could be anything you like it to be.)	The patient saw the gun lying on the floor but did not incorporate it in his story. The gun is an aggressive object and the fact that the patient avoids it suggests the possibility that he may have difficulty in handling aggression.
She started out in life	The figure in the picture is seen as a female. This is not sufficient grounds to assume that the patient identifies himself with female characters, since many males have difficulty in recognizing the sex of the figure in the picture. Nevertheless care should be taken to note how sexual situations are dealt with in the pictures that follow and particular attention should be paid to the roles with which the patient identifies in those situations.
the same as any other child,	Here the patient feels it necessary to compare the heroine with other children. The fact that he feels it necessary to make this comparison suggests the possibility that all may not have been well with him physically, emotionally, or socially. In view of the data obtained thus far, it is likely that his remark is determined by poor social relationships in childhood.
worked hard after graduating from school and found contentment quite a while.	Hard work and education are prerequisites for happiness.

Later on in life she ran into some trouble which she found hard to overcome,

This is very much like the theme in Picture #1, where the hero was well on his way to success but something turned up to interfere with complete happiness and successful accomplishment.

and is very much in despair.

This is the second occasion in which frustration is followed by the inner state of despair.

The outcome of her life will depend a great deal on the courage which she must have to overcome her present predicament.

Here the patient changes his role from storyteller to commentator. It is as if he were exchanging his role of patient for that of therapist. The latter is obviously more satisfying to him because it is of higher status value and places him in a position which is definitely higher than the one which he holds. Furthermore, this sentence does indicate that the patient has, at least, an intellectual appreciation of the fact that if change is to take place in one's condition then it is up to the individual himself to instigate that change. His statement that the heroine needs courage to overcome her difficulty suggests the possibility that the patient himself does not as yet have the courage to overcome his own problems.

Her interest in people and faith in people, I would say, must increase to a great degree in order for her to again find the happiness which she had before.

Apparently the patient has had difficulty in social relations and his reaction, like the heroine's, has been to withdraw from them. However, the patient does see the need for adequate social relations but probably has difficulty in establishing them.

I'd say that the outcome of her life is uncertain as a great deal is up to her.

The patient feels somewhat overpowered by the difficulties he has experienced in social relations and he has begun to doubt that he can pull himself out of his difficulties by himself.

It's up to her to pull herself together and face it. If she didn't she could continue on in the present state of mind

The patient reiterates that it is up to the individual to help himself overcome his difficulties. He also cites the alternative if he does not " pull himself together."

and possibly never again obtain the happiness which she had.

It is as if the patient were thinking aloud and verbalizing the alternatives which exist for him.

(That was good. Can you tell me what might be the trouble she ran into?)

This question was asked to determine the specific nature of the difficulty of which the patient spoke.

More or less feeling ejected by people. More or less ran into someone who hurt her deeply

(Note that here "ejected" means "rejected.") The "difficult situation" is one in which he has been rejected by others. Thus the hypothesis which was developed concerning his social relations on the basis of Pictures #1 and #2 is now borne out.

and that many of her ——— she feels that her friends feel she is no longer worthy to associate themselves with.

The patient is not certain whether the friends have actually rejected him or whether he only interprets their behavior as indicating that they have rejected him. The patient's concluding remarks reflect his feeling of inferiority and sense of worthlessness.

Summary Picture #3: The patient regards hard work and educational training as the means of attaining the happiness he desires. He has found social relations quite difficult because he feels rejected by others. He feels very inferior to others in his social group. However, he has at least an intellectual appreciation of the fact that if anything is to be done about his difficulties, he must do it himself. But presently he feels incapable of acting on his own. It is also suggested that the patient may have difficulty in dealing with situations involving sex and aggression.

TAT PROTOCOL

ANALYSIS AND INTERPRETATION

PICTURE #4

Looks to me like an average couple who get married and find great contentment

This is the second story in which the hero finds contentment through marriage, suggesting the possibility that the patient regards marriage as a prerequisite to contentment and happiness.

until he became despaired and discouraged in his work.

Inner states of despair and discouragement.

In the stories to Picture #1 and Picture #2 the patient spends most of his time discussing plots that involve successful accomplishment. In the stories to Picture #3 and Picture #4 the patient has begun to spend more time discussing failures. The change in theme may be a result either of the pictures themselves and the situations they depict or it may be a result of the fact that the patient is growing more and more secure in his relationship with the examiner. He need no longer affect a high status role but can begin to reveal his own problems and difficulties. (That the second hypothesis is tenable is revealed by the fact that the later stories do tend to deal with deeper and more personal material than the earlier ones.)

In the stories to Picture #3 and Picture #4 the hero's success occurs in the past and is short-lived. The patient spends a good deal more time in these stories discussing the difficulties involved in the present. But, more significantly, in discussing the present the patient is more concerned with feelings and inner states (usually of despair and discouragement) than with the objective situations that stimulate and produce these feelings. Thus it is likely that his frustration tolerance is low and that he is quick to see a situation as one involving conflict and one in which he is apt to fail rather easily. Such an attitude may stem from a series of earlier severe frustrations.

At the present time it is beginning to interfere with their home life

The despair and discouragement are quite severe and debilitating.

and she is trying to give him self-confidence enough to continue on in the field he was in. She looks like an intelligent person who can help to regain his self-confi-

The hero does not overcome his lack of self-confidence by himself, thus reinforcing the suggestion offered in Picture #2 that the patient does not feel that he can overcome his difficulties by himself. The patient, like the hero, requires a nurtur-

dence and for both to find happiness again.

ant person to help him in overcoming his difficulties.

It should be noted that the patient did not include the seminude figure on the wall in his story. This is a possible clue that the patient tends to avoid any object that stimulates sexual material.

Summary Picture #4: The patient is discouraged and lacking in self-confidence. He does not feel that he can overcome his difficulties by his own efforts. It is likely that he requires a nurturant person to help him. It is suggested that his frustration tolerance is low and that he is apt to evaluate most situations in terms of how frustrating they may be to him. It is further suggested that the patient is unable to cope adequately with sexual stimuli.

TAT PROTOCOL

ANALYSIS AND INTERPRETATION

PICTURE #5

Say she's a woman with one child

The patient limits the family constellation to just mother and child. By limiting the number of people in the family the patient does away with possible interference from the other members of the family, father and siblings, and thus has his mother all to himself. It was suggested earlier in Picture #2 that mother-son relationships are important. Here we have additional information to support our hypothesis.

and she has gone to the room where the child is studying and much to her despair

Again " despair " is one of the heroine's first reactions and this time in a situation in which the events do not follow the usual or expected course. In this story it is not assumed that the patient has identified with the female in the picture but that he has identified with the child. On the basis of the data obtained from the other stories, it is suggested that in this story the patient is describing his mother.

has found that the child is not in the room and possibly out playing

The mother despairs because the child is out playing instead of studying, as she probably wished the child to do. Insofar as the child is concerned, need play-mirth replaces need understanding.

as such children do when that age.	Apparently the patient feels that it isn't right for children to act contrary to their mothers' wishes and therefore he excuses the child by saying " as such children do when that age," namely, they are children and must be excused for their indiscretions. Or he may wish to indicate to the examiner the period in his life when such behavior did occur, namely, in childhood.
She will undoubtedly look for the child and bring him or her home	The mother feels that study is more important than play and brings the child home. Even at that age, when most boys are out playing, the mother insisted that the patient devote himself to his work and forego other pleasures.
and explain to them,	The mother apparently did not punish the patient physically but tried to correct his behavior by verbal methods.
him or her, that he should continue to do their work	In this sentence the patient feels it necessary to indicate the sex of the child. He alternates, however, between male and female, and between singular and plural pronouns. This confusion may stem from two factors. The first possibility is that the picture may have stimulated some personal problem which the patient may have experienced in the past and he hopes to deceive the examiner by not identifying the sex of the hero correctly and thus keep him from learning the content of the problem. Secondly, the confusion in the sex of the child may reflect the patient's confusion with regard to his own sex role. There was other evidence in Picture #3 that the patient may identify with female figures. Combining this evidence with the present data, which suggest con-

fusion as to his own sex role, it appears that the sexual area is fraught with problems for the patient.

to achieve their role in life.

Evidently the mother had set certain goals for the patient to attain. Thus it is learned that the mother is the original source of the patient's level of aspiration.

Undoubtedly she will explain to the child in a way that he will continue studying.

The mother is successful in getting the child to return to work and he does so without resistance.

(How does the child feel when he has to come back from play?)

Since the patient did not discuss specifically the hero's feelings with regard to the mother's action, it was considered wise that these be probed.

The child is not too studious but one who can get along.

The patient does not answer the question directly. It is, however, interesting that he does not express hostility against the mother even when pressed.

The last comment also reflects the inferiority feelings of which we had evidence before. It is also an expression of the fact that the patient doubts that he could achieve the goals that his mother had set for him.

From the total story it can be further inferred that the best way for the son to obtain his mother's love is through hard work and successful achievement, preferably in an academic role.

Summary Picture #5: Mother-son relationships appear to be extremely important. The mother appears to have been a demanding person who deprived the patient of the opportunity to play with boys his own age and insisted that he devote himself to his work in the hope that he would achieve his " role in life." Apparently the patient himself did not feel capable of achieving the goals which she had set for him. Nevertheless, he conformed to her wishes without resistance. It is also suggested that the patient has some difficulties involving sex.

TAT PROTOCOL   ANALYSIS AND INTERPRETATION

PICTURE #6

Say this young man in the beginning of his life was blessed, not blessed, say born into a home which could give him the proper education, possibly higher, higher education than average.

Despite the fact that the patient changes his mind and uses "born" instead of "blessed" his first choice is highly significant. It indicates how highly he values educational training. He regards it as a "blessing." Note that it is not just "proper education" that he desires but education that is "higher than average."

Through school he was an honor student who would do honor to anyone he was connected with. He has gone into life and has made a success of business

Again the success experience occurs in the past. Furthermore, achievement brings honor not only to the patient but also to anyone with whom he is connected. Thus by great achievements he becomes accepted by others.

but is now having trouble

The inevitable "but" and the "trouble" which occurs in the present.

explaining to his mother or making her understand what he wants to do.

It is interesting to compare the son's behavior in this picture with his behavior in Picture #5. In the latter the mother did all the explaining to the son and the son, without resistance, carried out her wishes. In the present story the son is doing the explaining to the mother. This difference in behavior is explained as reflecting the change in the patient's attitude toward his mother as he grew older. He has progressed from a submissive individual to a person who attempts to be more independent and assertive. Apparently he feels that he must consider his mother's feelings when planning a course of action because he does take time out to explain to her what it is he wants to do.

I'd say that they split up before this due to an argument and he's trying to make her understand his side of the story as well as her own.

The patient implies that there has been at least one other attempt to convince his mother of what he wants to do. One wonders therefore why it was that he could not stay away after this first attempt was unsuccessful. There are two possible hypotheses: first, as suggested above, he does not want to hurt his mother's feelings and secondly, he is so attached to her and so insecure in his new role as an independent and assertive individual that he is afraid to do anything without first getting his mother's permission.

The patient also provides information which reveals that he regards his mother as a very dominant and stubborn person who wants to have her own way at all times. She cannot appreciate her son's desire for autonomy and wants him to carry out her demands. In other words, she still wants to keep him as a little boy.

I'd say that he is a man who is strongheaded without realizing it and one that will go ahead when he's found the argument of no avail.

The son never convinces the mother because she is so obstinate. Apparently the patient regards being "strongheaded" as a negative trait because he feels it necessary to apologize for such behavior by suggesting that the hero is "strongheaded *without* realizing" it. Thus if the patient does do anything contrary to his mother's wishes, he feels quite uneasy and uncomfortable at the time.

Furthermore, it should be noted that the hero does not carry out his plans in the present but in the future. Combining this fact with the suggestions made earlier on the basis of the previous stories, that the patient appears to be lacking in assertiveness and self-confidence, it is suggested that the patient has a strong need autonomy but it is doubtful that he does satisfy this need.

Summary Picture #6: The patient has a strong need autonomy or desire to establish himself independently of his mother. However, he experiences a good deal of uneasiness and discomfort when he attempts to act according to his desires. It is doubtful that he can ever separate himself from his mother. His mother appears to be a very dominant woman who wants to run her son's life. It is also suggested that the patient places a good deal of importance upon education as a means of attaining his goals and he believes that successful accomplishments are means of facilitating the development of adequate social relationships.

TAT Protocol	Analysis and Interpretation
Picture #7	
Looks like father and son. Son has through hard work of his own made a great success in life.	Further evidence of the patient's energy, drive, and high level of aspiration.
His father couldn't give him very much support to begin with	The father is characterized quite differently from the mother. While the mother may have been dominant, she was definitely concerned about her son. But the father, according to his son, did not live up to his obligations to support his son. Thus it appears that one of the reasons why the son was not able to attain the goals he desired was his father's inability to give him the necessary financial aid.
and the son has become very independent because of his success	Successful accomplishment leads to independence.
and does not wish to have a great deal to do with his father.	The patient's attitude toward the father is quite different from the one he expressed toward his mother in the previous story. In the previous story he returned to the mother to explain his behavior to her; in this story he rejects his father after having been successful. Therefore it is suggested that the son prefers or cathects the mother more highly than he cathects his father.
He's one who will go his own way and not bother a great deal about his father's feelings in any way.	Again, this is quite different from his reaction to his mother. He is quite concerned about his mother's feelings but he is not at all concerned about his father's.
He may or may not find a great deal of happiness because of it.	Apparently the patient is not completely convinced that he can go through life rejecting his father.

Summary Picture #7: The patient's father appears to have been unable to support the patient financially. Because of this, the patient was unable to attain the educational training he desires so much and which he regards as a prerequisite to success. As a result, he tends to reject his father. However, although he does reject his father, he is quite uncomfortable about it. Previous hypotheses concerning the patient's drive and level of aspiration are also substantiated.

TAT PROTOCOL	ANALYSIS AND INTERPRETATION

PICTURE #8

This young man, early in life was wounded with a gun in an accident.	This is one of the few stories in which there is any indication of aggression. But two important factors should be noted: first, the aggression is not very intense and secondly, it is directed against the hero. Rarely, if at all, does the hero in any of the stories express aggression. Thus it is suggested that the patient regards himself as one who is usually the focus of aggression and secondly, that he himself rarely expresses any overt hostility.
He is now about high school age	Education appears to be so important to the patient that he reckons chronological age in terms of scholastic progress.
and when seeing the gun in what appears to me to be an attic, he is recalling in his own mind a vision of what was done to him at the time of the accident. I believe that it is something which he will recall more than once in his life.	The patient may have experienced a traumatic event in the past and he may be referring to it in this story. This should be checked in the stories that follow. One of the important factors to be noted, however, is that the patient does engage in autistic thinking and that he tends to be perseverate on situations in which he has been involved in the past. He may possibly be particularly concerned about those situations in which aggression has been directed against him.
I don't think he is one to bear a grudge for it	The patient says that he is incapable of any malice at all.
as he is understanding and forgiving.	He is kind, forgiving, and accepting.

A MALE PATIENT STARTS THERAPY

I'd say that he'd go on to live an average life.

This last sentence is the patient's means of complying with the instructions to tell us something about the future. The patient appears to be so concerned about the past, and so involved in thinking about the past in the present, that he almost forgets to tell us about the future. It should be noted that in almost every story the patient tells us something about the past, present, and future in what appears to be a very forced manner. It is suggested that this approach reflects the patient's desire to conform very closely to the rules set down by those whom he regards as superior and to behave in such a manner that he will be absolutely right in all that he does. By not straying from the rules, he does not leave himself open to criticism. These hypotheses should be checked not only against the patient's approach to the other stories, but also against the manner in which he deals with his drives and social relationships.

Furthermore, the approach which the patient has adopted in relating the events that occur in the stories does not indicate that the patient is a very creative individual of superior ability who has had the advantage of advanced educational training. Creative and bright subjects do not usually state explicitly the period of time with which they are concerned. Their style is smooth and free flowing and the time factor is reflected in the tenses of the verbs. The stories are usually more complicated and not as descriptive as those of other patients. Consequently, combining the data obtained from the patient's approach to the stories with the clues regarding his intelligence as obtained from an evaluation of his vocabulary, it is suggested that the patient is of average intelligence.   On the basis of this evaluation, it is doubtful that he can achieve the goals he desires.

Summary Picture #8: The patient is himself unable to express much aggression.   He regards himself as being the focus of aggression.   While others may be hostile toward him, he does not retaliate in kind but " turns the other cheek."   He perceives himself as a kind, accepting, and forgiving individual.   It is possible that he may have experienced some traumatic event in the past and that this story is based upon it.   This should be checked against the data which follow.   He also appears to follow rules and regulations very carefully.   On the basis of the clues in this test regarding the patient's intelligence, training, and ability, it is doubtful that he can realize his high level of aspiration.

TAT PROTOCOL	ANALYSIS AND INTERPRETATION
PICTURE #9	
I'd say they started out in life somewhat of a poor home.	The home environment is uncongenial. The " poor home " may refer to the financial conditions of the home or to the way in which the home has been managed. The former has been already indicated in Picture #7.
They got to an age	Apparently the behavior which the patient is about to describe is the behavior which occurred at a later stage in his development and was probably quite different from the pattern of his behavior in his earlier years. Note how this supports the hypothesis that was developed by comparing Picture #5 and Picture #6. In the first of these he told us how the boy reacted when he was young and in the second he told us how he would have preferred to behave when he grew older.
where they felt that they should run away, to get away from it.	At this later age the patient felt that he should reject his home.
They have ended finding they could not find happiness by running away and	Rejecting the home and running away is no solution because the men do not find satisfaction. Note how similar the

are very undecided what to do.

reaction of these men to their home is to the patient's reaction, noted in previous stories, where a break from home seemed imminent. In the previous stories (Pictures #6 and #7) it was also doubted that the patient could effect an adequate adjustment away from home. Thus, although the patient may desire to leave his home and be independent of his family, he is not sure that he will be able to find the satisfaction he desires away from home. He is in conflict. On the one hand he cannot stay at home because it does not satisfy his needs. On the other, he does not want to leave home because he is afraid that he will not find happiness elsewhere. He therefore stays at home and the conflict is unresolved.

A group of men who have taken to the road, who will continue on for the rest of their lives traveling but never reaching their goal.

The patient seems quite pessimistic about ever resolving his problem. He is extremely doubtful that he will ever achieve what he wants. However, it is interesting to note that he may have some specific goal. It is not a meaningless chase.

(That was good but can you tell me what their goal was?)

This question was asked to determine whether there was any specific goal.

To find beyond their reach more or less a home suitable for them.

It is still impossible to determine exactly what kind of home he wants, since the word "suitable" does not give us very much information as to what specific needs must be satisfied. Nevertheless, note the hopelessness that the patient expresses with respect to ever achieving the goal he desires.

(Yes, but can you tell me what was wrong with their home?)

Another probe for more specific information.

It was poorly managed and they were not given proper attention.

This is an important bit of information. It is a crucial part of the picture that has been missing up to now. It is a necessary clue for understanding many of the dynamics involved in the patient's problems and difficulties. Briefly, what the patient tells in this sentence is that due to the uncongenial environment at home his need for recognition was frustrated. In other words, he felt rejected at home. The rejection theme in this and other stories helps to clarify and support many of the factors that were indicated previously.

(1) It reinforces the belief that the patient is playing a role in the test situation and that his use of "big words" and "desirable" plots are attempts to attain recognition from the examiner. By playing the role of a capable individual, by using "big words" and "desirable" plots, the patient hopes to satisfy in the test situation needs which have been frustrated in the past.

(2) The reason why many of the patient's stories deal with his aspirations and why many of these are on a fantasy level can also be better appreciated. One of the reactions to frustration and rejection is to retreat to fantasy. Since fantasy life is so completely unstructured, the individual who fantasies reigns supreme and he can determine what shall and what shall not occur. Thus in his fantasy life he achieves all that he is unable to achieve in reality. He becomes the honor student who would do honor to anyone with whom he is associated; he also becomes successful in business and thus must be recognized by others (Picture #6).

(3) The reasons why several of the heroes in the earlier stories achieve their goals without aid can also be better understood. Since he is not recognized at home and is not given the attention he

desires, he feels it incumbent upon him to prove to those at home that he can be successful without their aid.

(4) The reasons why he has constructed situations in which there is a mother with only one child can also be better appreciated. If the others reject him in real life, then he will reject them in fantasy and thus obtain the love and affection of the one he desires.

(5) The reasons why education appears to be such an important factor are also more apparent. An adequate educational background would have provided him with the necessary skills and means with which to establish himself independently of others. Furthermore, it is possible that he may have been rejected because of poor scholastic attainments.

(6) The reason why he despairs when he thinks that he cannot get the solution to a problem by himself, as in Picture #1, is a little more obvious. No one else will help him when he gets into difficulty. More significantly, he feels that they might reject him because his inability to solve a problem indicates weakness.

(7) Having experienced rejections early in life, he desires aid from a nurturant person to help him overcome his difficulties, as in Picture #3.

(8) Not having been completely accepted at home in his youth and adolescence, and therefore not having received sufficient love and affection, the patient was not in an environment in which he could develop sufficient ego-strength so that he could establish and maintain his independence without anxieties. In view of his earlier rejections, he has become somewhat dependent and submissive.

Summary Picture #9: The patient regards his home environment as having been uncongenial. He feels that his home was poorly managed and that he did not receive the proper attention. Thus, in essence, he felt rejected. This is an important clue to the dynamics involved in this case. Although he would like to leave home, he is afraid that he will never find the conditions which are necessary for the satisfaction of his needs.

TAT PROTOCOL

ANALYSIS AND INTERPRETATION

PICTURE #10

This one could start in the cradle.

A very literal attempt to comply with the instructions to tell us what happened in the past.

They're average people to begin with who have completed schooling.

The schooling which the characters have had appears somewhat irrelevant, since it does not play an important role in the plot. But once again it reflects the importance which the patient attaches to education — even "average" people have an education.

They did not know each other before, that is when they were younger and have only met and taken up an acquaintance which both find very interesting to both of them.

It should be noted that the relationship between these two individuals is kept on a very superficial level. It is only an "acquaintance" which is very "interesting." There is no expression of any deeper emotional ties. But there is some satisfaction which the hero does derive from this relationship.

I believe that they will continue to go together for a length of time and in middle age marry

The courtship is unusually prolonged and the marriage is quite delayed. Several of the factors, indicated previously, which might play an important role in this regard are the patient's dependent attitude with regard to his mother, and his inability to establish himself away from home, and his problems with regard to sex.

and find a great deal of happiness in each other's companionship.

There is no expression of love or any real emotion even after marriage. Their happiness revolves about their "companionship." Thus it is suggested that the patient is as yet not ready to establish any emotional ties in a heterosexual relationship.

Summary Picture #10: The patient is quite hesitant about establishing any emotional ties with a member of the opposite sex. It is suggested that his dependent attitude with regard to his mother, his inability to establish himself independently of his family, and his problems with regard to sex are several of the important factors which militate against his being able to effect an adequate heterosexual adjustment.

TAT PROTOCOL	ANALYSIS AND INTERPRETATION

PICTURE #11

Looks like, I believe they're animals walking along looking for food.

When evaluated directly, "looking for food" is a reflection of the patient's need nutriance. On a deeper level of interpretation, however, it is suggested that the search for food reflects the patient's dependent needs. Many psychoanalytic studies of psychosomatic patients, especially those with gastric disorders, have indicated that food frequently plays an important role in the dreams of these patients. Stated very briefly, the psychoanalytic point of view on this matter is that since the mother is the original source of satisfaction for the child's hunger drives, the striving for food in psychosomatic patients with gastric complaints is an indication of the patient's desire to re-establish the earlier satisfying relationship with the mother. Thus food in these cases is a symbolic reflection of the dependent strivings or need succorance in the patient. This line of thought has been followed in interpreting the present story.*

The lizard was asleep and heard them going by. He

This is the second picture in which there is aggression expressed in the story.

---

* It should be noted at this point that the writer did not suggest in his final report that the patient was suffering from ulcers. There was no attempt to determine the exact symptomatology in this case. However, when it was learned that the patient did have ulcers, the dynamics which might have been involved in its development could be found in the report based on the TAT.

awoke, looked out and saw the animals and decided to use them as a meal for himself. After chasing them for quite a distance he caught one or two of the three and returned to his former hiding place and slept off the meal.

(Picture #8 was the first.) Once again the aggression is not expressed by the figure with whom the patient identifies but against him. Thus it is again suggested that the patient does not express any aggression overtly but rather that he regards himself as the focus of aggression. Furthermore, there is no counteraction or retaliation on the part of the patient to any aggression directed against him. His defense in this case is to retreat as fast as he can. It is also interesting that the small animals never succeed in satisfying their needs, just as the patient himself never succeeded in satisfying his. Compare this story with the one regarding press rejection in Picture #9.

Summary Picture #11: The patient is a dependent individual who probably has difficulty in expressing any overt hostility. In situations involving aggression, it is more likely that he will be the focus of aggression than the one to express it. When he encounters aggression, he is more apt to retreat than to fight back.

TAT PROTOCOL

ANALYSIS AND INTERPRETATION

PICTURE #12

The man leaning over the boy is one who at one time or other has studied hypnotism and is putting what he has learned into practice.

The protagonist in the story to this picture is the hypnotist. Nevertheless, it is assumed that the patient identified with the figure of the boy and not with the hypnotist. Clinical experience with this picture has shown that when patients tell stories to it which involve some psychotherapeutic procedure, they reveal their attitudes to the therapist and the therapeutic situation. Since some patients believe that hypnotism is an integral part of psychotherapy, it is assumed that our patient will reveal his attitude to therapy in this story.

At the present time he has put his subject to sleep and is making him rest peace-

Note that the patient has taken a very passive role in this situation. The hypnotist has done everything so far with

fully. If he continues properly with what one might call an experiment on his part the boy will awaken and continue on in normal life.

very little cooperation from the subject. Since the subject is so peaceful at present, it is suggested that the patient has begun to derive some benefit from treatment. The patient seems somewhat uncertain about the therapist's abilities. He is concerned lest the therapist not conduct the therapy properly and do the subject harm. But there is an element of hope in his concluding remarks. This reflects the patient's hopefulness that he will be cured by therapy and that he will lead a normal life.

Summary Picture #12: In view of the patient's dependent feelings, indicated previously, it is interesting to note that he has chosen a passive role in therapy. He is hopeful that the therapist will be able to cure him but it is doubtful that the patient will actively participate in therapy.

TAT PROTOCOL

ANALYSIS AND INTERPRETATION

PICTURE #13

Before the tragedy which now has entered the home of this young man

This is an "original" story using the term "original" as it is applied in the Rorschach.

and his mother, they both led a normal life.

Clinical experience has shown that men of the same age as the patient usually perceive the woman lying on the couch as the wife, fiancee, or girl friend of the hero. Or she might be a prostitute. In a large number of cases the stories revolve about sex. This patient's story deviates from the "norm" and this deviation appears to be significant. The fact that he sees a mother figure where most individuals see a sexual object suggests, once again, that mother-son relationships are exceedingly important. On a deeper level, this is suggestive of an unresolved oedipal situation. Furthermore, by not discussing the sexual factors that might be involved in this picture, it is suggested that the patient has had difficulty in effecting a mature heterosexual adjustment and that he shies away from sexual material.

Upon returning from school he has found his mother dead upon her bed, from an illness which she had been suffering from for quite some time.

This statement suggests that the patient has a good deal of repressed aggression against the mother. A frequent technique used by most patients who cannot express their aggression directly against the people to whom they feel hostile is to have them die in the stories because of natural causes or as a result of an accident. They achieve their ends, therefore, without suffering guilt. The act was committed by an external force over which they had no control. Thus it is suggested that it would be wiser to describe the patient's attitude toward his mother as ambivalent in view of the fact that previous stories have indicated that she is also positively cathected.

When the boy finally adjusts himself to a new home, which could be with friends or relatives

It is rather interesting to note that the hero does not express any real feeling because his mother has died nor does he mourn her very long. No sooner does she die than he begins to adjust himself to a new home. Only because the patient uses the words " tragedy " and " adjust " is it suggested that he did feel badly. The lack of feeling following the death of the mother reinforces our hypothesis regarding the hostility that is directed toward her.

he will again find interest in school and complete whatever education is necessary and lead a life of his own.

The cause of the hostility is now evident. The mother does not permit him to lead a life of his own. Thus if she dies he can proceed to become an independent person in his own right. Furthermore, it should be noted that education, once again, is an important prerequisite to success or to being able to lead a life of one's own.

Summary Picture #13: Mother-son relationships are exceedingly important. It is suggested that part of the patient's conflict involves an unresolved oedipal situation. His attitude toward his mother is best described as ambivalent. His hostility toward her appears to be based on the fact that while she is alive he cannot " lead a life of his own."

TAT PROTOCOL	ANALYSIS AND INTERPRETATION

PICTURE #14

I don't get the darkness in the home and light outside — that's what got me —— All I can say, he may be one who in the past has studied astronomy and is now looking up at the sky. He may possibly continue along this line,	Education results in the selection of a profession. Because of the fact that the profession is a scientific one, and because the patient, on the basis of the other stories, does not appear to have any " scientific curiosity " which would lead him into science, it is suggested that his choice has been made on the basis of the prestige value that it has for him.
and some day work for someone in that line and possibly some day become a well-known astronomer	Although he is willing to serve an apprenticeship to one who is superior to himself, he hopes some day to be successful and famous in his own right. The fact that he uses the word " possibly " indicates his doubt concerning his ability to achieve his goals.
or astronomist	A neologism due to lack of knowledge of the correct word. Note once again the desire to use " big words."
in his own right.	The desire to be autonomous and independent of others.

Summary Picture #14: Very little new material has been gained from this story. The patient's high level of aspiration, his desire for independence, and his doubt concerning his ability to achieve his goals are evident once again.

TAT PROTOCOL	ANALYSIS AND INTERPRETATION

PICTURE #15

God, what is this supposed to be —— I know, it's a graveyard, but that's all I can say . . .	The patient's comment and his long delay may reflect that the picture is so difficult as to tax his creativity, or it reflects the anxiety which the picture has stimulated in him. From the story that follows it appears that the latter is the more

He is a man who has worked hard all his life.

tenable hypothesis and the anxieties revolve about the death of the mother.

High energy level and strong drive.

Through his hard work he has fulfilled his ambitions,

Need achievement.

which were never realized by the loved one which he is now visiting.

This statement is a little abstruse. It is not clear whether the " loved one " did not realize her own ambitions or did not live to see the hero realize his ambitions. One possibility is that the " loved one " led an unsuccessful life and the hero achieved the success which the " loved one " herself could not achieve during her own lifetime. The other possibility is that she died before the hero achieved his goal. If the first hypothesis is correct, then it is suggested that the " loved one " may have lived through the patient and driven him on to great heights in order that she might enjoy, albeit vicariously, the successes which she was unable to enjoy during her own life. If the second hypothesis is correct, then the patient feels that the time may be short and that he had better achieve his successes quickly in order that the " loved one " will be able to give him her love in return for his good work. Otherwise she may die and it will be too late.

The loved one should have been a greater part of his life

The relationship between the " loved one " and the patient was not completely satisfactory.

but was not because of the work which he had himself so wrapped up in. I believe he now realizes this and knows that although he accomplished what he set out to do in his work he never fully appreciated or enjoyed her company.

This is the first instance in the set of stories in which hard work has some negative value. The hero is so involved in hard work that he does not have the time to enjoy the love he really wants.

He may or may not again return to the work which he has been doing in the past, for he will always realize in his own mind no matter what work he may enter that he missed something in life which is much greater than success itself.

There are several important factors indicated in these remarks. First of all, the patient cannot be motivated to work hard unless there is a constant source of love available. It is his need for acceptance and love that is motivating him constantly. Secondly, his primary need is for love and affection and his high level of aspiration is only a means of attaining this love. He is not interested in science or a profession because of any insatiable curiosity or desire to help humanity. He aspires to great heights (and they need not be in any specific field) because he believes that through great achievements he will receive the love he desires. Thirdly, another conflict in which the patient finds himself can be better understood. This conflict may be described as follows: In order to achieve the love and affection he desires from his love object, he must work hard, but if he works hard then he loses all the valuable time during which he might get more and more of the affection he desires. However, if he spends all the time trying to gain the favor of the " loved one " he may actually lose her love in the long run because he believes that he must be successful if he is to win and keep her affection. Furthermore, there is additional pressure put on the patient. He seems to feel that the " loved one " might die before he has achieved his great heights. If this happens, then all his efforts would have been for naught and he will lose forever the source of his love and affection.

(That was good, but can you tell me who might the loved one have been?)

This question was asked to determine specifically who the " loved one " is.

Probably his wife or mother.

The mention of " wife " is discounted since it is apparently camouflage to deceive the examiner. To mention the mother alone would have been to give himself away completely. The mother, then, is the " loved one " whom the patient wishes to satisfy. It is interesting that " wife " and " mother " do occur together. This suggests the possibility that the patient's desired mate is one who will satisfy the same needs as the mother does. (Note the description of the mate in Picture #3 and how similar she is to the characterization of the mother in most of the other stories.)

Summary Picture #15: The patient's high level of aspiration appears to stem from his desire to receive love and affection from his mother. He feels that by successful accomplishment he will win her love. However, he also feels that by working hard to achieve great goals he does not have sufficient time to win her favor. Thus he is in a situation which remains unsolved. It is also suggested that his desired mate is a mother-figure. Ambivalent feelings with regard to the mother were also indicated.

TAT Protocol	Analysis and Interpretation
Picture #16	
The picture I see in front of me is a young man and his mother.	When given a completely unstructured situation, the patient immediately begins to structure it in terms of a problem with which he is deeply concerned, namely, mother-son relationships. It should be noted that throughout the story to this card the mother plays a dominant role.
She has in the past through her hard work	The mother, like the patient, is a driving and energetic person. It is possible that the patient has developed his own drive because of her influence and such evidence is available from a previous story (Picture #5).
given him the education and the background to go on to be an average successful man.	The mother, unlike the father (Picture #7), is a hard-working individual who is a source of support to the patient. She aids him in the attainment of his goals.

He, through gratitude to her, unintentionally may devote most of his life to her,

The patient feels very strongly that he must repay his mother for all that she has done for him. The use of the word "unintentionally" is interesting. On the one hand it indicates that the patient felt quite helpless in reacting the way he did to his mother. That is, it was only "natural" for him to desire to repay his mother for all that she has done for him. On the other hand, it may be that he feels that it is necessary to apologize to the examiner for acting the way he did. That is, he realizes that he should not have been so completely concerned about devoting all his life to his mother. Thus by using the word "unintentionally," he attempts to indicate that it was not his "fault." (It should be noted that in a previous story, Picture #6, the patient also apologized for the hero when the latter was in conflict with the mother.)

and possibly miss the happiness which he may have found in companionship with friends, both men and women.

The devotion to the mother is so complete that he is unable to establish adequate social relations with any others.

He does not regret doing anything for his mother

The patient has subjugated himself completely to fulfilling his mother's needs. On the basis of Pictures #6, #9, #13, and #15, one doubts if he "does not regret doing anything for his mother." It is therefore suggested that, at best, his feelings toward his mother should be characterized as ambivalent. However, in view of the fact that in most of the stories involving aggression the hero rarely expresses the aggression, it is suggested that the patient suppresses the hostile feelings which he has toward his mother.

as he realizes that if it was not for her devoting so much

Since the mother has been so good to him, he feels obligated to repay her in

time and energy towards his welfare that he may not have been the man that he is to-day.

His mother is one who is selfish

kind. He feels that if he achieves anything at all, it is primarily his mother's doing.

From what follows it appears that the patient did not mean that she is " selfish " but rather that she is not selfish. Nevertheless, it is suggested that this slip of the tongue is significant and probably indicates his covert feelings regarding his mother and one which he would not have desired to make public. This slip of the tongue confirms in some measure our hypothesis stated above regarding his ambivalent feelings toward his mother.

and encourages him to go among friends and find as much happiness as he can.

The patient now defends the mother. Even though he does not go off to make friends, he wants it known that it is not his mother's fault. He would like us to believe that she really wants him to go off and make friends, and that his lack of social success is primarily his own fault and due to his own inadequacies. Thus he appears intrapunitive. It should be noted how the mother's behavior in this picture differs from that described in the earlier pictures, in which she tried to keep him away from friends (Picture #5). Possibly the mother has come to realize the harm she has done to her son and she would like to have him change in certain directions.

She would like him to marry

The motivation for marriage does not come from the son but rather from the mother. Apparently she has planned a good part of his life.

if he feels that he has found the proper mate for himself.

The mother's desire that he marry is bound by a very important qualification. The patient may marry provided " he has found the proper mate for himself." Thus, although his mother wishes him to marry, she does not relinquish completely her hold on the patient. No doubt the mother has had much to do with the setting up of the standards which her son's mate must meet before she can be considered a " proper mate." Furthermore, by this qualification the patient also reserves the privilege for himself to reject any possible mates. He can continue to delay marriage, ostensibly because he has not found the " proper mate," while in reality the standards he has set for this mate may be as unrealistic as his high level of aspiration, and also because mother-son ties are so strong.

And to build a life of his own.

The mother probably feels that it is about time that her son should become independent of her or, more likely, the patient would like his mother to feel that it is about time he became independent of her.

(How does he feel about being obligated to his mother?)

This question was asked in an attempt to elicit any deeper feelings which the patient may have had regarding his attitude toward his mother.

Even though he may marry while his mother is still alive

Although the patient does not answer the question directly, it was not considered wise to continue probing in this direction, since too many anxieties may have been stirred. His answer does imply the doubt which he has concerning the possibility that he will ever get married.

he will see to it that she is always provided for to the best of his ability.

His sense of duty and obligation is so strong that he will continue to care for his mother even after he is married.

Summary Picture #16: The patient feels completely obligated to his mother for all that she has done for him; it is quite obvious that he feels duty-bound to take care of her now and even after he has married. It appears that his mother may have changed her attitude with regard to her son. While she kept him from associating with others of his own age group in the past, she now wants him to participate in social groups. In view of the patient's manner of dealing with aggression, it is suggested that the patient does not express his hostile feelings toward his mother but rather suppresses them. In the main he is intrapunitive.

TAT Protocol	Analysis and Interpretation

PICTURE #17

This man was born in the circus life and brought up in it. He has been taught by his father to do tricks which he himself has done in the past.

This is the first time that a father has been mentioned as having helped a son. In view of all the material that has been gathered from the previous pictures it is doubtful that the patient is referring here to the actual relationship which existed between himself and his father. It is therefore suggested that the patient's discussion of the father in this picture indicates the kind of father he wants — namely, one who will teach him how to become superior. Another possible interpretation is that the father in this story represents a special role in the family which the patient would like to have.

He is now about 26 years old

Exactly the same age as the patient.

and is earning his living doing the tricks, I should say performing the tricks which his father has taught him. He like his father will stay in that type of life as long as he may live.

After having been taught by the father, the son is now capable of taking over the father's role completely. In other words, he is able to replace him. Combining this story with the data gathered from the previous ones, we have all the factors necessary to complete the picture of an unresolved oedipus complex. There is hostility against the father, a very strong relationship with the mother, and finally a desire to replace the father.

It is interesting to note that the patient has selected the circus and the performing of tricks as a means of earning a livelihood. Such activity provides the hero with a good many opportunities for the satisfying of his exhibitionistic needs and also provides him with a good deal of praise, approval, and recognition which he desires. Thus if the father had been the type of man the patient wanted him to be, the patient could have achieved all that he desired.

Summary Picture #17: The patient wants a father-figure who would be a source of support to him and who would provide him with the necessary means with which to achieve the goals he desires. On a deeper level, it is suggested that one of the patient's problems revolves about an unresolved oedipal complex.

TAT PROTOCOL

ANALYSIS AND INTERPRETATION

PICTURE #18

He returned home from work as always. He had supper with his wife and children and then went to visit some friends which he knows in a nearby tavern.

In general the patient's characterization of the heroes in the previous pictures was interpreted as a reflection of the manner in which the patient perceives himself. From these stories the patient appears to perceive himself as a kind individual who does not bear grudges (Picture #8), he is hard-working (Pictures #2, #7), he is a dutiful son who does not avoid his obligations to his mother (Picture #16), he avoids sexual objects (Picture #4), and he avoids aggressive objects (Picture #3). From these traits, the patient appears to be an ideal person who has few negative traits. Most of the behavior that he attributes to his heroes has positive value. If his heroes commit any wrongs at all they usually do so without intending malice. This is the first story, however, in which the hero strays from the straight and narrow path. It is therefore quite important that the effects of this hero's behavior be studied, since it may provide us with the necessary clues as to why the patient constantly considers it necessary to confine himself to " proper " behavior.

During the course of the night he drank quite heavily. Without realizing the danger he put himself in, he

The hero gets into trouble without meaning to do so. The money which the hero has exposed is interpreted as having certain symbolic significance for

exposed to the eyes of others a large sum of money.

the patient. It is interpreted as meaning power to him because having money means being wealthy. On the basis of the previous stories, it is suggested that the power he wants would permit him to be independent.

On the way home he is attacked from behind but because of his condition he was not able to protect himself properly. He was beaten and robbed of the money which he had on him and lie there

Again aggression is directed against the patient. Note that he does not fight back.

until someone took him to a place for treatment.

Another person is again called upon to help him out of his difficult situation. Thus, when the patient is in difficulty, he needs another's aid to help him overcome his problems. He cannot handle his problems alone.

As most of these cases are never solved, he will lose the money which he has so foolishly exposed and will never do it again.

The hero has lost his wealth forever. Thus we see that the patient conforms to acceptable behavior all the time because he is afraid that if he does not he will get into difficulty and lose all that he has worked to attain. Therefore it is best that he be very moral, that he stay on the straight and narrow path, and thus not get into difficulties.

A deeper psychoanalytic interpretation of this story seems relevant. Money, to this patient, may not only be symbolic of power but also of the penis. Thus by exposing his money (and it is interesting that the patient uses the word " exposes " in this story) to the group of his male friends, he is symbolically exposing himself and demonstrating to them that he is as good or as masculine as they. But when he does so, he is attacked and robbed of his wealth or masculinity. This story therefore suggests the patient's fear of castration. Briefly then, the patient feels that he dare not demonstrate his masculinity, be assertive, or enter into competition with other men since they might become aggressive against him — or castrate him.

Summary Picture #18: The patient is afraid to stray from the straight and narrow path or to behave contrary to what he considers to be morally acceptable behavior. To leave the confined boundaries of this path would be to leave himself open to attack. Therefore, in order to avoid difficulty, he conforms to all the mores and high standards of society in a very careful manner.

TAT PROTOCOL   ANALYSIS AND INTERPRETATION

PICTURE #19

———— This picture was drawn by a man who, whom from his childhood has studied painting and has reached the stage where he has gone in for the modern type of art.

Although the patient has difficulty in developing a story to this picture, he does not discard the picture. To discard it would mean that he has failed and that would be a severe blow to his ego. It is therefore interesting to note what he does with this picture. He avoids the content of the picture and proceeds to discuss the artist. He also chooses to call it an object of "modern art." Thus he has a rationalization for his obvious difficulty. Among some laymen, modern art is completely enigmatic and meaningless. Only the artist himself can understand what he has attempted to portray. Therefore, since the patient has been presented with a picture of modern art, it cannot be expected of him to understand what is going on. Furthermore, by mentioning "modern art" the patient manages to indicate that he knows such an art form exists. It is suggested that the patient regards this evidence of his knowledge of modern art as an indication of good breeding and good educational background and thus his status and prestige are both increased.

The drawing which he has made will in the future be

The patient's drive and strong need for successful accomplishment appear once

hung in art galleries for many visitors to come and look at and praise.

He will undoubtedly continue through hard work to go on to greater heights.

(That was a good story but can you make up a story about the picture itself?)

I can't figure out what it is supposed to be. I see a chimney on top, snow on the outside of the roof and windows. I can't understand what that is supposed to be in the sky. I can't make a story out of it.

again. This time, however, his desire for recognition is also included. This corroborates our earlier hypotheses that the patient is seeking praise, approval, and recognition by means of accomplishment.

Note how the patient reacts to praise and recognition. It heightens his level of aspiration and spurs him on to greater and greater achievement.

This question was asked to bring the patient back to the picture itself.

Future research involving this picture might well be focused upon two major problems. The first is the content of stories told to this picture. Clinical experience has indicated that the severity of the psychological disturbance is negatively correlated with the degree of solidity of the formal structure that is developed to this picture. Thus, at one extreme, " normals " see a house and, at the other, schizophrenics frequently have difficulty in recognizing any form at all. It is suggested, therefore, that one might, depending on the research, develop a scoring system for this picture which would be comparable to the F+ in Rorschach testing. The interpretive significance of this datum in the TAT might very well be the same as in the Rorschach — as an index of ego-strength (see S. J. Beck, *Rorschach's Test,* Vol. II, p. 20, New York: Grune and Stratton, 1945). Thus it is suggested that because the patient could mention only discrete parts of the picture and not bind them together into a whole (e.g., " house "), that this may reflect the weak state of the patient's ego.

Summary Picture #19: Additional evidence has been obtained from this picture concerning the patient's high level of aspiration and his desire for praise, approval, and recognition.

TAT PROTOCOL   ANALYSIS AND INTERPRETATION

PICTURE #20

He starts off in childhood as an average boy does. He may or may not have completed grammar and high school.

This is the first time that a hero appears who has not had very much of an education. It will therefore be possible to compare what he thinks happens to a person who does not have very much of an education with what happens to a person who has all the education he desires.

He is at the present time a man of about 35 years of age.

The hero is much older than the patient himself. It is suggested that the patient is apparently going to tell us what he thinks his future will be, since he, too, does not appear to have had much education.

He's the type that depends a great deal upon his friends to help him when he is out of work.

Only adequate education does not lead to much success and even failure. Therefore, the hero becomes dependent upon others for aid but, as has been observed previously (Pictures #6 and #7), the patient would much rather regard himself as an independent and self-made man. Thus it appears that he drives himself on to great heights in order that he will not be forced to depend upon others for aid.

He will not rise to great heights as he has not the initiative to do so.

The hero does not have energy or drive and therefore he will never amount to much. Thus, in order not to come to the same end as the hero, the patient had better work hard.

He will get along but he will never be satisfied

Just to " get along " is a completely unsatisfactory situation for the patient.

because he has missed too much.

To what this comment refers it is hard to say, unless the patient means that he missed too much education.

(That was good but can you tell me what it was that he missed?)

This question was asked to find out what it was that the patient meant by his concluding remarks.

Put it this way. He is the type of man who would like to have risen to greater heights but feels as though he cannot because of his lack of education to do so.

This confirms several of the hypotheses which we have developed previously. The patient believes that education is a prerequisite to achieving great heights. Not having had this education, he feels that he will never amount to much and therefore will become dependent upon others — a situation which he cannot tolerate. It therefore appears that this story contains the patient's real fears.

Summary Picture #20: The patient fears that because of his lack of education he will never amount to much and therefore will become dependent upon others. This would be quite an unsatisfactory situation for the patient because he prefers to be independent and successful.

Final TAT Summary

This patient is a dependent and submissive individual who has experienced severe rejection in his home and in social groups outside the home. As a result, he has been continually frustrated in his need for recognition and constantly deprived of the love and affection he desires. He has fantasied a good deal as to the means through which he might be able to satisfy his frustrated needs and he has tried, albeit unsuccessfully, to achieve the role he desires. At present, he attempts to deny his dependent and submissive tendencies, which have forced him into an inferior position socially. But he finds it difficult to become the assertive and independent person about which he has fantasied because he cannot break old family ties and overcome old behavior patterns. He also fantasies of the day when he will become highly successful and thus achieve superior social prestige and with it all the love and recognition and affection which he lacks at present. But here, too, the patient is frustrated. He believes that he lacks sufficient educational training, which he regards as a prerequisite for successful accomplishment. The patient therefore finds himself in the midst of an insoluble frustrating situation. On the one hand, he has grown dissatisfied with his present role in life and, on the other, he feels incapable of doing much about it.

The patient regards himself as a " kind " person who does not " bear a grudge " against anyone. In many ways he attempts to be a faultless individual who cathects only the highest of ideals and always behaves in the most correct fashion. He tries to achieve this ideal state by avoiding any situation which might stimulate him to act in such a way that others might disapprove of him. He rigidly conforms to the codes and rules of behavior which are set down by others and highly cathected by society. In this manner he denies his own individuality and hopes to become more acceptable to others. However, by behaving in this manner he falls far short of becoming the independent and assertive person he has set up as his ego-ideal.

In social groups the patient is constantly beset with feelings of inadequacy and inferiority. He has been rejected so many times in the past that he anticipates rejection in any new group that he enters. The patient places a great deal of emphasis on status roles in social situations. He believes that people are accepted or rejected in social groups and are accorded positions of high prestige because they have been successful in their chosen fields. He therefore believes that others reject him because of his lack of education and because he has not attained any measure of success. At times, however, the patient attempts to overcompensate for his feelings of inadequacy by erecting the façade of an intelligent and capable person. He cannot maintain this role over a long period of time and he handles it quite ineffectively. He does not compete with others nor assert himself in social groups for fear that they will aggress against him. He is more apt to carry out the wishes of others than strive to satisfy his own desires. In order to maintain good social relationships he avoids situations that might stimulate aggression. In situations where he is the object of aggression, he will more readily turn the other cheek than retaliate. His own feelings of hostility are suppressed.

Because the patient feels that only by successful accomplishment can he achieve the recognition he desires, the specific field of endeavor is of no consequence provided it has some social status. He is very involved in all that he does. He feels that he has so very much to lose or so very much to gain in everything that he undertakes that he regards every frustration as equivalent to failure. At such times he despairs. He becomes extremely discouraged and although he would like to be a counteractive individual, he is not. He has a low frustration tolerance and every failure is a severe blow to his ego, since to him it indicates that he may really be as inferior as the rejections which he has experienced from others have led him to believe. He would like to solve all his problems without asking others for aid, since he feels that he must prove to himself and others that he is a capable person. Moreover, he is afraid that others will regard his inability to solve a problem as a reflection of his inadequacy and therefore continue to reject him. However, the patient is as yet unable to go off by himself and to do things by himself since he functions best when he knows that a source of affection and encouragement is constantly available to him.

The patient appears to be unable to effect an adequate heterosexual adjustment. He avoids all stimuli which might evoke any sexual material and it is apparent that for him any discussion of sex is tabu. There is a suggestion that he has some feminine traits and that he is confused as to his own sex role. It is further suggested that his ties to his mother are so strong that they also have a negative effect upon his attitudes concerning marriage.

The patient describes his home environment as being quite uncongenial. His father appears to have been an inadequate person who was unable to support the family. The patient has a very low regard for his father. He is hostile to his father because he did not provide the patient with the necessary financial aid to attain the goals he desires. However, in view of the fact that the patient's creativity and organizational ability on the TAT is about average it is doubtful that the patient has the necessary training and/or ability to achieve the success he desires. On a deeper level, it is also apparent that the patient rejects the father because the patient himself would like to take the father's role in the home. The patient's siblings are also no source of comfort to him. He regards them as rivals for his mother's affection. Of all those in the family, the patient's mother appears to have been the most significant figure in his life. From his description, she appears to be a domineering and selfish person who set the standards which the patient was to attain. In his youth the patient complied passively with her requests and carried out her wishes without resistance. As he grew older, however, he began to think about breaking his ties to his mother, but he has never been successful in carrying out his intentions. Although overtly he still regards his mother with a great deal of affection, on a covert level he feels quite hostile to her because she has deprived him of his independence and she has not always been the source of love he desires. He feels that he has been deprived of this love because he has not been very successful in life. He therefore spends a great deal of time fantasying about how different his relationship with his mother would be if he were to become successful. If he were successful, he would be able to care for all of his mother's needs and give her all that she has missed in life. In return he would receive the love and affection he has had to do without because of his inferior status and inadequate achievement. But since his realistic inadequacies (lack of education and training for a position of high social status) keep him from achieving his desired goals, he becomes discouraged and intrapunitive. Although he may never become successful, the patient still feels obligated to care for his mother and even though he marries he will always be concerned about her needs.

In view of the patient's uncongenial home environment and rejection in social groups outside of the home, it is obvious that the patient did not grow up in an atmosphere conducive to the development of his individuality and independence. Lacking in his youth the experience necessary for the development of ego-strength, the patient has been unable to take advantage of the opportunities and situations which must have presented themselves and on the basis of which he might have established a more adequate adjustment. He appears to have been unable to tolerate the anxiety which would develop during the transitional period between the breaking of old dependent ties and his establishment as an independent member of society, able to satisfy his own needs and achieve the goals which he might set for himself.

Insofar as therapy is concerned, the patient appears to have an intellectual appreciation of the fact that if any change is to take place in his present condition, he must attempt to effect such a change by himself. He is also quite anxious to establish good social relations. However, it is evident that he does not have very much insight into his problems and that he will require a good deal of support before he can attempt to effect a more adequate adjustment. He seeks a nurturant person to help him overcome his difficulties. In view of his dependency and desire for a nurturant therapist, there is the danger that he might find too much satisfaction in the therapeutic situation and thus become even more dependent. Furthermore, therapy might also be impeded by the fact that the patient does attempt at times to assume a superior role in a social situation and he will therefore not discuss problems and difficulties which reflect his own shortcomings, for fear that he will lower himself in the eyes of the therapist. However, this will be overcome as he begins to feel more secure in the therapeutic situation.

Notes from F. A.'s Case Folder

This patient was started in therapy after his initial interview with the psychiatrist. No social history was obtained from the patient. At the time of the patient's first visit, his condition was diagnosed as " Psychoneurosis: Somatization." The patient had been in therapy for a total of nine hours at the time of this TAT protocol. The following notes, abstracted from the patient's case folder, summarize the data that are available.*

The patient is the fifth of seven children. Three brothers and one sister are older than he and two sisters are younger than he. The parents treated all of them " fairly and equally." The patient feels that he is different from all the others in his family; that the others are so much brighter and so much more alert, while he is dull and has difficulty catching on to things. The patient feels that his family does not have confidence in him.

The patient's oldest brother, who is similar to his father in that he is quick-tempered, teases the patient unmercifully. The patient says he

---

* After reading the case folder material, it will be noted that many of the statements made in the analysis and interpretation of the TAT protocol are not indicated in the patient's verbalizations by the time of the ninth hour. This is not an uncommon finding. One can hardly expect a patient to verbalize all his deep problems so early in therapy. The statements made in the psychologist's report were, however, supported by the psychiatrist treating the case.

frequently bites his tongue so that he won't say anything in order that his brother will not be able to laugh at him.

The patient's father has been unemployed for several years now. By the time of the ninth therapeutic hour, the patient did not speak specifically of his attitude toward his mother.*

At 5½ years of age the patient started school. He failed two classes and left school when he reached the seventh grade. After leaving school he worked at various odd jobs until he entered the Army.

The patient was in the service for three years but did not see active duty. He complains that he became nervous and developed ulcers during his military career. He was discharged on points.

Self-consciousness and lack of self-confidence had troubled the patient for many years before he was drafted. He explained his feelings as follows: " I guess it's because of my lack of education." He feels insecure in making friends and meeting new people. He doesn't know what to talk about to them. He frequently spoke about his need for people to do things for him — to help, support, and guide him. In speaking of his social relationships, the patient also said, " I can't stand criticism. I get very sore about it."

The patient masturbated as a youngster and experienced a good deal of guilt because of it. He stopped masturbating when he realized " it was foolish." He has not had sexual relations. He has been going with a girl for the past half year but " it's not very serious." The patient feels that " religion and sin should not be discussed with strangers."

At present the patient is employed as a carpenter's apprentice. In talking about his job, the patient said, " I like to get things done right away. I don't like to have things unsettled."

The psychiatrist had a little difficulty establishing rapport with the patient during the first therapeutic hour because the patient felt ill at ease in his presence. The psychiatrist writes, " Sitting in the therapist's office the patient feels that he is inferior because I am more educated than he and he is nervous and anxious." Since the first therapeutic hour, the patient has had only one gastrointestinal upset. He is still being continued in therapy.

----

* During the fourth therapeutic session, the patient spoke of his love for milk. He said that he drinks over a quart of milk a day because it made him " feel sleepy, warm, comfortable, and cozy." At this point the psychiatrist could not resist noting in his report the parenthetical comment " mother's milk." His interpretation was not given to the patient.

CHAPTER 9

A MALE PATIENT SEEKS JOB TRAINING

The Case of A. R.

This patient is a 37-year-old married male veteran who is presently unemployed. His parents are both living and he is an only child. He was tested by a psychologist to determine whether he could successfully undertake a job training program. The TAT protocol was sent to the writer for analysis and interpretation. The psychologist who administered the test did not use any technique for estimating time nor did he use any inquiry.

TAT PROTOCOL

ANALYSIS AND INTERPRETATION

PICTURE #1

This is a little son or a little boy

In referring to the boy in this picture most patients speak either of " a boy " or at most " a little boy." This patient repeats the word " little " twice. Our first clue, therefore, is obtained from the first phrase. By assuming that the patient has identified with the boy, the phrase is interpreted as meaning that he regards himself as " little " psychologically — i.e., that he is inferior or else does not count for much. Or, he may be " little " physically — i.e., small in stature.

The fact that the patient alternates between " son " and " boy " and possibly means to substitute the latter for the former suggests the hypothesis that the patient may have experienced or is experiencing difficulties in his relationship with his family — specifically, he may not feel as a son.

that is looking at his violin and he don't know just what to do about it,

The patient begins his story to this picture by identifying the boy and then he continues by discussing the hero's activity in the present. There is no discussion of the past or of what " led up to " the scene in the picture, as was request-

209

ed in the instructions. The patient may have avoided any discussion of the past. It may have stirred too much anxiety in him to verbalize these past events and consequently he chose not to speak of them. Another possible reason for his inability to discuss the past may be that his ability to conceptualize may be poor and he is therefore bound to the stimuli in the picture in a very concrete fashion. We shall have to await the additional data from the other stories before we can suggest which of these two possibilities seems to be the more tenable.

The patient's grammatical error in this segment — his use of " don't " instead of " doesn't " — should also be noted. Such incorrect use of language may indicate that the patient may not have had much education or it may be a clue to a more serious defect in social communication.

The last significant datum in this section is that the hero in this picture is indecisive. This reflects the patient's own indecisiveness.

whether to continue playing or whether he's realizing that some day he will be a great violinist.

The hero here is confronted with two alternatives which in terms of the remainder of the story remain unresolved, thus reflecting his incapacity to resolve his situation. One of the alternatives in the segment here is an activity. The other is a fantasy. The first will take more energy than the second. Consequently, it will be important which of these two the patient finally selects.

The use of the word " realizing " is rather interesting. To " realize " means " to make real." The patient seems to use this word to refer to a fantasy activity. Thus, it suggests as one hypothesis that the patient " makes real " his desires in fantasy and that he may have recourse to fantasy because reality is so frustrating to him. In his fantasy he achieves and is successful in something he may not be able to do in actuality. In addition to this interpretation, one should also be aware of the inappropriate term " realizing " and that this may reflect not only poor educational background and possible difficulties in communication that are consistent with serious defects in ego-structure, but because the word is " on a higher level " than a similar one he could have used, it suggests the possibility of upward social mobility. The last point is consistent with the fantasy regarding success.

The outcome is   Judging from the previous sentences, one might have expected the patient to discuss how the two alternatives presented previously were resolved. But no, the patient turns to the outcome and then does not give an ending to the story. Thus, just as the patient did not speak of the past, so he cannot speak with any certainty of the future, and he is limited to the present. The present for him is unclear and composed of alternatives from which he cannot make a selection. His time perspective is therefore a very limited one. He appears unimaginative. The " unknown " factors of the past and future may be too confusing or too disturbing for him and therefore he avoids them.

it's up to him it's up to him whether he'll be a success or not.   This statement suggests that the patient believes that a person's success or lack of it depends on himself and, by implication, that one should not rely on others to achieve success. It is important to evaluate this statement of the patient, for if the patient really has accepted this idea then it may be regarded as a sign of independence. There are two reasons why it is not regarded as such. First, if the patient were an individual capable of independent action this would have been woven into the story in such a fashion that it would have to be inferred from the behavior discussed. Secondly, the patient's statement has the tone of a comment — as if he were talking to himself, goading himself on.

If he's got it in him to make a success, well, he'll do it.

The patient's doubt and uncertainty concerning success is indicated by the " if." Furthermore, it is not simply " up to him " as indicated above, but he also has to " have it in him." This may well be a rationalization for not achieving success — he may not " have it in himself."

This last statement is also a datum in support of the hypothesis that the subject may regard himself as inferior (or " little " psychologically) because he is not certain whether he has it in him to achieve success. Note also how the initial optimism of the patient (" he'll be a great violinist ") has now been toned down, suggesting the patient's own pessimism.

Summary Picture #1: The patient is an insecure and indecisive person who is confronted with alternatives that he is unable to resolve. He feels inferior and very likely seeks in fantasy what he cannot achieve in reality. Although he manifests need achievement in this story, and feels that it is " up to himself " to achieve his goals, he seems to be pessimistic about it. He avoids the past and future and has a narrow time perspective.

TAT PROTOCOL

ANALYSIS AND INTERPRETATION

PICTURE #2

In this picture here it seems that the field is being turned over for the plantation of certain crops.

The patient's approach to the material in this picture deviates from the " norm." In general, patients start their stories either by referring to the people in the picture or they may make some general comment suggesting that the picture represents a " farm scene." This patient does neither. He avoids the people and refers to a detail in the picture — the field. Even the field has no person acting upon it — " it is being turned over." This behavior suggests his avoidance of interpersonal situations — a retreat from them. The individuals in the picture may have stimulated certain fantasies in him concerning people whom he knows and this may have been the stimulus for his avoidance.

The reader may also have been aware of the fact that the patient in his story to Picture #1 referred only to the behavior of the hero and did not speak of any interaction with other people. Only briefly at the beginning of the story to the first picture did he imply a relationship with others (when the hero was referred to as a " son "), and then this was changed. Furthermore, he also emphasized how much success depended on himself and implied that it did not depend on others. This material reinforces the interpretation with regard to his avoiding people and difficulty in interpersonal relationships.

Another significant item in this segment is the use of the word " plantation." Obviously " planting " would have been the more appropriate word. Why, then, the word " plantation "? It is hypothesized that the patient may have viewed the scene as a plantation and when he came to refer to the crops this word intruded upon his thought processes when it was inappropriate. Such behavior, suggesting poorly integrated thought processes, is regarded as a reflection of rather poorly integrated ego-structure.

In view of the patient's use of the word " plantation," it is suggested that the misuse of the word " realizing " in the story to the first picture is not primarily a result of poor educational or intellectual background. This is further bolstered by the subject's vocabulary level in this and other stories.

Seems like the mother might be there looking to the distance and looks like either his sister or his lady friend is holding a couple of books ready to perhaps go home again.

At this point in the story the patient has not indicated very clearly who is the hero in the story. Only because the patient refers to " *his* sister " and " *his* lady friend " do we infer that the main character in the story is the man. The fact that the male is referred to so indirectly suggests that he feels he does not count for much. Furthermore, the women are engaged in activities which take them away from the hero. This again suggests that one of the possibilities for inadequate social relationships is that he feels rejected by others.

The intensity of the patient's indecisiveness is reflected in the last sentence when the younger woman is " perhaps " going home again. Thus even in describing her activity he cannot be definite.

The fact that the young girl in the picture may be either a lady friend or his sister suggests the hypothesis that there might be certain incestuous drives present which are disturbing to the patient. However, we know from the brief history (p. 209) that preceded this protocol that he is an only child. Thus we can discount the fact that he is talking about his own sister. The more interesting detail is that he speaks of a "lady friend." We know from the history that the patient is married. Then why does he refer to the younger woman as a "lady friend" and not his wife? This suggests that the patient's marital relationship may be unsatisfactory.

Well, seems like the man is looking to the distance and sees somebody coming or

There is still no interaction between the people in the story. The hero's behavior in the picture has no relationship to

looking at the, at the landscape.

And the lady on the right here seems to think of perhaps some day she'll look into the distance.

the activities in which the others are engaged.

In the second sentence of this story the patient had referred to the woman against the tree as " the mother " but here he refers to her as " the lady on the right " — substituting the personal with the impersonal just as he did in the story to Picture #1 where he changed from " son " to " boy." These data suggest that he is confused about family relationships.

Note also the bizarre quality of his overqualified statement " the lady . . . seems to think of perhaps some day she'll look into the distance." He perseverates on the theme of " looking into the distance " and this is so idiosyncratic that it is difficult to hypothesize what the meaning of this phrase is for him. (The phrase may refer to a sort of hopefulness, if by looking into the distance he means the future.) It should, however, be noted that both the male and the mother engage in the same activity of " looking into the distance "; this may be evidence for identification with her.

That girl there I don't know. I don't know. I don't know what she's thinking about. Perhaps of a future with the young man.

After perseverating on his denial with regard to what the girl might be thinking of, the patient finally develops an idea. It should be noted that it is *she* who is considering a future with the young man and he does not tell us what the man's attitude in this situation is. It is therefore suggested that the patient has assumed a very passive role in this relationship.

The outcome would be that there may be something independent to the work that they're doing, that they will be doing and this farmer here.

Something may be in the offing but it is unclear as to what it may be. Despite the fact that the patient is very disjunctive it would have been worth while to conduct an inquiry with this patient at this point. Not only would such an in-

quiry have the value of possibly revealing the significance of some of his idiosyncratic statements, but during the
course of this inquiry it would also have
been possible to determine how severely
disturbed the patient is. Unfortunately, no such inquiry was conducted.

In the above analysis attention was paid
primarily to the subject's use of language and the content of the story.
However, attention should also be paid
to the sequence which the subject follows in his story. He refers to the field,
the " mother," the " sister," the " man,"
the " lady on the right," the " girl," and
the " outcome." Each of these is not
only referred to as a disparate unit without any direct interaction, but when an
object is referred to once it is not left,
but returned to later. Thus the patient's organizational capacity is poor,
his personality integration inadequate,
and his ego-structure weak.*

Summary Picture #2: The patient's thought processes are disorganized,
confused, and poorly integrated. His language behavior gives evidence
of idiosyncratic use of words. He is concrete in his approach to the material. The patient is confused as to his family relationships and has difficulties in social interaction. Evidence for rejection and feeling separate from others was also suggested.

TAT PROTOCOL

ANALYSIS AND INTERPRETATION

PICTURE #3

Well, this seems to be a fellow that seems to have been
tormented in some way and
beaten

The patient regards his environment as
hostile and actively aggressive against
him. He feels tormented and beaten.

---

* It is impossible for the purpose of this manual to have an extended discussion of personality integration and language and thought process. Such information, however, is important for understanding the remark made above. The
reader who is not too well acquainted with this area is referred to: Kasanin,
J. S. (ed.), *Language and Thought in Schizophrenia*, Berkeley, California: University of California Press, 1944; and Rapaport, D., *Organization and Pathology
of Thought*, New York: Columbia University Press, 1951.

and is at a point of exhaustion.

The aggression from the environment must be quite severe, since the hero is now " at a point of exhaustion." What is the patient's reaction to all the aggression that had been directed against him? Passive. He does nothing to counteract the aggression.

The outcome of this would be rather relief from what was bad.

All the patient can develop in telling about the future is relief from his difficult situation. But note that no energy has been expended in attaining this relief.

Note that the patient has not mentioned the gun in the picture. It is interesting that in the preceding story he referred to most of the details in the picture but in this one he avoids the gun. It is suggested that this reflects his inability to deal adequately with his own aggressive needs and this would be consistent with the passivity indicated above.

Summary Picture #3: The patient is a passive individual who regards his environment as aggressive and hostile. He feels beaten and tormented. He does not counteract the hostility he experiences, but hopefully seeks relief. It is also suggested that he has difficulty in dealing with his own aggressive needs.

TAT Protocol

ANALYSIS AND INTERPRETATION

Picture #4

This picture seems to relate to a couple about to be separated for some time, for what reason, maybe that he's going off to war or has troubles on his mind, maybe he has folks, would like to do things for his folks and do things for his lady friend, it seems that way.

In this segment there is additional evidence of ego-weakness. Note that several possibilities for the development of a theme are thought of but no single one of them is selected for further development. As a matter of fact, the patient selects two possibilities. Here he seems to spend more time on the possibility that the couple is about to be separated because he wants to do things for his " folks " and his " lady friend." This suggests that he may still be tied to his parents and consequently unable to establish a mature marital relationship. The unsatisfactory nature of his marital life is also indicated by his referring to the girl as his lady friend.

And, well, the outcome of this, well, it's in the balance.

The patient is unable to solve the situation described above and once again this suggests his passivity, indecision, and weakness.

Well, it's in the balance in another way if it's war waiting if he'll be back or not or if it's lonely to be away from her or not.

Now the patient refers to the other theme and once again he is concerned with alternatives which remain unresolved. It is interesting to note that above he was considering what he could do for his folks or his lady friend, but here he is concerned primarily with himself. He is concerned about himself and whether he can tolerate being away from her.

He has a job to do and he wants to go ahead and do it.

Which of the various situations described previously is the " job " he wants to do is unclear. This statement is offered almost in desperation. It is as if he may be so completely dissatisfied with the state of affairs he is in that he wants help.

One general comment is in order at this point. Four of the patient's stories have been analyzed; in two of them (Pictures #2 and #4) his stories appear incoherent, confused, and badly organized; and in the other two the patient's ability to communicate his ideas and his organizational ability are somewhat better although not perfect. In the two disorganized stories there is one common factor: In both of them the patient is concerned with a situation involving his family and his " lady friend," while in the other pair he is concerned with a single person. This is another bit of evidence which helps in clarifying one of the sources of his problems.

Summary Picture #4: The patient finds himself in conflict between satisfying the needs of his parents and satisfying the needs of his wife. Apparently he has not evolved any plan for resolving this conflict. He is concerned about his life and whether he can tolerate separation from his wife. He may be so completely dissatisfied with his present state of affairs that he wants help.

TAT PROTOCOL	ANALYSIS AND INTERPRETATION
PICTURE #5	
Well, this picture seems just like a lady to be inquisitive	Since there are obvious age and sex differences between the patient and the figure in the picture, and because of the patient's inmaturity, referred to previously, which would result in his identification with children, it is suggested that the patient had not identified with the woman and that the story will not reflect his own needs, etc. Instead, it is assumed that the story reflects his attitude toward his mother or women. The mother in this story is "inquisitive." This is much too strong a word to use for the action that follows — "to see how her children are." If that was all she wanted to do, then it would have been sufficient to say that "she opened the door" or "she looked in." Since the word is a strong one and since it also has negative overtones it suggests the intensity of his negative reaction to the behavior which is regarded as prying. The patient's hostility to the mother is also reflected in the sarcastic remark "just like a lady."
	It is significant that his hostility is not expressed directly toward his mother but appears only indirectly in the way in which he characterizes the female figure.
and wishes to see maybe to see how her children are.	In this section the patient has the mother play the role of a solicitous parent.

If they have fallen asleep or if everything is in order.	We cannot interpret this section without considering the data obtained from the previous one. Combining the hostility toward the mother which was evident above with the mother's solicitous behavior in this section, it is suggested that what the mother may consider to be maternal behavior is perceived by the patient to be her means of dominating him and therefore he resents it. He cannot be alone.
The outcome is not definite yet.	On the face of it this story does not appear to be very complex; nevertheless the patient has difficulty in developing a specific outcome for it. The outcome which " is not definite yet " may refer to his relationship with his mother which, as in Picture #4, was " in the balance."

Summary Picture #5: The patient perceives his mother's solicitous behavior as her means of dominating him. He resents her behavior but he has not yet developed any means of dealing adequately with it.

TAT PROTOCOL	ANALYSIS AND INTERPRETATION
PICTURE #6	
This young man has some words with his mother.	The conflict between mother and son is expressed rather directly in this story but note how the patient describes it. The mother and son are not having an argument but the " young man *has some words* with his mother." Thus the aggressive quality of the conflict is toned down.
They have both set their minds.	Both mother and son appear to be stubborn individuals. Since the patient's mind is " set " against his mother's, the possibility is suggested that we may have underestimated the patient's ability to assert himself and to fulfill his desire for independence and autonomy. Therefore the hero's reaction to the situation as it is described will be extremely important for our analysis. If the hero follows through on whatever his

mind is " set " on, then many of our earlier hypotheses will be negated, since he will have shown more independence than we have given him credit for.

She wants to have him do something.

He perceives the mother as a domineering individual. This datum supports the hypothesis developed on the previous story as to how the patient regards his mother.

He has other plans;

This suggests the possibility that the patient may be capable of developing plans; at least he thinks he is capable of developing plans, but note that he speaks of them in general terms and he does not tell us what his plans are.

whether they are foolish plans or not remains to be seen.

Note that the " foolish plans " to which the patient refers are his own and not his mother's. It is almost as if he were telling us what his mother or others thought of his plans. He is somewhat defensive about his plans and he appears to be pleading for a chance to try them out.

The outcome, well, there may be mutual understanding through heartache and joy.

Note that the outcome does not refer to his going ahead with his own plans but to the relationship with the mother — mutual understanding. This is evidence once again of his being tied to her.

Summary Picture #6: Additional data have been obtained suggesting that a conflict does exist between mother and son. She appears to be a dominant individual who refuses to permit her son to go ahead and do what he wishes. He appears to be unable to effect a separation from her and to carry out his plans on his own.

TAT PROTOCOL

ANALYSIS AND INTERPRETATION

PICTURE #7

Seems like this father and son here. His father's trying to give him some advice on the venture that the son may wish to do. Just giving him some fatherly advice.

Father-son relationships do not appear to be as strained as mother-son relationships, which were discussed in the previous picture. Father-son relationships may be better because, as this story indicates, the father is more tolerant of the son's plans than is the mother. It is difficult to say from the choice of the word " advice " whether the father is advising the son how to attain his goal or whether he is dissuading him from attaining his goal. The father, unlike the mother, does not make any plans of his own for his son.

Note the patient's use of the word " venture," which reflects his level of aspiration. It is not a mere job that the patient is interested in but something more important — a venture. (The patient's need for achievement was previously indicated in Picture #1.) In previous stories the patient alluded to the plans which he has but never does he speak about them specifically.

Well, the venture may be a number of things, might be a number of things, a number of things.

When the patient comes to elaborate upon the " venture " he perseverates on the phrase " number of things " but no definite information is obtained. The content of the comment is similar to the patient's behavior in previous stories, where he entertained several alternatives but was unable to select from amongst them one for action.

Another comment with regard to " venture " is that it implies risk or doing something the outcome of which is uncertain. This may reflect his need excitance or desire to prove himself. In either case it would add to the patient's prestige if achieved.

Well, the outcome is, well, I feel they'll both be satisfied with whatever is being undertaken.

The planned activity is not described but the patient concludes by pointing out that both parties are " satisfied." This satisfaction may well be what he desires rather than the opportunity to go out on his venture.

The stories to Pictures #6 and #7 should be compared with the story told to Picture #4. In the first two stories the patient describes situations involving parent figures and both of these stories are concluded with "satisfaction" or "understanding." In Picture #4, which involved a "lady friend," however, no such positive state was attained. It is therefore suggested that one of the factors involved in the patient's poor marital adjustment is the fact that he has not detached himself emotionally from his parents.

Summary Picture #7: Father-son relationships appear to be better than mother-son relationships because the father advises the patient in his ventures and does not have any plans which he tries to enforce upon him. It is suggested that the plans he has may be grandiose and also that one of the factors affecting his marital relationship is his emotional involvement with his parents.

TAT PROTOCOL   ANALYSIS AND INTERPRETATION

PICTURE #8

Seems to be a crude operation on a man. Doesn't seem to be an experienced doctor, if you could call it a doctor since I think he's experimenting in a concentration camp. What the boy's doing in this picture I can't see.

There is insufficient evidence in this story to determine with whom the patient has identified. On the basis of similarity with previous material (Picture #3), however, it is hypothesized that he has identified with the man on the table. Consequently, it is suggested that the patient regards his environment as hostile and constricting ("concentration camp"). The aggressor, it should be noted here, is a male.

The patient's inability to organize the figure and ground aspects of this picture reflects his poor integrative capacity.

Clinical experience has indicated that where the patient identifies with the figure that is being operated upon, the theme of the story is often associated with the patient's castration fears.

Summary Picture #8: Although it is difficult to tell with whom the patient has identified in this story, it is hypothesized that he perceives his environment as hostile and constricting. Additional evidence was obtained regarding his poor integrative capacity. Castration fears are also indicated.

TAT PROTOCOL

PICTURE #9

Well, there's a bunch of fellows that's been taking it easy in the fields. Looks like they're hiding away from the sun, with their hats over their faces with no definite plans in sight. Well, it seems that they're just resting and just taking it easy and not really thinking of anything in particular.

ANALYSIS AND INTERPRETATION

The story here involves a good deal of passivity. Energetic persons usually will conclude by having the men rise in order to do something. This does not occur here. In view of the material obtained previously with regard to "plans," it is therefore suggested that these plans are likely in large measure to be fantasies of things he would desire to do but does not because of his passivity.

Note also that although Stories 8 and 9 are brief there is much less confusion in thought process than was observed in other stories.

Summary Picture #9: The patient is a passive individual whose plans are primarily on a fantasy level.

TAT PROTOCOL

PICTURE #10

This is just between the mother and, well, son. Seems to be youthful enough for being a son.

ANALYSIS AND INTERPRETATION

Most of the stories to this picture by other individuals usually refer to a situation between a husband and wife or between a man and a woman in a heterosexual relationship. In this story the patient refers to a scene between the mother and son. The patient himself appears to be somewhat uncomfortable in this situation. The patient's discomfort before calling the boy a " son " is indicated by the use of the words " and, well," and also by his rationalization that the male figure " seems youthful enough for being a son." His behavior thus far indicates that he regards mother-son relationships as particularly meaningful. This hypothesis was suggested previously on the basis of the earlier pictures.

And I don't know the boy's going away and don't know whether he's coming back

Again, when the patient is involved in telling a story concerning a relationship with the mother, the alternatives appear and the thoughts are unclear. Interpreting the content of his remarks, they involve either the relationship with the mother or a possible rejection of her.

and they're glad to see each other after a long absence.

The patient picks up the second of the two possibilities and expands on it, thus suggesting that his ties to her may be stronger than his capacity to leave her. It is possible that too much anxiety may be provoked if he left her.

The outcome can be heaven or hell.

Even though the two persons are happy to see each other the happiness does not last very long, as indicated by the content of the outcome.

All depends on which way the wind blows.

The outcome does not depend on anything the patient can do. In view of previous data, he does not feel capable of doing anything about changing the unsatisfying situation that exists between himself and his mother. He therefore relies on fate. The patient apparently lacks the ego-strength to grapple with the situation and to resolve it in the way he desires.

Summary Picture #10: The patient is ambivalent about his mother but it appears that the ties keeping him with her are stronger than his motivation to leave. The relationship is therefore a trying one and he does not rely on himself to solve it.

TAT PROTOCOL

ANALYSIS AND INTERPRETATION

PICTURE #11

Well, the picture seems to be at the top of some steep mountains where there seems to be a bridge there and it seems like somebody is running. Seems like the

The major theme here is escape from a threatening environment. Or, interpreting the prehistoric monster symbolically, the patient may be running away from his own instinctual drives.

arms are swinging although it's too much for plain walking. Might have been some rocks that have fallen. Also seems like a prehistoric monster coming off of there, some cave in the side of the hill there.

The outcome is maybe death, maybe freedom.

It is interesting to note the dichotomy here. The outcome is not merely death or life but death or freedom. This indicates the importance the patient attaches to freedom, very likely because he lacks it in his present constricting environment.

Summary Picture #11: The patient is running away from a threatening environment and his instinctual drives. He would seek more freedom than he has now but it is doubtful whether he achieves his goal.

TAT PROTOCOL

ANALYSIS AND INTERPRETATION

PICTURE #12

Seems like a boy is very sick there and lying on a bed perhaps in a coma or needing quite a bit of rest.

In view of the patient's strong passivity indicated in the previous stories, it is assumed that he has identified with the boy and that the description here suggests that the patient may himself feel ill and in need of a rest.

The man that's bent over him, well, is kneeling on the bed and tries to see if there is any life in the face or he's half asleep or what.

The older male figure takes an interest in the boy. Comparing this story with the others in which he referred to women, it is apparent that relationships with older men may be better than with women.

The outcome of this may be OK. Well, it may just mean a good rest and that's all.

Despite the severity of the condition described previously, the patient feels that all he needs is a rest.

Summary Picture #12: He feels ill and believes that a rest will cure his troubles. Relationships with older men seem to be more positive than with women.

TAT PROTOCOL

ANALYSIS AND INTERPRETATION

PICTURE #13

This picture here is of a young woman, might have been a young couple.

It should be noted from the patient's use of the word "might" in this sentence that he prefers to leave the relationship between the two people in the picture somewhat indefinite. Furthermore, he does not refer specifically to the male in the picture at the beginning of the story. His purposes in doing so may become a little more obvious from the material that follows.

Somehow she might have taken some poison,

The content of this section of the story is definitely aggressive. Since the story represents a situation between a husband and wife, it is suggested that his aggression against his wife is indicated. However, note two rather interesting factors which appear in this section. First, he leaves all of the factors which might have led up to the woman's act quite indefinite by using the word "somehow," and secondly he has the woman take poison herself and thus the male in the picture is not implicated at all. It is suggested that the use of the indefinite word "somehow" and the fact that the woman commits the aggressive act by herself reflect the patient's inability to cope with his own aggressive impulses. Not being able to express his hostility openly and directly, he creates a situation in which he achieves his own ends (i.e., doing away with his wife) without in any way implicating himself.

The fact that the woman has died in this story aids us in appreciating the dynamic factors that might have been involved in the patient's opening remarks to this story. Since he does feel aggressive toward his wife and since he does not care much for his relationship with her, he left their relationship somewhat indefinite at the start and said they "might have been a young couple." In addition, by not referring to the man in the picture before the act has occurred he avoids responsibility for the act.

and he is delirious about her death. He's emotionally upset about it. That's all I can see on this.

The hero's reaction to his wife's death is quite severe. On a superficial level it is suggested that his reaction reflects the upset he would experience after being separated from her. However, on a deeper level of interpretation it is suggested that the severity of his reaction at her death is a manifestation of what he experiences with regard to the aggressive act that has been committed in the story.

The outcome for them all will be trying.

The outcome to this story is quite illogical when considered in the light of the preceding circumstances that occurred in this story. Obviously the outcome cannot be trying for *them* if the wife has already died. It may be, however, that his guilt regarding his aggressive impulses toward his wife is so intense that he cannot end the story with her dead and therefore he must revive her.

Finally, since the patient does not deal directly with the sexual content of the picture, it is suggested that he also has problems in this area.

Summary Picture #13: The patient feels quite hostile toward his wife. However, these feelings stimulate a great deal of guilt in him. Difficulties in regard to sex are also indicated.

TAT PROTOCOL

ANALYSIS AND INTERPRETATION

PICTURE #14

This is a silhouette of a person looking out of a window. The outcome may be whether he'll be able to, I don't know. I can't see any-

The patient's production to this picture is descriptive. He is severely blocked when he is about to describe the hero's activities and the outcome of his behavior. Clinical experience has indicated

thing. Well, he's looking into space.

that a fairly common factor which disrupts the thought process in stories to this picture is thoughts of suicide. It is therefore suggested that the patient may have suicidal thoughts.

It should be noted that the patient uses the phrase " looking into space " here. This is similar to the phrase " looking into the distance " in Story 2. The behavior here suggests that the patient uses this phrase in order to avoid discussion, aside from any other idiosyncratic meaning this may have for him.

Summary Picture #14: It is suggested that the patient has suicidal thoughts.

TAT PROTOCOL

ANALYSIS AND INTERPRETATION

PICTURE #15

This is a cemetery. A cemetery. Perhaps of all the boys that were killed in the war amongst the tombstones. The man seems to have, wonders whether it was all worth while or not. That's all I can see.

The patient, we know from the brief history at the beginning of the protocol, is a veteran. Consequently, it is suggested that this theme refers to his concern with the value of the war.

The man may be just a visitor or that's about all, may be by the side of his loved ones. Real tragedy. The outcome at his age would be no outcome at all.

The second theme to this picture refers to the dead ones as " loved ones." This suggests both his positive and negative feelings toward his family. Furthermore, since this is a " real tragedy," it reflects his reaction to the possible separation from them — i.e., it would be tragic and there is no outcome.

Summary Picture #15: The patient has both positive and negative feelings toward his family. Losing them would be a tragedy for him.

TAT PROTOCOL

ANALYSIS AND INTERPRETATION

PICTURE #16

Well, the outcome would be all right for me in time. Time takes care of everything.

When the patient is presented with the blank card he does not develop a story to it but becomes autobiographical. The extent of his personal involvement is so great that he is unable to utilize his resources for imaginative purposes.

The fact that the patient starts by speaking of the "outcome" suggests that he is concerned about the future but he is optimistic regarding it. Although his last sentence in this section might, on the face of it, suggest that there is passive reliance on "time," the material which follows indicates that he is actually doing something about it.

At present I feel well, I do feel quite nervous and it's beyond my control.

The statement that he feels well "at present" suggests that he has probably gone through more serious periods of his disorder but his capacity to control whatever it is that is involved in his "nervousness" is inadequate.

However, I'm trying to help myself in every way; keep myself busy and occupied and do what I can find.

The patient is actually trying to help himself to overcome his difficulties by engaging in activities. Keeping busy and occupied may be techniques for avoiding inner feelings and thoughts.

The patient feels that he can overcome his difficulties by busying himself with his work. It is obvious that this is an inadequate means of dealing with his problems and that at best he is treating his own superficial symptoms and not the underlying causes of which he may still be unaware.

I get tension or I feel warm all over and sometimes I have to take a long walk and just walk and walk and walk until it breaks off of me, and, well, I don't like noise. I don't like noise, it seems to irritate me. I like to be by myself. I do enjoy things I like to do. I like to work alone.

Here we have an enumeration of the patient's symptoms — extreme tension and irritability — and again how he tries to cope with these symptoms by motor activity. In addition, his preference for solitude and his avoidance of social situations is also indicated. This corroborates earlier hypotheses of how difficult he finds social interaction at the present time.

I think I can hold my own against anybody.

This assertive comment does not flow naturally from the earlier statements. His behavior here is similar to free association with himself as the theme.

The content of his statement suggests that the patient is measuring himself up against others and in so doing he implies the challenging nature of the situation. There is also a positive tone about this statement but it has to be evaluated carefully, depending upon what means he utilizes to establish this positive self-regard.

Well, I'm experimenting on different things at home, you know, gases and things and so on. My one ambition is to help the blind to see. I believe I have an idea to do that but I'm not trained enough to accomplish this and I want to work on other things as general electricity and power and so forth. Anything along these scientific lines I enjoy, but, well, I guess that's about all I have to say.

Here the patient becomes more specific about some of the activities through which he keeps himself occupied. Note that the plan is somewhat grandiose but at the same time the patient is realistic in that he says, " I'm not trained enough."

Two of the interests in this section are rather interesting in terms of the material presented previously. His interest in helping the blind to see reminds us of his statement in Picture #2 where he spoke of " looking into the distance." Visual activities are strongly cathected and probably strongly eroticized by the patient. Amongst other things this may suggest voyeurism or the possibility of being an " all-seeing " individual. His speaking of power in this section is also interesting, for the previous material suggests that he is anything but a powerful or strong individual. Consequently, this interest may be a means of compensating for his own felt inadequacy or desire to have power over others as others have had power over him.

Summary Picture #16: The patient's illness is of some duration. He feels better now than he did previously but he is still tense and irritable and unable to control his " nervousness." He tries to occupy himself in activities and this suggests that he may be trying to avoid disturbing thoughts. His interests are somewhat grandiose and they appear to be means of compensating for his own inadequacies. His feeling of self-regard is positive but it appears to be based on the grandiose ideas in part.

TAT PROTOCOL	ANALYSIS AND INTERPRETATION

PICTURE #17

This fellow seems to be dangling down the rope, like an athlete. He shows quite a bit of muscles and seems to be enjoying his work.

The content of this story is consistent with the patient's associations to the previous card. On the previous card he indicated that he feels best when he is working on something he enjoys and the production to this picture is a continuation of that theme. Note that the patient perceives the figure in the picture as a strong athlete and that in Picture #16 he indicated his own strength by saying, " I think I can hold my own against anybody." In view of all the data collected up to this point which indicate how weak the patient is in dealing with his psychological problems, one should note his desire for strength.

His outcome I guess would be quite bright because he seems to enjoy what he's doing.

Note that the outcome is definitely bright when the hero works alone and at a job he enjoys. Contrast this outcome with the outcomes that the patient develops to stories involving interpersonal relationships. When the story involves an interpersonal situation there are usually two outcomes — one extremely good and the other extremely bad. By contrast this story highlights the difficulties that the patient has experienced in social situations and how uncertain and inadequate he feels in such situations.

Summary Picture #17: The patient feels inadequate in interpersonal relationships and derives his satisfaction from situations in which he can work alone. The desire for strength is also indicated.

TAT Protocol	Analysis and Interpretation

PICTURE #18

| This fellow here is being grabbed by someone. I just see the hands, don't see no face or anything. | The patient describes a situation that involves press aggression, which suggests that the patient regards his environment as hostile. It should be noted that after the patient describes the attack his production becomes essentially descriptive and rather banal. Clinical experience has indicated that one of the factors that may be responsible for such evasiveness may be the fact that the patient may perceive such an attack from the rear as a homosexual attack. |
| Whether he's imagining he's being grabbed by someone or whether someone is actually in back of him, more than one person, it is hard to tell. You see another arm sticking out from beneath his. | Here the patient cannot decide whether the perceived aggressive environment is fantasy or reality. It is suggested that this is an indication that the patient himself has begun to question whether the aggression he has perceived in his environment is real or not. The fact that he has begun to question his perceptions is regarded as a positive sign in this case, for on the basis of his earlier confused thought processes it might have been suspected that his disorder was more severe. |

Summary Picture #18: The patient regards his environment as hostile to him but he does nothing to counteract this aggression. It is suggested that his story to this picture may reveal his fear of homosexual attack. The patient attempts to distinguish between reality and irreality and this is regarded as a positive sign in this case.

TAT Protocol	Analysis and Interpretation

PICTURE #19

| This picture here it's all confused. There's so many things here that could be out on the ocean someplace. It's not quite clear what it means. That's all I can make out of it. | As has been pointed out elsewhere in this manual, severely disturbed patients frequently have difficulty in perceiving a solid structure in this picture. This reflects the patient's weak ego-structure and internal confusion. |

Summary Picture #19: There is additional corroboratory evidence available in this production concerning the patient's weak ego-structure and his internal confusion.

TAT PROTOCOL	ANALYSIS AND INTERPRETATION

PICTURE #20

| This is someone, that's a man, a man leaning against a post, a little light, I guess, and, well, he's just resting there, perhaps thinking of his chores during the day or perhaps his near future, I don't know, maybe looking for a job, and maybe wondering what he should do next. | The patient engages in passive and ruminative activity. He is concerned about the immediate and the more distant future. |
| Doesn't seem like anywhere in particular to turn. | The patient is incapable of selecting a goal and he is incapable of formulating any plan of action to achieve this goal. It is unlikely that he will be able to rid himself of his present difficulties and to develop goal-oriented behavior without outside aid. |

Summary Picture #20: Once again the patient's passive and ruminative activity have become evident. The patient is incapable of selecting a goal for himself or of developing a well-formulated plan for achieving his goal. It is suggested that he will be unable to get himself out of his difficulties without outside aid.

Final TAT Summary

Mr. A. R.'s record reveals a good deal of pathology and simultaneously some evidence of positive personality characteristics. It appears that his illness is of some duration and although he " feels better " now, he is still irritable, tense, and unable to effect adequate control over what he describes as his nervous feeling. He seeks to overcome his present condition by occupying himself with tasks and doing things he enjoys. His plans, however, are overambitious and grandiose and are related to his desire to be more controlling of his environment. His ego-structure is quite weak.

This patient's thought processes are often disorganized and confused. He gives evidence of idiosyncratic use of words but there are no neologisms. He is unable to integrate material and resorts to dealing with concrete events and objects. When confronted with a problem situation he thinks of several possibilities or alternatives for action but is unable to select one from amongst them on the basis of which he will go into action. Such behavior is especially manifest on those occasions when he deals with situations involving his mother and/or his wife. When dealing with less stressful and anxiety-provoking material, he is much more organized and, although not necessarily imaginative, for he is too involved with himself and the solution of his difficulties, he appears to be better integrated. He also gives evidence of being able to differentiate between reality and irreality and this augurs well for his adjustment.

Emotionally, Mr. A. R. is the sort of person who avoids the expression of feelings. To have feelings would bring him in too close contact with other people and this he seeks to avoid, for the outcome of such relationships is such that he is not likely to achieve the satisfaction of his needs. He is beset with ambivalence — he may desire warmth and the satisfaction of dependent needs but this he fears may result in rejection or in becoming so dominated by others that his own plans and ideas would be denied.

He feels particularly ambivalent toward his mother or mother-figures. On the one hand, there is a desire for a close relationship with her and on the other he wants to break the ties with her. The former, however, is stronger than the latter. Too much anxiety may be provoked at the possibility of leaving and despite his desire for independence he succumbs passively to her demands with inner feelings of hostility toward her that remain unexpressed. He sees his mother as a solicitous, inquisitive person who is domineering and stubborn, and who has little if any regard for his needs. He has no means of coping with this situation and anticipates a trying relationship with her for some time to come. He wants acceptance and understanding with her but the price for this seems to be a constricted environment and loss of freedom. In general, it may be said that he is quite confused about his relationship to his mother.

His relationship with older adult males is a more positive one. He feels that they are more understanding and can be helpful to him in realizing his plans.

His relationship with his wife, as one might infer from the discussion regarding his mother, is particularly bad. He is caught between the desire to satisfy his parents' requests and needs, and those of his wife. This, too, remains unresolved and in view of his strong ties to his mother it is apparent that his wife's needs are the ones to suffer. He does not regard his wife as a wife but as a woman with whom he has a more superficial relationship. He feels quite hostile toward his wife and he has difficulty in dealing with this hostility, for it stimulates guilt. Another aspect of his difficulty with his wife is that heterosexual relationships (since the relationship with his mother plays an important role here) are disturbing to him — he is disturbed about sex and confused about his own sex role.

His reaction to the disturbing relationships described above is to withdraw from them — in part, this is a resultant of his inability to deal adequately with them and in part a feeling that he is not completely accepted and possibly even rejected by the others in his environment. In general, he regards his environment as hostile and aggressive but does not actively indulge in changing it. He is quite passive in this regard, has difficulty in dealing with the aggression, and submits, hoping that a solution, positive or negative, will be found as time passes. He tries to deal with his tension by engaging in activities that interest him or by diffuse motor activity.

The patient has a low energy level. He feels tired and seeks rest. The desire for such relaxation is probably motivated as a means of seeking release from the tensions described above and withdrawal from interpersonal relations. At the same time, he is motivated to achieve and to work in constructive areas. He feels best when he is working at something he enjoys and as a result of these activities he feels ready to compare himself with others. His interests lie in working in scientific areas. His goals in these areas are somewhat grandiose and dynamically they appear to be related to his desire for the power that he lacks realistically and are a means of making up for feelings of inferiority. Despite the value of a work plan and the gratification that he gets from work, it is unlikely that he will be able to find the opportunity for channelizing his energies constructively without outside help.

Notes from the Case Folder

The following is a summary of the data that were available concerning A. R.'s history and diagnosis.

This 37-year-old patient is an only child whose birth was not planned. His mother said, " I don't want this child." At present the family appears to be a closely knit unit and the patient is said to be equally devoted to both his parents.

The patient had a rather protected environment in his youth and, according to his mother, made friends at school but was not allowed to play in the street. He is said to have a fine sense of humor, and throughout his army career his mother encouraged him to foster this. His mother does not consider him nervous or high strung. The veteran likes to read but has confined his reading to technical novels. He attended high school for three years and, prior to his induction into the service, he owned an electrical appliance store and spent most of his adult civilian years working on inventions. He is said to be ambitious and he has purchased some lots which he hopes to utilize for a new business. He is now married to a girl to whom he was engaged for three years.

The patient had fifteen months' military service with six months in the European Theater. He had no combat experience. He was hospitalized after an accidental gunshot wound (the record says it was self-inflicted) in the leg. Following hospitalization, he was noted to be depressed, suspicious, uncooperative, and showing little spontaneity. He talked of people trying to pry into his secrets and to gain information about his inventions. He was returned to the Zone of the Interior with a diagnosis of schizophrenia, paranoid type.

In the psychiatric hospital the patient received twenty insulin shock treatments. During hospitalization he was observed to appear moderately dejected, frequently with a frown on his face. When questioned he would state that he had a generator invented which would run without fuel. He was discharged when his symptoms were in remission.

Following the patient's discharge from the service, he registered at a school for electrical engineering to be trained as a technician. He attended the school for nine months and then dropped out because the course was "too fast" for him. At that time he complained of tenseness, crying spells, difficulty in concentrating, and difficulty in understanding the instructions. For the four months since he left school, he has loafed at home.

At present there is no evidence of psychosis. Auditory hallucinations are denied. Patient is clear and coherent. No blocking is noted. He does not socialize, preferring to remain with his family, which is the limit of his social activity. He is eager to resume training.

Psychiatrist's diagnosis: Schizophrenia in remission. Feasible for training.

CHAPTER 10

A SCHIZOPHRENIC BEFORE AND AFTER INSULIN SHOCK AND PSYCHOTHERAPY

PART I: BEFORE THERAPY

Starting with this chapter, and with only one exception (Chapter 11), a series of protocols obtained from patients before and after different kinds of therapies is presented. There are three purposes in presenting these records: First, to continue with a description of various personalities as they are manifested through responses to the TAT. Secondly, to indicate the usefulness of the TAT in studying the therapeutic process. Thirdly, it is hoped that a study of pre- and post-therapy protocols obtained from the same person will stimulate thinking about the *integrative* as well as the disintegrative processes of personality. Clinical psychology has for so long been steeped in psychopathology that the " catabolic " functions of personality have been emphasized at the expense of the " anabolic " ones. Further research is sorely needed in this area. The reader may find it worth while to read the pre-therapy protocol and then develop hypotheses as to what changes he would expect. Finally, the reader should be cautioned not to generalize from the single cases which are presented as to the values or shortcomings of the therapeutic procedures that the patients experienced. The cases were not selected as representative of the different therapies.

The Case of S. Z.

The patient is a 28-year-old unmarried male. He is the second of five children. His four siblings are girls. This patient was tested with the TAT by a psychiatrist * who was interested in the test and who was just starting to learn it. No time was indicated.

TAT PROTOCOL	ANALYSIS AND INTERPRETATION
PICTURE #1	
He started to play — I guess he got disgusted with it because he couldn't play well, wishing that he could play well — looking lovingly at it,	The story starts with the hero beginning an activity but as the story continues we find that the activity is not completed. The hero is self-critical because he cannot play well. He cannot " master " the

---

* The author wishes to express his appreciation to Dr. G. Schauer for sending him S. Z.'s protocols and the protocol on the organic which is presented in Chapter 11.

238

wishing that some day he could master it — and then again he may not want to practice.

instrument (frustrated need dominance) and is dissatisfied. It is as if there were a drive or desire to play the violin but because he was unable to reach the standards he had set for himself and because his frustration tolerance is low, he gives up.

Note that the active behavior of the hero — practice, play — is usually rejected or stopped, while the more passive ones, " wishing," " looking lovingly," and later " sits back and watches," are indulged in, thus reflecting the patient's passivity. It should also be noted that the hero looks " lovingly " at the violin and thus indicates that he can express tender affect. The question is whether this affect can be expressed only toward inanimate objects (or what these objects may represent for him) or whether he can also express such affect toward individuals.

Finally, the story indicates that the patient is confronted with a series of alternatives from which he cannot select one for a course of action — an indication of a weak ego.

After that he may pick the violin up and play again or he may sneak out.

The complete story as told by the patient does not include any human figures other than the hero. The question then arises as to why must the hero " sneak out." To " sneak out " suggests that the patient does not have complete control over the situation. One possibility is that parents or others demanded or requested that he play the violin. There is not sufficient evidence here to support the hypothesis. On the contrary, the drive is internal — the hero does wish he could play, he looks lovingly at it, etc. Consequently, it is hypothesized that the sneaking out is a means of getting away from the object which stimulates a drive that he cannot satisfy. It is almost as if he had given the violin a personality and the demands were coming from it and the best way to avoid these demands was to sneak out. It therefore reflects poor control over his own drives as well as the low frustration tolerance and irrationality of the situation.

Then again he is dismayed at something. He wants to play very much and feels that he is not quite good enough. Therefore he just sits back and watches.

The hero uses the word "dismay" correctly (but what he is dismayed at we do not know) and from his vocabulary level in the other stories he may be of high average if not superior in intelligence.

Once again he indicates that because he feels that he is not good enough he yields and becomes passive. Note that he concludes his story not by "sneaking out" but by watching the violin. Thus the cathexis for this situation is very strong. Furthermore, there is a controlling aspect to his final act, for he does not look at the violin but watches it.

Summary Picture #1: The patient feels that he is not good enough to actualize his desire. Being unable to master a situation, his need dominance, which is high, is frustrated and he seeks to escape the situation. He has poor control over his drives. He is beset with a series of alternatives for action. He does not accept the active ones but the passive ones.

TAT PROTOCOL

ANALYSIS AND INTERPRETATION

PICTURE #2

Right over here you . see probably a farmer. A horse plowing the fields. A sister, maybe a girl friend, a teacher. On the right his mother is watching.

Throughout almost all of the patient's production to this picture, up to the time he was requested by the examiner to make up a story, he either identifies the figures in this picture or describes them but does not, with one minor exception that will be referred to later, develop a story that relates the interaction of the characters. It is hypothesized that either the figures themselves or his difficulties in social situations generally stimulate thoughts which are anxiety-provoking or tension-producing and thus result in concrete behavior.

Note that sister and girl friend are descriptions of the same figure, thus indicating some incestuous wishes. This person is described as a teacher. She has more status than he does as a farmer. And he may either cathect women with intellectual capacity or feels that he can learn from them.

Finally, the mother exerts a controlling influence on the situation.

In the background his own home, a barn — .

It is unclear whether he was continuing with his enumeration here or whether he thinks of his house as a barn.

He is in the valley — the others are up. He seems to have a strong back.

The first sentence here indicates that in comparison with the women he feels lower than they or inferior to them. This fits in with the second sentence where he points out the man's physical strength which, it is hypothesized, is in contrast to the girl's mental ability, since she is a teacher.

The girl seems to be a single girl — countrified. The woman seems to be sort — a wife of a farmer — and yet you can tell she is hard working; she probably had some children.

Continued description of the figures. Note that the girl is described with a single word, while a lengthier description is given of the mother — thus suggesting that she is a more significant figure for him.

In the background you see some water, where they catch fish. In other words: they live on the land and out of the sea — from fish.

The patient leaves the figures to turn to the background — an avoidant reaction probably based on his difficulty with the mother and girl friend. The reference to food here may well reflect unsatisfied oral needs.

(Can you make up a story?) He probably was talking to his girl friend, the teacher. His mother came to tell him to go back to work and not idle away the time. The girl is dismayed — walking away. Mother doesn't want them

After some coaxing by the examiner, the patient can develop a story which includes interaction. This indicates that under proper stimulation the patient can utilize his imaginative capacity. But note that the content of the story indicates that the mother interferes with the patient's opportunity to engage in

together — at any rate, not now, as he has to work.

heterosexual contact. She is domineering and emphasizes the importance of work. The patient, however, does nothing to prohibit the interference.

Summary Picture #2: The patient feels that his mother is a hard-working but domineering person who interferes with his opportunity to establish heterosexual contact. He does nothing to prohibit this interference. His relationships with her and with women in general are tension-producing and interfere with his thought processes. He cathects women who have intellectual status. He feels inferior to both his mother and other women. Incestuous desires and oral needs are indicated.

TAT PROTOCOL

ANALYSIS AND INTERPRETATION

PICTURE #3

I can't quite make out what this is. It might be a pen knife or a toy pistol.

The patient has difficulty in identifying the revolver off at the side. He sees it as a " pen knife " or " toy pistol." Both of these are smaller and less aggressive than the object represented. Consequently, it is suggested that the patient may have difficulty in dealing with his aggressive needs. It should be indicated that the knife has castration as well as aggressive connotations.

He's probably tired and crying, because somebody may have scolded him — or just resting. And then again, he was naughty and knows that he shouldn't have done bad and he is sorry and cries in the corner like anybody else would — when they're small.

The punishment theme is the one he focuses upon. Thus, twice so far (cf. Picture #2), he indicates that he and others in his environment do not get along well. The important added factor here is that he feels guilty over what he has done.

(Can you tell me how it ends?) He finished his good cry, forgets all about it, gets up, goes to sleep and does whatever he pleases.

(When the patient completed his story he said he wanted to explain something.)
I do not know what's wrong

The patient's comment has interesting didactic value. Often when one is interpreting a story such as this, and interpretations regarding sexual behavior are

with me. Probably my sex life. I think I should be castrated. I masturbate in bed and every time I think someone gets a child. They change the sheets every time and I think something is going wrong.

made, the skeptic asks for validating information which may or may not be available in the remaining TAT stories. Sometimes such information may be available only through experience or, in the case under study, only through the course of a good many therapeutic sessions. Here, however, the subject himself verbalizes his problem for us. One might have interpreted the patient's story as indicating the behavior he has described on the basis of the " naughty " behavior, the guilt, and the fact that he goes to sleep and " does whatever he pleases." The beginner in TAT interpretation should be cautioned against making such interpretation, for the temptation to make it is very strong and many errors are possible. Persons well trained in TAT interpretation and those who are well grounded in psychoanalytic literature and practice will probably be more successful. To be sure, such persons have probably been aware of the fact that the patient's story to Picture #1 might have been symbolic of the penis and the patient's difficulty with the violin might have been regarded as his difficulty in controlling or, as he put it, " mastering " his sexual drives. For purposes of this manual I have generally tried to avoid such symbolic interpretations unless there was direct evidence in the case.

Summary Picture #3: The patient feels very guilty about masturbating. He feels that he should be punished, even castrated, for it. He thinks someone gets a child every time he masturbates.

TAT PROTOCOL

ANALYSIS AND INTERPRETATION

PICTURE #4

This may be just a drawing or a picture on a wall. It doesn't seem to be real. The

Obviously, the patient was presented with a picture. It is probable, however, that the picture stimulated fantasies

girl in the background is a calendar or something.

The man seems to turn away from her affections. It looks like he doesn't even want — he might like her, but in his mind he might have another picture, perhaps the girl on the wall. Just like me. It's a case of loving, and the other not loving the one.

(Can you tell me how the story ends?) That's what I can't figure out. He seems to have been disillusioned. He had a strong face — character and determination. The girl seems to have charm. The girl in the background may be his fantasy — or a girl in real life. He is not looking toward it — it looks behind him. It may be his past.

(Can you tell me a story?)

He might be frustrated and might not see eye to eye with the girl that loves him — because of that fantasy, he might have —

(Can you tell me the outcome?) That's the outcome: he can't see her way! It's kind of similar to me!

with such intensity that he was unable for a while to differentiate reality from irreality.

The hero rejects the woman's affections because he has another woman in mind. But judging from the last sentence it appears that his love is not returned.

The girl who interferes with his relationship is someone from his past. He is unable to detach himself from her.

The reader may no doubt have observed that during the course of this and other stories the patient is coaxed several times either to tell a story or to develop an outcome. Although this is usually not good procedure it may be necessary with such patients. The examiner can only trust his sensitivity in such instances.

The patient cannot develop an outcome because the relationship with the girl in the past, fantasy or reality, interferes.

(The patient associates then to an episode of confusion he had during a dance, while under the unaccustomed influence of a couple of beers. After the dance he may have had intercourse with a girl, who may have been his girl friend. He fears that later on he may have committed incest with his mother.)

The patient's association after putting down the picture indicates that incestuous wishes directed toward the mother are interfering with his capacity to form an adequate heterosexual relationship. This biographical datum supports the hypothesis suggested previously regarding the patient's difficulty in differentiating reality from irreality.

Summary Picture #4: The patient's incestuous wishes directed toward his mother interfere with his capacity to effect an adequate heterosexual adjustment. The patient has difficulty in differentiating reality from irreality.

TAT PROTOCOL

ANALYSIS AND INTERPRETATION

PICTURE #5

This woman opens the door — comes into a room. From her eyes and face she seems amazed that the room may have changed some — even if it didn't change, it doesn't seem to her mind that it's the same as it was when she left. The whole picture is the face — everything else seems to be altogether different. She sees a change — is surprised of something, or afraid of something. (The patient is asked for an outcome, but he is unable to give it.)

There are two possibilities here: either the patient is describing his mother as others usually do in reacting to this picture or he is describing himself. If he is describing his mother here he sees her as a fearful woman. Support for the second hypothesis comes from the behavior he describes in his last comment to the previous picture. His ego-structure is so weak that it affects his sense of reality.*

Summary Picture #5: The analysis of this story suggests that the patient regards his mother as a fearful person or that his ego-structure is so weak that he has difficulty in maintaining his sense of reality.

---

* The reader who is interested in a more extended discussion of the dynamics underlying this point is referred to E. Weiss, *Principles of Psychodynamics,* New York: Grune & Stratton, 1950.

TAT PROTOCOL	ANALYSIS AND INTERPRETATION

PICTURE #6

Some fellow leaving home, having an argument with his mother —	This story is in contrast to some of the stories he told previously in which the hero did not assert himself in relation to the mother. In this story there is direct evidence of conflict and a desire to leave the mother.
he is very sorry he hurt her.	The patient is sensitive to the mother's feelings and he reacts with guilt.
She is looking away, doesn't want to express her feeling — he wants to tell her how sorry he is, but it just won't come out of him.	Neither the mother nor the son expresses her or his feelings — they are inhibited. From the description of the mother here it appears that the models he has had for identification may well have been inadequate insofar as learning to express his feelings is concerned.
(Can you tell me how the story ends?)	
I might have gone home and might have had some intercourse with my mother — I hate to think of it — I always threw that thought out of my mind.	The patient is obsessed with incestuous thoughts regarding his mother.

Summary Picture #6: The patient is unable to express assertive or hostile feelings toward the mother. He is sensitive to her feelings and reacts with guilt when he takes an active role with regard to her. Both he and his mother are unable to express their feelings. He is obsessed with incestuous thoughts.

TAT PROTOCOL	ANALYSIS AND INTERPRETATION

PICTURE #7

A father is giving his advice to his son. Probably the son has done something wrong or is discouraged, and feels guilty. The father has some experience in life and gives him advice what to do and	This is the first story in which an older male figure appears. In contrast to the other stories which involve females, the relationship here is a positive one. Although the patient feels guilty, he is able to seek advice and he may possibly take it. This augurs well for prognosis or it

to make things better for himself.

(Can you tell me how the story ends?)

The son takes the advice and is happy about the whole thing after it blows over.

may be a reflection of his present positive attitude to his therapist.

It might also be an indication of his having had more positive relationships with his father than with his mother.

Summary Picture #7: The patient's relationship with older adult males is more positive than it is with women. This augurs well for adjustment to a male therapist. The patient is discouraged and guilt-ridden.

TAT PROTOCOL

ANALYSIS AND INTERPRETATION

PICTURE #8

I see some surgeons cutting open a man's body — a rifle on this side here — left side — a light shining down on — this boy. I had that vision, if they could bring me up to A-40 they would chop my arms and legs off — to little pieces, and from there I would get another life — and in that life I would meet my girl. It would be like being born again!

(Can you tell me how the story ends?)

This man dies — and actually his soul is in another person (points to the boy).

The patient starts by referring to the picture but his own fantasies are so intense that they intrude. Note that the sequence at the beginning of his production is fragmentary — this disruptive thought process is usually an indication, as pointed out previously, of internal problems breaking through. The defenses are weakened. Once again the patient tells us symbolically what it is that is disturbing him — castration wishes.

In the light of the previous data indicating the guilt which is related to his sexual behavior and his incestuous wishes, it is suggested that the patient manifests here a desire for castration as a means of expiating his guilt. And note that having paid penance he would be able to start all over again.

It is also likely that the closer relationship with the older male figure in Picture #7 was a means of protecting himself against his sexual desires.

Summary Picture #8: The patient has strong guilt feelings which he seeks to have alleviated through punishment. He hopes for castration and then another opportunity to live his life over.

TAT Protocol	Analysis and Interpretation

PICTURE #9

A bunch of fellows that are working. Probably have some time for themselves. Taking it easy and resting — blocking off the sun from their eyes. They seem to be all pretty friendly to each other. It could be a picnic, like one time we had a picnic in Connecticut. If it was not for the grass and the attire they have on, I would say it was a beach. (Can you tell me how the story ends?) After a while they just get up and start walking around — and start to work again, I guess.

In this story we find that a relationship with peers is dealt with as a positive one. The men are " friendly." Note also that here too the patient interpolates a personal memory, indicating his inability really to maintain psychological distance from the stimuli.

It is worth noting that the figures " start to work again." This suggests that the subject may be an energetic person who is inhibited by all the restrictions pointed out above.

Summary Picture #9: The patient has a friendly attitude toward peers. His activity level is inhibited by the restrictions discussed previously.

TAT Protocol	Analysis and Interpretation

PICTURE #10

Well, this seems to be a picture of a mother and a — or a — a mother and dad who saw each other again after a long absence. Or it could be two — lovers who finally found each other. Or it could be — both of them closing their eyes not to see each other. Then if you look at it from a distance: the man has sort of only half of his face. You can't see the rest of his face. And the

In view of the material obtained previously regarding the patient's feeling toward his mother, it may be suggested that the hesitancy and delay after speaking of the mother might be a result of his thinking of himself here but this was censored and later altered to father and then lovers. Although the defense may be an inadequate one, he does have some defense.

The sex drive and desire for approbation in this area is strong but note that he

woman seems to have no chin — and there is a hand — left hand — here, probably of the woman.

(Can you tell me how the story ends?)
I guess after filling the face — I suppose they both open their eyes and look at each other — as if they can see each other. The woman on the bottom seems to have no eyes at all. They open their eyes and see each other. Depends what they see in the other person.

cannot deal properly with it because the thought process is disrupted.

Note also the emphasis in the story on the eyes. It is suggested that this emphasis is related both to the controlling aspect of seeing a person (as indicated in Picture #2) and to his concern that with open eyes people may see through him— i.e., become aware of that which stirs guilt in him.

It is hypothesized that the possibility of a relationship depends on the evaluations that are arrived at.

Summary Picture #10: The patient's sex drive and need for a relationship to satisfy this need are strong but frustrated. His guilt makes him aware of whether or not others are watching him.

During the second test session when the patient was to be presented with Pictures #11–20, the patient was negativistic. He finally agreed to take the test provided he was permitted to tell his stories in verse.

The examiner was often unable to follow the patient; therefore, the blanks in the record are the examiner's omissions and not pauses.

It is quite impossible to do a detailed analysis of the " stories " that follow, for the material, in general, is so idiosyncratic and autistic. The reader, however, may wish to note two major items: that the patient's ego is on the one hand so fused with the environment that he cannot differentiate between self and others, as in Picture #12, and how he tries to establish his own ego identity, as in Picture #19.

PICTURE #11

I see the ground - - - a'brown
The rocks, the cliffs - - - -
- -

I see the bridge that man does cross
And all in flames — the rocks, the moss
And all the men and creatures, still
- -

I see the smoke up in the air
As it goes circling near and clear
It's just another partition now
And may be a tree or just a cloud.

The rocks, the walls are also brown
And brown is the one I have to crown
For ground's is the crown and brown is the crown
And ground is the one I will have to be.

The creature on my left is brown
Although some tale (tail?) it has found
But brown is the ground, it'll touch the ground
And that's the spot that is for me. - - -

PICTURE #12

One creature here I see is man
The other one is just a pose.
They are both brown in suits and soles
And they're the ones that you'll have to crown.

One lying down and one kneeling beside.
But they're both one — deep inside
And you do know as well as I
Just what I mean when I say " inside."

Inside is on the outside below
Where brown is ground and that's where we go.
The one inside and out will have to know
To be together out on the ground.

That is why I am here to say
All these things I have to say.
This is not my place, I cannot stay
My knee is the one that gave me - - - haste.

And you all know what I mean with this.
It's just the thing you cannot miss.
The ground is brown, that's where I go,
Me — myself, and all you know.

PICTURE #13

A man I see with woman down
With breast apart and one arm down.

Two books upon the table brown
The man's right hand is on his brow.

The two are browns and they reach the ground,
For ground is brown, and ground is ground.
The picture on the wall is sound.
The chair upon the floor is ground.

(What happens in the picture?)   I can't say.

The light upon the table is grounded
By two poles which are carved by a good workman —
And he knows his business well.

The night is black and the sides will light
But the light will shine when you put the plug from behind.

(The patient is asked for a story.)

I have to do it that way.
But that is wrong.   I'll have to say,
The light is grounded,
And it cannot stay.

PICTURE #14

I see a man coming out of the night
Like Lochinvar, and as bold as a knight

He sees the day is breaking for him
And he knows he will be on the ground with - - - kim.

The window panes are just a flaw
And they're brown, as brown as the floor.

And the ground is brown, and I am brown
For the brown will win and the ground is him.

He looks upon the outside longing.
He knows he finds the one belonging.
And in this one he knows he shall
Be the only one — his gal.

PICTURE #15

I don't think I'd like to say anything on this.
I would like to pray, too - - - and that's all! —
I would like to pray.

I see his hands are in front in prayer,
And locked together in the shape of a tear.
His arms are bent, like two legs spread,
And his cloak is black but he has no head.

I know his face — he is not mine.
Mine is just the one I own.
The one I own I cannot give
To any other who shall have this gift — no: this rift.

PICTURE #16

I see upon this sheet of paper
A blank. But there is something I would like to say:
I find some designs upon this paper,
For paper it is and it can be torn.
The designs I see cannot be described,
For all I know, it's brown outside.

PICTURE #17

This man I see is going up a rope.
His right hand is above the left,
His left knee is above the right.
His soles are even and they are both flat,
Except the left which is flatter yet.
And on his crown - - - -
        (turns card upside down)
                he knows he's down
And turned upside down.
For then he is going down to the ground.

But the face he has is not mine
For I own my own
And my own is all
Is all the one I know.

The other within me is the one I've loved
From the time I have seen her in her black cloak.
But she is brown and there she is
Down to the ground - - - round —
The earth is round, that is why I live on the brown.

The rope is hanging from above,
And he goes head first; rather, soul first
Down to the ground
Where it is brown.

He is part of a pillar of stone
And things he must be, are all of stone.

His hands, it seems, like he has no fingers.
But the reason for that is that he is just a ringer.
(ringer: baseball — mop wringer — the tail makes a rink)
A ringer is a monkey too
Just between who and who - - - -

PICTURE #18

- - - - - - - - - -

This man he has two hands on him,
The hands have four fingers which are not his one-ly one
The tie is like a river going down
And pointing in that direction of the ground.
The knot is just around his neck
And the hand to the right he may not own.

There is a man in the picture being pulled down by the one he loves.
- - - Actually he is being pushed down from above. —
And that's the way he wants it, and that's the way she wants it,
— Because they are in love — THEYTS
T S is not my name.
It's just that I want to have it framed.
So I let you know who I am,
When you come down, so we shall know.
That's all for now - - - - - -

PICTURE #19

(The patient is asked to tell a story in prose.)

In this picture I see two eyes at sea.
They do not have a color there,
But when I come down to the ground
I shall know what and how they be there.
— Should I turn it upside down —
It'll be the other way around.
So you see it makes no difference
How you tap upon the floor or ground.
I am myself and that is all.
My name you say, and I say too, can be spelled two ways:
It's ABEL and ABLE *
That's the first name but the second is the same.

---

* The patient mentioned his own name. To maintain the patient's anonymity this has been altered in the text. This does not change the meaning.

That's what the picture is: just a jumble
And that's what I *was*
But now I see my way clear
I know why I am here
My second name is Z . . . . . . y *
Spelled Z . . . . . . y *
But the first name does not mean that
I am two in one
For one is down and the other will be there in brown.

PICTURE #20

I don't see anything here, because I cannot see the face,
And the light, I don't know if it is a light,
And the pole or lamppost, I cannot see what that is.
The specks in the background may be anything.
The only thing I see is ground,
And that color is the brown. —

Final TAT Summary

Mr. S. Z. is a patient with very weak ego-structure. Inner drives, especially sexual impulses, are strong and strive for expression. He is too weak to control them. While he may not act out all of them, they interfere with his thought processes and sense of reality. He cannot, at times, differentiate whether his thoughts, stimulated by sexual drives, are only thoughts or whether they are references to situations that actually occurred in reality. This stimulates intense guilt and a desire for punishment in order to cleanse himself of his guilt. His guilt is so intense that he is quite aware of others' reactions to him and this may be manifest in suspiciousness. His thought processes are never well integrated. At best, when confronted with a situation he conceives of several alternatives to action. More often his thought processes are confused and autistic. Instead of being object-oriented, he is involved with his own drives and obsessive thoughts which, as indicated above, take on the status of reality for him.

The patient is a sensitive person who does have some desire to achieve and to manifest his own individuality but he is unable to utilize his energy to satisfy these tendencies. His frustration tolerance is very low and when he encounters obstacles he becomes negativistic and tries to escape. But there is no escape, for he takes his thoughts with him. Socially, the patient feels quite inferior to others.

---

* See footnote on previous page.

His mother appears to the patient as a hard-working, domineering person who is unable to express her feelings. He is sensitive to her feelings, does not assert himself against her, and is strongly tied to her. She interferes with his capacity to establish a positive heterosexual relationship not only by virtue of her dominance, to which he reacts passively and in a conforming manner, but also because of his intense incestuous drives which he verbalizes. These drives stir intense guilt from which there is no relief. The fact that the incestuous feelings are so intense also keeps him from establishing a relationship with her that would satisfy his dependent needs.

The patient cathects women with intellectual ability but he feels inferior to them. His strong ties to his mother interfere with his heterosexual adjustment. In the sexual area, it should also be pointed out that the patient feels guilty about his masturbatory activity. He believes that someone gets a child every time he masturbates. The guilt in this regard is so intense that he desires castration and the possibility of a new life so that he may start over.

The patient is capable of establishing more positive relationships with adult males and this augurs well for his capacity to establish a psychotherapeutic relationship with a male therapist. Relationships with peers are also more positive than his relationships with women.

PART II: THE SAME PATIENT AFTER THERAPY

When the patient had been close to completing a series of insulin shock treatments, the following TAT protocol was obtained from him.

The psychiatrist who administered the test briefly describes the patient's behavior as follows:

" Rapport was good throughout the test. Patient's behavior in the test situation was not characterized by any evidence of unusual behavior. His responses were coherent, without circumlocution. He stated he was speaking a little more slowly than he usually did because he still felt a little ' groggy ' from the insulin shock treatment administered during the morning."

To avoid too much repetition with the analysis of the first protocol, only major similarities and/or differences will be pointed out in the material presented below.

TAT PROTOCOL	ANALYSIS AND INTERPRETATION
PICTURE #1	
Little boy looking at violin.	The " little boy " suggests feelings of inferiority.

Probably told by mother to practice. He would rather play ball.

The "probably" reflects some uncertainty but note that it does not appear with too great frequency in this and other stories.

A conflict between the press dominance of the mother and the need playmirth of the patient is indicated almost at the start of the story.

Looking at it in a way which seems to indicate that it might be something else, like a baseball or football.

Note that the patient wishes that the violin would be "something else" but there is no distortion of the violin into another object. Thus, the patient has the capacity to control his own needs and this is consistent with increased ego-strength.

He will continue to look at it in that way for a few minutes and then start practicing. When he gets into the swing of it he will begin to like it and forget all about baseball.

The patient overcomes his own desires and gives in to the mother's demands. Furthermore, the patient enjoys what the mother requested of him.

Mother had just come in a few minutes ago to see if he was practicing and to tell him to get started.

The patient returns to the press dominance from the mother and in this manner emphasizes for us the manner in which he regards her.

Note that the patient referred to the past, present, and the future, and that the story is fairly well organized with the exception of the last sentence, which should have come at the beginning rather than at the end. His thought processes here, if they are a sample of what is to follow, are not so confused as in the previous protocol — another sign of better ego-structure. Finally, the story here did involve a social situation, and the patient is not as involved here with his own feelings and needs as he was in the first TAT.

Summary Picture #1: The patient regards his mother as a domineering person. He is in conflict with her but acquiesces to her demands. He has the capacity to control his own wishes and does not distort reality in terms of his autistic desires. His thought processes do not appear to be as confused as they were in the first TAT protocol.

TAT PROTOCOL

ANALYSIS AND INTERPRETATION

PICTURE #2

I see a girl with books. Young man stripped to the waist working on a farm. Young woman leaning against a tree and a farm building and furrowed ground. Water is in background, probably the sea.

The structural aspects of the patient's story to this picture are quite interesting. The patient describes the various parts of the card (in the segment at the left). Later, he discusses, albeit minimally, the interaction between the characters, and finally he tries to interpret their behavior and motivations. Here one observes levels of integrative or abstract behavior. The more integrated the personality the more capable is he of starting with the abstract level, but the patient here builds up to it. The fact that the buildup does appear suggests that the patient still has anxiety with regard to the situation depicted and that he may try to control it by compulsive behavior.

The woman leaning against the tree just finished talking to the young girl.

Interaction occurred between the women but no additional information is provided.

The older woman is probably the man's mother. One with books will walk away and the fellow will start working and the mother will do her chores.

A relationship with the older figure is indicated. The three figures engage in different activities but they do not interact. Note that the hero in both the first and second stories engages in an activity — something that he did not do in the first TAT protocol.

Can't tell from expression what their feelings are. Woman on tree seems to have a superior, smug look as though she's the boss.

The mother is now characterized directly as a " superior, smug " person, reflecting the patient's negative attitude toward her. In the previous protocol he described her behavior but here he is capable of describing her personality and expressing hostility toward her.

Girl seems to look wistful. Something she wants and can't have. Probably wants to marry the fellow but the mother needs him to do work.

The younger female is described in more positive terms than the older one. Consequently, it appears as if some of the ties to the mother have been loosened somewhat. Note, however, that the patient still takes a passive role with regard to the two women; both want him for different purposes but the patient does not state his choice. He seems, therefore, to have become more active physically, as indicated in the practicing on the violin (Story 1), but not more assertive in interpersonal situations.

I think they will eventually get married and be very happy.

The conflict alluded to above is not resolved in the story and the patient jumps to the future. This, plus the change in style ("I think") and the fact that the marriage occurs in the future, reflect the wishful nature of the state. One should not overlook the optimistic note that occurs in the story.

Summary Picture #2: The patient is unable to assert himself in a social situation involving both his mother and a marriageable female. Need sex and need affiliation with the latter appear stronger than previously, and ties to the mother appear somewhat weaker. The patient is capable of expressing hostility toward the mother, and characterizes her as "superior," "smug," and "the boss."

TAT PROTOCOL

ANALYSIS AND INTERPRETATION

PICTURE #3

A little fellow, tired, late at night, has just finished playing with a toy of some kind. He is tired of it and very sleepy. He fell asleep with his head on the chair.

The first part of the story here, as in the first protocol, is interpreted as referring to masturbatory activity. The intense physical fatigue here may be related not only to masturbation but also to the fatigue that he experienced at the time of the test, since he had had an insulin shock treatment earlier during the day of the test. This last point is not emphasized too much in this analysis since the hero in the two previous stories did engage in physical activities.

His mother will come in and send him off to bed.

Again, the mother takes the dominant role. The patient does not initiate the activity himself.

Might be a pocket knife.

The instrument on the side might be an aggressive object or a castrating one.

Just sleepy, no dreams. Unusual position but it's 'way past his bedtime and he's so sleepy he could sleep anywhere. He is 10 or 12 years old and has a brother and sisters but they are sleeping, too, in their own rooms.

Note the organization of the story. After completing the reference to the mother, the patient had a brief but fairly well-organized story. After this, however, he returns to the pocket knife and the boy. This breaks up the organizational level of the story but it is still not as confused as during the first protocol.

The reference to "no dreams" in this segment may be an allusion to the fact that there will be no more associations after this picture as there were after his first story to this picture.

The patient belongs to a family here, and he does not refer only to himself as he did the first time.

Finally, in contrast to the previous story, no overt reference is made to guilt. Dynamically, however, the fatigue may be related to guilt.

Summary Picture #3: The patient is physically quite fatigued. The fatigue is related to masturbatory activity and guilt. The fatigue may well have been emphasized as a result of shock treatment earlier during the day. The mother again assumes an active role and the patient is unable to initiate the activity to satisfy his needs.

TAT PROTOCOL

ANALYSIS AND INTERPRETATION

PICTURE #4

Man and woman in background. Woman in back. Woman is pleading with man. He won't listen. Pin-up girl is in back. The other woman is pleading — he doesn't want to have any-

Although there is no specific mention throughout the story of why the relationship between the man and woman should break up, there is a clue in the fact that "woman in back" and "pin-up girl" are interpolated amongst his references to the couple. What she

thing to do with her, doesn't want to go out with her. Been going together, but he wants to break it up. They were good friends. He doesn't want to hurt her feelings. She's trying to bring about a compromise where he won't leave. His face shows emotion. He's got to make a decision. She's trying to delay his decision. Woman always wins out. They will be married.

stands for — mother and/or sexuality — may be the disturbing element.

In the remainder of the story the conflict between the man and woman is described. Note that he is sensitive to the woman's feelings but is unable to assert himself and finally he conforms to her demands. Although he does not make the decision, the couple gets married. This suggests that the possibility of a heterosexual relationship is not as disturbed now by what the picture on the wall represents as it was before therapy.

In the analysis of the story to Picture #2 it was suggested that the desire for marriage was strong but if the desire were really strong then the content of the story here should have been different. Consequently, it is suggested that the desire may well be there but it is not as strong as first implied.

Summary Picture #4: The patient's desire for a marital relationship is not very strong. There is still some interference as a result of ties to the mother. The patient is a sensitive person, but unable to assert himself or express hostile feelings toward marriageable women. He conforms to their demands passively.

TAT PROTOCOL

PICTURE #5

Woman coming into a room. Looks surprised at what she sees. Hasn't seen this person for a long time. She's surprised. The person is a brother or sister or a good friend. Someone had told her she had a visitor but she didn't know whom to expect. She'll recover from her surprise, greet him, it's her son. They'll tell each other how

ANALYSIS AND INTERPRETATION

The strength of the relationship between mother and son is well indicated in this story. Here the patient himself poses the various alternatives as to who the visitor might be — and then he ends up by deciding it is the son. The final sentence in the story and the surprise element in the body of it suggest that the story may be related to the patient's anticipated return home.

they feel, where he has been,
and things like that.

Summary Picture #5: The patient looks forward to his return home
from the hospital and to the reunion with his mother.

TAT PROTOCOL	ANALYSIS AND INTERPRETATION

PICTURE #6

Elderly woman, young man (long pause) . . . woman staring. The boy is looking down displeased. She has a vacant stare as though she doesn't understand something. Something he had said or done. (long pause) He has a coat on because he is leaving in a hurry. His mother is displeased at what he is going to tell her, she senses it. Waiting to hear it. He's going away on a long trip or not going to be home, joined the army perhaps. Not glad to leave her. Woman is trying hard not to make an emotional scene. Leaving because something he has to do . . . duty. They love each other. Loves her and hates to leave her. To her it seems strange for him to leave because she thinks of him as a little boy. She loves him very much. A very good mother. She will cry but he won't change his mind.

The content of this story would suggest a good deal that is positive. The patient is capable of developing a story in which the son does leave his mother. This is in marked contrast with the stories that he has told thus far and therefore it may be regarded as indicating a good prognosis for breaking ties with the mother. In doing so, however, one should not overlook a significant aspect of the story. Most of the story refers to the mother's feelings. He is quite sensitive to her feelings and her feelings are quite intense, as are his. She does not want him to leave and he does not want to leave her. Consequently, although the content may be hopeful from a prognostic point of view, just how much one can count on this is another matter. It is also interesting to note that the patient has the hero leaving for the army — it is his " duty." It is as if he has to develop a duty that is higher than what he may conceive of as being his duty of staying with his mother. Another positive indication is that he " joined " the army — suggesting some action and volition on his part — some understanding that if he doesn't do this on his own before discussing it with his mother, then he may never get around to doing it. Finally, it should be noted that he sees the mother as regarding him as a " little boy." Leaving her is evidence for growing up.

It should be noted that the patient describes the mother in this story as a "good mother." This is in contrast to the "smug" mother in Picture #2. Note that the context in which the good mother appears is one in which the hero acts out his desires and the "bad" mother appears where the mother interferes. This suggests that when he is frustrated in his desires he becomes hostile but when he can fulfill his desires, then he is not.

Summary Picture #6: Despite the patient's strong ties to his mother, his feeling that she loves him, and his desire not to hurt her feelings, he has the desire to break this relationship, grow up, and become a man. He may not be happy to do so but he feels the need to do so. The hostility toward the mother apparently stems from the fact that she interferes so much with his desires and regards him as a "little boy."

TAT PROTOCOL

ANALYSIS AND INTERPRETATION

PICTURE #7

Father and son. Father is telling him different things. Boy is about 18 or 20. Father should tell him facts of life. Father has seen and gone through a lot of things. Son turning everything over in his mind. Will come to some decision of his own about father's advice . . . plans for future, or perhaps about the girl he's going out with, the type of life he should lead with her. Father seems serious, the son is grim about being talked to in this way. He figures he knows enough, nobody should tell him what to do.

During the first part of the story the patient has the father telling him things about life. As a matter of fact, he regards this as the father's or older male figure's obligation. But all he desires apparently is information. He does not want decisions made for him. Toward the end of the story when it is possible that someone is attempting to direct his life, then he begins to object, for "he is grim." The patient wants to make his own decisions and is therefore regarded as tending to become more assertive.

Note that this is the first story in all that were obtained for this patient thus far in which "should" behavior appears. This, it is suggested, reflects a growing feeling of the obligation that others have to him and a greater striving for independence.

The content of the story may refer not only to the patient's father but also to his attitude toward the therapist. He has all the information he wants from him, and note that it refers to plans for the future and heterosexual behavior, and now he wants to make up his own mind.

Summary Picture #7: The patient wants only information from older male figures — father or therapist — and when they try to direct his behavior he objects. He is tending in the direction of more assertiveness. This is also evidence of a growing feeling of the obligations that others have to him and a greater striving for independence.

TAT PROTOCOL	ANALYSIS AND INTERPRETATION

PICTURE #8

Picture of boy and rifle. Background shows consequences of what can happen — a dangerous operation. An accident — surgeon is operating on boy who was shot with rifle. Young fellow will be O.K., he will pull through. Dangerous weapons should not be used.

Aggression as manifest in the accident results in the operation. Aggression therefore results in punishment. Two factors should be noted here — the optimism with regard to the recovery and the conscience as manifest in the last sentence, which is moralistic. This suggests that he has not necessarily integrated his impulses but suppressed them.

Summary Picture #8: Aggression results in punishment. There is evidence for optimism and suppression of impulses.

TAT PROTOCOL	ANALYSIS AND INTERPRETATION

PICTURE #9

Hard day's work, it's summer. They're taking a break after work, or it's lunch. I don't know which. Young man in foreground is part of group but he has no hat. They're all laborers in a field. That's all there is.

The new aspect of this brief story is his description of the young man. Although this " young man " is " part of group, he has no hat "; thus he is still different from the other men. Nevertheless there is still some identification with men. The patient's energy level is regarded as not too high, for although they are laborers they are not even at work.

Summary Picture #9: The patient identifies with men but still feels somewhat different from them. Energy level is not very high.

TAT PROTOCOL	ANALYSIS AND INTERPRETATION

PICTURE #10

Two people, man and wife, hugging each other. Just finished a kiss. Telling her how much he loves her. Married a long time. Still like each other this way. He seems happy. Girl's expression is happy. All is well. Everything will continue to be all right.	In this story the patient refers to a heterosexual relationship in a positive fashion. This suggests that the patient may well be more capable now of adjusting on a more mature level than he was when he first told his story to this picture. In view of the data obtained to Picture #4 and others, it appears that he will be prepared to enter a heterosexual relationship provided, as one of several conditions, that the woman does not dominate the relationship.

Summary Picture #10: The patient gives evidence here of being able to express positive emotions in a heterosexual relationship. In view of previous data, this is dependent upon whether or not he feels forced into the relationship.

TAT PROTOCOL	ANALYSIS AND INTERPRETATION

PICTURE #11

Stone wall and bridge going to other side. Cliffs in background. Prehistoric monster coming out of cliff in cave. Someone fleeing across the bridge. Another monster on this side of the bridge. Rocks and stones . . . path that leads to bridge was covered up by stones. Monsters pushed the stones down. A human form fleeing across the bridge, afraid of the monsters. Bridge leads no place, ends in a blank wall.	This story reflects fear and pessimism with regard to controlling inner impulses.

Summary Picture #11: The patient is fearful and pessimistic concerning his capacity to control his inner impulses.

TAT Protocol

Analysis and Interpretation

PICTURE #12

An old man and young fellow. Old man kneeling on bed, fellow is sleeping. Old man made sign of cross over young man, blessing him. Father and son. Youth might be dead and priest is giving him last rites. Looks more like father and son. One of those times when a father feels tender toward his son. Will walk away. Son will eventually wake and know nothing about it.

There are two alternatives in this story — either the young fellow is dead and the old man is a priest or it is a tender scene between father and son. The first may well reflect the patient's depressive mood, and the second his desire for a positive relationship with the father.

Summary Picture #12: Evidence for depressive mood and desire for positive relationship with older male figures are indicated.

TAT Protocol

Analysis and Interpretation

PICTURE #13

A picture of a woman, breasts showing. A man standing beside bed with one arm up to his eyes. She might be dead. He is mourning for her. Chair at foot of bed. Had been sitting there reading or dozing off and his wife made a noise and woke him up — a dying noise. She is dead and he will be unhappy.

In contrast to the story told to Picture #10, here the relationship does not have a very happy ending. One of the reasons may be that the picture here is too overtly sexual for the subject. Nevertheless, what is apparent is that adequate heterosexual relationships for the subject are rather difficult to attain.

Hostility toward the female figure is indicated.

Summary Picture #13: Difficulty in heterosexual situations and hostility to the female figure are indicated.

TAT Protocol

Analysis and Interpretation

PICTURE #14

A fellow in dark room. Looking out of window, sil-

The patient appears to be quite a sensitive person. It is interesting to note, in

houetted against light background. Room is dark and it's light outside. Looking up at sky or clouds, admiring beauty or looking or gazing — thinking. After a while, he'll probably walk away and go to sleep.

view of the analysis of the first protocol, that he can be alone and not be troubled by obsessive thoughts and guilt.

Summary Picture #14: The patient is a sensitive person. He has the capacity to be alone and not be troubled by obsessive thoughts and guilt.

TAT PROTOCOL

PICTURE #15

A lone figure in a graveyard. Lot of monuments and hands in prayer — just clasped — very thin face — hollow eyes.

Someone he loved very much is buried there. It could be a man or woman. Unusual to be alone at night in cemetery. Had mixed feelings, reminiscences, and on the spur went to see the grave of his beloved. In silent prayer, felt better inside. After a while he will go away and maybe come back again sometime.

ANALYSIS AND INTERPRETATION

The story here reflects the patient's capacity for a strong attachment and his ambivalence regarding it. The new datum is that the patient may well find solace in prayer.

Summary Picture #15: The patient has strong attachments and feels ambivalent about these. He may well find solace in prayer.

TAT PROTOCOL

PICTURE #16

This one needs a lot of imagination. I am thinking of what my mother is doing now. She's in the kitchen shelling peas. Probably near the sink preparing to make

ANALYSIS AND INTERPRETATION

When confronted with the blank card, the patient reverts to his mother — again indicating his strong attachment for her.

supper. A radio is playing
. . . it's an Italian story to
which she always listens
while she is doing her work.

Summary Picture #16: The patient's strong attachment to his mother is
indicated here.

TAT PROTOCOL

ANALYSIS AND INTERPRETATION

PICTURE #17

I see a muscular fellow letting himself down by a rope
in a corner outside of a
building. Letting himself
down from the roof. It's
kind of unusual, he's barefooted. Maybe it's a rope in
a gym. He feels he can
climb down easily because
it's easier going down than
going up and he has already
reached the top and is coming down. He is smiling triumphantly.

This story reflects some pleasure in accomplishment. It may well reflect his
feeling that the worst is over.

Note also that the patient has become
more realistic since, when he observes
that the hero is barefooted, he changes
the scene to a gym.

Summary Picture #17: The patient has pleasure in accomplishment. He
is quite realistic and feels that the worst is over.

TAT PROTOCOL

ANALYSIS AND INTERPRETATION

PICTURE #18

A man, probably asleep. I
see four fingers on his shoulder and an arm. Holding
him back. Another hand
under his armpit, you can
see the wrist and the cuff of
a shirt. He might have been
drinking and fell asleep.
Some fellows are trying to
push him into a taxi and
take him home. It is a dark
night. They will get him into a taxi, give his address to

It should be noted that the patient is
quite passive here and the " four fingers " and " arm " are first seen as holding the hero back but they later are seen
as assisting the hero. This suggests that
press dominance is converted into press
nurturance.

the driver, who will take him home.

Summary Picture #18: The patient is quite passive here. He is dependent on others for help.

TAT Protocol	Analysis and Interpretation

PICTURE #19

A snowbound cottage or a house. Two windows, two small lights which look like eyes, and a chimney. Looks like someone's home because the lights are on. There are two other windows, you can see the reflection of the light outside. A windy day, snow drifting, fantastic figures in the background which are snowdrifts.	Note that the first time the patient was presented with this picture, he was unable to develop a coherent structure. This time, however, a structure is developed. The one pathognomic sign still remaining is the mention of eyes but here, to be sure, they do not figure for much since they only "look like eyes." Yet this suggests the presence of some feeling of guilt. Note that the patient is reality bound and is not disturbed by the "fantastic figures" since they are snowdrifts.
Nothing is going to happen.	The patient in this statement seems to be trying to reassure himself after describing the difficult environmental conditions. It is a counterphobic statement.
People inside will some day be able to get out when they are no longer snowbound.	The "people inside" do nothing to get out but seem to be waiting passively until such a time when the environmental conditions change. The outcome, nevertheless, is optimistic.

Summary Picture #19: The patient's ego-structure is better now than previously but there is still evidence for guilt feelings. Although the environment is difficult he does not engage in activity to solve it.

TAT Protocol	Analysis and Interpretation

PICTURE #20

| A man sees an electric light. In background is a tree. Light throws reflections, it's a windy night. Fellow in a park has a date and is waiting for someone. Maybe he | The first theme concerns itself with anticipated rejection. Such concern may be a consequence of his strong desire for company, in itself a good prognostic sign, as indicated in the second theme. Note also that the male plays the domi- |

got stood up and is thinking of the girl he is waiting for. No, he's not stood up, just got there too early. It's a rainy night and he's looking forward to company with pleasure. She will come and they will go to a show, a dinner, and have a good time.

nant role and this again appears in a theme where the heterosexual relationship turns out to be a positive one.

Summary Picture #20: The patient has a strong desire for heterosexual affiliation and because it is so strong he anticipates rejection. Again, where the male plays the dominant role, the heterosexual relationship is a positive one.

Final TAT Summary

In contrast to the first TAT protocol, the patient's ego-structure, after combined insulin shock and psychotherapy, is better integrated. He gives evidence of a stronger capacity to control his drives. He does not distort reality in terms of inner needs but is rather object-oriented and quite rational. His thought processes are not as confused as previously and although he still at times entertains several alternatives for action, this too is not as characteristic of the patient as it was previously. There is evidence to suggest that impulses that were previously quite disturbing to him and which he still has difficulty in integrating, now tend to be suppressed.

There are also changes in his perception of interpersonal relationships. He still regards his mother as a domineering person who loves him and regards him as a little boy. Although he still is inclined to conform to her demands, he is nevertheless aware of his conflict with her and he is more desirous now of asserting himself against her. He is still quite sensitive to her needs and he still does not want to hurt her feelings. The desire to be independent of her, however, is strong and despite the pain involved he wants to leave her. To be sure, he may still be held back from acting on his desire because of his passivity. Evidence for strong ties to the mother is present but incestuous feelings are no longer verbalized.

The patient now manifests a stronger desire for a heterosexual relationship than previously and interference from the mother is not as effective as was found in the first TAT protocol. However, he gives evidence of hostility to women and an attitude that women are domineering. Although he tends to conform to domination, he resents it and feels more adequate if he takes the initiative and asserts himself. He is concerned that he may be rejected but hopeful that a good relationship can be effected.

With men the patient also appears to be more assertive. He may listen to them but he wants to make up his own mind. He identifies with men but is not completely secure in his masculine role with them.

The patient also appears to be more energetic in the second protocol than in the first. He has more capacity to engage in constructive activities and to take pleasure in accomplishment.

Mr. S. Z. feels that the worst is over and anticipates his return home.

Notes from the Case Folder

The patient is a 28-year-old unmarried white male. There is no history of mental disease in the family. The father is described as a domineering, complaining, and nagging person. He had one previous marriage before marrying the patient's mother. The mother suffers from a kidney ailment and is described as " nervous." The patient has four siblings, all girls, who are living and well.

The patient was the second of five children born to an immigrant family. He spoke his parents' tongue until the age of six, and then he first started to speak English. He is said to have had difficulty in toilet training and had enuresis until seven. The patient is reported to have been exceptionally calm during family arguments. He graduated from high school at the age of 18 with average grades. There was occasional truancy and he was somewhat slow in expressing himself. For two years he took some courses in college.

He masturbates with moderate guilt feelings to date; he is shy and passive toward females. He has carried on a fantasied love relation for the past five years with a casual female acquaintance. He engaged in homosexual play at seven and nine without any consequence later on. He had a vision of " the light " and affective experience of a religious nature at the age of 13.

The patient was inducted into the Army in 1942 and discharged " on points " four years later. He never went AWOL, he was never wounded, but he did have several attacks of malaria. After his discharge, the patient held an unskilled job but was studying for a more skilled occupation.

Prior to hospitalization the patient talked and acted queerly at home. He spoke of having visions. Two days after this occurrence he was found preaching in a neighborhood store. He became violent when stopped and was taken to a local hospital. Upon admission to the institution at which he was tested, the patient thought he was Jesus Christ. He was agitated and had delusions of reference and unworthiness. He had to follow " rules " and " orders." He escaped from the institution after the first month and returned in two days.

The patient was presented to a psychiatric staff meeting one week after the first record presented above was obtained. The psychiatrist's notes are as follows:

" Throughout his hospitalization he showed schizophrenic ideation and affectivity. However, clinically he was noted to have marked fluctuations in the degree of 'insight' and in his accessibility for psychotherapeutic attempts. In his negativistic phases he verbalized his behavior as 'self-willed' or 'I have to follow a rule, which tells me . . .' Though sufficient rapport could be maintained during these days by the examiner to have him cooperate in interviews and test procedures, his cooperation was markedly colored by his negativistic attitude. During his days of greater accessibility and better 'insight,' psychotic ideation could be elicited without difficulty; however, it is remarkable how well this patient is able to handle his ideation and how well psychotherapeutic rapport can be maintained."

After about a year of hospitalization during which the patient had shock therapy and several psychotherapeutic interviews, the patient no longer had any delusions, his behavior in the hospital improved, and he was discharged.

CHAPTER 11

THE PROTOCOL OF A DETERIORATED ORGANIC

Psychologists are rarely, if ever, called upon to administer a TAT to a deteriorated organic, because there is usually little concern with the psychodynamics of such a patient's behavior and there is little desire or need for psychological material that might help either in differential diagnosis or psychotherapy. Such a case is presented here, however, to provide the reader with additional material that may serve a useful purpose in developing a frame of reference for analyzing all types of TAT protocols. Specifically, the case here illustrates an extreme of disorganized thought processes, concreteness of approach, perseveration, misperceptions, and delusions.

The report on the patient stated: "The patient is a 52-year-old male who was dilapidated in appearance and who talked in a very rapid, indistinct, and unintelligible manner, using words which at times sounded like dysarthria. He was quite delusional and incoherent, but cooperative during the examination and in the ward." The patient had syphilis of the central nervous system.

PICTURE #1
Boy with violin here.
One cord short
   "   "   "
   "   "   "
   "   "   "

Four over there, see
Bust
Little boy there, one eye shut one open
there
Face kind of crooked over there
White cloth on table over there
Two wires short there
(What do you think happened before
the scene you see in the picture? What
is going on at the present time? And
what will the outcome be?)
One eye shut, one half open (demon-
strates, grimaces)
His mouth is crooked.
Is he a patient here? Looks like the boy

on the yard who played baseball on Sun-
day.
He is sitting down — doing nothing.
Face crooked
He is sick.

PICTURE #2
—— Hmmmm!
He straightened the horse there
Two women, one watching, one faces
this way.
One house and barn
The horse looks that way (illustrates by
grimace)
Bushes, hill, house, lake
The horse's harness is not right, the ring
should be that way.
He has no shirt on, the horse isn't mov-
ing.
Farm there, half an acre
Stable there — half an acre, half an acre.
There is another horse pulling a plow.
Slaves working for nothing — 1865 —
slave days
Looks like old Kentucky, old Kentucky.
Half an acre, half an acre, half an acre,
half an acre.
It's during slave days, slave days, slave
days, slave days
Mississippi, Mississippi, Mississippi
(points at girl's face and at furrow)
That's the slaving days, slaving days,
slaving days. (points at farmer)
Mississippi, Alabama, Georgia, Ken-
tucky, slave days.

PICTURE #3
—— Hmmm!
He fell over and can't get up — fell on
back. That's where he sleeps (points at
bed)
(talks about a crib, points out position of
bed in his room)
It's a prison bunk there.

He has his other hand hid against his face.
Prison walls over there
Can't go back to bed there —
One leg up, one leg rolled short
One hand — here is the other — can't see it.
He looks sick.
(repeats) Those were slave days (refers to last picture.)

PICTURE #4

— Love match — love match — love match
He looks this way, she looks at him.
She is nigger — this part (points to his lips)
There are white niggers.
A young girl, middle age, with nice brown hair is back there
Sitting — she (in foreground) has black hair.
She has no stockings on — bright gown — he has an army shirt on.
Two glass frames, one here, one there.
Love match
Look at eye lashes, up that way (illustrates with grimace)
Eye pencil, nothing but night gown, no splits on, left leg over right knee.
Love match — love match — she loves boy friend (laughs)
Black finger cover, see here
Nigger woman (disapproving grimace)

PICTURE #5

That takes you way back — way back — way back
One table, sitting room, table — corner up, comes up
That takes you many years back.
Books here, seven books, seven books here
Oil light, oil light (studies it closely)

(laughs) Pumpkin flower vase, pumpkin flower vase
See there — eyes there, it's not cut right, it's not cut right, it's not cut right.
Eyes and nose are not cut right (perseverates on face in vase)
A sitting room, one table folded down the side
Old timer (laughs)
Old time clock, old time clock, old time clock
Seven books

PICTURE #6
Grandmother and son there
All grey hair — grandmother
He has a handkerchief in hand
He has a felt hat in hand
Grandmother and son
She looks out of window — straight down
One lapel there, not pressed on right
Collar is messy on right, creasing there, collar on left side is flat
The grandmother there, grey hair, she is 80, he is 40.

PICTURE #7
Hmmm — (laughs silently)
The picture is painted
He has one square lip and there — hmm (surprised) one round
That's Grant there, Grant, Grant
Many years back
His hair is not painted right.
The car there, black (laughs)
Hand painted, hand painted, say it's hand painted, hand painted, hand painted, hand painted.

PICTURE #8
Operating, operating, cutting open, operating
Old time rifle, old time rifle
Old time shotgun

Operating room
Shadow there, shadow (points out light
beam in picture)
Old time shotgun
Boy here, young boy
White here, black (points out light re-
flection on his hair)
Right shoulder is higher than left.

PICTURE #9

(laughs) The old Civil War
1, 2, 3, 4 there, woods (laughs) — one on
his back — on belly —
Civil War, way back (laughs)
Laying it there (points out legs across
picture, describes their position)
Civil War — 1861.

PICTURE #10

That picture isn't painted right (points
to deep shadows)
That's back there.
Austria-Hungaria — the picture is Aus-
tro-Hungaria — the faces.
(Talks about abnormal sex practices)
Egypt — they do it this way
The woman does it that way (puts finger near buttocks and then in his mouth
— expresses amused disgust)
(Talks unintelligibly — incoherent, irrelevant, marked speech defect — doesn't
enunciate consonants and slurs syllables
unintelligibly. Laughs irrelevantly, grimaces. Inability to sustained attention.)

PICTURE #11

—— (studies picture)
Two mountain snakes
Five heads there (points to rocks)
One buffalo — there
It would be in old Africa.
(Talks about elephants, leopards, lions,

in a dramatic fashion with grimaces —
unintelligible)
Other people engraved in stone there
Footpath
——

It was taken in Africa.
A rhinoceros — Christ!   It's a big baby
That's the buffalo
Two mountain snakes there
Cobra snake eats only pork
Wouldn't eat buffalo

PICTURE #12
Hypnotizer, hypnotizer
Army cot, army cot, army cot, hypno-
tizer (laughs)
One leg is up there, right leg
He's hypnotizing him.
Outcome, outcome — one leg up there,
left leg —
Hypnotizer

PICTURE #13
—— sleeping here —
Choked murder (points to woman's
neck)
(indicates posture of man)
He choked her — choked her.
His hand is cut off — fingers cut off.
(points to invisible fingers of man's left
hand — gesture of cutting off his fingers)
Murder
Oil light, oil light, oil light
14th century back (laughs)
Hand made table and chair
Fingers

PICTURE #14
—— (laughs) ——
He is ready to jump
Commits suicide (laughs)
He is going down on the ground and be
dead

(Tells story of man falling and not breaking *one* bone)

PICTURE #15
(laughs) A graveyard — a graveyard
Protestant and Catholic graves together
Three crosses here, they are Protestant
Graveyard
Says prayer in the graveyard
Catholic tombs — crosses
Graveyard — says prayer
He doesn't have a Bible in his hand ei-
ther.
Some Protestant preacher

PICTURE #16
That's a blank — blank.
No picture at all — blank, blank
That's 16 by 28
Can't see anything there to do.
Blank, blank, blank
One finger mark, right there, right there,
right there, right there

PICTURE #17
Steeple deck — steeple deck
He paints a sign — steeple deck — paint,
paint, paint, paint
Cable — 10 foot apart
Painter (?) — copper
Steeple deck

PICTURE #18
Back is murder
One by his collar, one by his arm
Kill him — murder, murder
You see four fingers, can't see the thumb.

PICTURE #19
(laughs) ——
Snow and water, snow and water, snow
and water
Window curtains, egg shaped
A bungalow

Pair of feet, head right there (points to
window in foreground)
Two females (watch?) (window in left
foreground)
Bungalow (laughs) — it's very small.

PICTURE #20
A big fence there — across the way — one
light up there — flash light
It's a person — there's a guard there
—— a colored guy up there, see there
(points to left upper part)
A female standing right there (left fore-
ground)
Fence there
An X there (right center)
Guy standing on guard there ——

CHAPTER 12

A MALE STUDENT BEFORE AND AFTER
CLIENT–CENTERED THERAPY

PART I: BEFORE THERAPY

The Case of Mr. Beri

Mr. Beri is a twenty-two-year-old student, married, and the father of two children. He came to therapy voluntarily because he was disturbed about himself.

TAT PROTOCOL

ANALYSIS AND INTERPRETATION

PICTURE #1

3″ (Groans) This is a boy who is playing the violin.

The groan may be a physical manifestation of the client's uneasiness. This may arise from general annoyance with the test situation or even with this test in particular; i.e., annoyance and uneasiness that arises from dealing with a task that is unstructured.

(Words lost) (Pause: 5″) Uh, when he was two, his parents decided that he would play the violin

Two significant factors are reflected in this sentence. First, note that the client indicates the age of the boy. Some people may suggest that the boy was young or when the boy was a child, but here the client states the hero's age precisely. Starting with this clue, one should attend carefully to similar factors in other stories to note how intense or characteristic such an approach is of the client. Is it so frequent that it can be characterized as compulsive?

which he didn't want to do. Uh, so now he's looking at the violin 'cause now he's about seven. Uh, he wonders how he's going to get out of it;

The hero may have objected " when he was two " but apparently had to comply, for when he is seven he is still confronted with the violin. Note that the hero takes a passive role with regard to the violin; " he's looking " at it and not really playing it as his first sentence in the story suggests, and furthermore he en-

280

gages in internal activity, "wondering," but takes no active role in getting out of the uncongenial environment.

he's decided to go into physics. 40″

The hero relies on himself, that is, makes a decision for himself but does not tell us if the interpersonal situation is resolved or if the boy does go into physics. Thus it is suggested that he may still feel dominated by his parents.

It should also be noted that the activity he decides upon, physics, is far removed from music. It is almost as if he were deciding to do something that would spite his parents.

The selection of physics also suggests intellectual aspirations and because of the precision in this area, it may suggest that his previous stated age of the boy is an indication of some compulsiveness.

Summary Picture #1: This client sees parental figures as dominating persons who get their own way. Their wishes are not congruent with his and he is passive in their presence. He seeks to engage in activities which differ markedly from their desires. He has intellectual interests and prefers situations that are definite and fairly well structured.

TAT PROTOCOL   ANALYSIS AND INTERPRETATION

PICTURE #2

1″ This is, uh, pseudo-American and, uh, she's going to get married tomorrow.

The client's reaction time to this picture is very brief. Almost as soon as he sees the picture he has two comments to make. Neither of these comments figures directly in the story that follows (just as in the story to Picture #1 when his first comment is that it is a boy playing the violin, although the boy really does not play it in the story). This suggests that the client is an impulsive person. Furthermore, note that the first comment to this picture is a critical one (it is assumed that the comment is about the picture as a portrayal of an American scene), and direct criticism of people is expressed neither in this story nor in the first. He is able to express hostility in a critical fashion of inanimate objects but not of superior figures. The reference to marriage, which would be scored as a fusion of both need sex and need affiliation, is not a strong theme in this story and does not appear as a strong need in the others that follow.

There's the father and the mother and the daughter, and the girl is my wife, my first wife.

After identifying the figures, there is a decrease in psychological distance and the client makes reference to biographical material. The decrease in psychological distance suggests weak ego-structure and this hypothesis is further corroborated by the fact that some of the sentences in this story do not follow logically one from the other — as in the sentence that appears in the next segment.

I took her home, she lived on a farm when she was young.

The biographical material presented above and here suggests that the client has been married once before to a farm girl. Just whose " home " is referred to here is unclear — whether it was his wife's home or the home he shared with his wife.

And she's trying to get the hell out of there.

After the interpolated comment the client returns to the heroine and indicates once again that the environment is uncongenial.

The mother and father are a good deal more muscular and the mother looks pregnant.

It is interesting that of all the possible characteristics he could have selected, the client selects physical characteristics which do not necessarily make them better parents. Furthermore, because a comparison with the daughter is intended here it suggests a feeling of being different from his parents and in this case it refers to feeling weaker and also having different interests.

It should also be noted that although the parents are both described as muscular there is no difference between the two with the exception that the woman has a child-bearing function, but does she have others?   (This point will be discussed later.)   Because the mother is described with emphasis on a masculine attribute, it is suggested that she may not have been a mothering or warm woman.

Uh, she's going away to school, it seems.

The referent for " she's " is obviously the girl but note that in terms of the structure of the story, it follows a description of the mother — another indication of the interference of the adequacy of the client's communication.

One should also note the tentativeness of the client's statement as reflected in the phrase " it seems."   It may well be that whenever the client has to take definite action he does so with hesitation.

She doesn't like it because she wants to get away from the farm,

The immediate referent for " it " is school.   Note that a negative cathexis is stated concerning school and the reason seems to be given, namely, he is not attracted to school because of what positive attraction it may have for him but because it gets him out of a difficult situation — just as in Story 1 there was no " buildup " regarding the boy's interest in physics, but it seemed to be selected because it was sufficiently different from music.

and, uh, she's looking over to the left where she sees a large cow.

Thus far in the story there is no interaction between the figures in the story. As a matter of fact the client's comments are primarily descriptions of the people.   When the heroine becomes a little more active she does not interact with the parents but sees an animal. This lack of interaction reflects the difficulty the client experiences with his parents.

The statement " a large cow " is a quite unusual one in the stories told to this picture. To understand this, the following interpretation is offered. The cow is a female milk-giving animal. As such the animal is quite different from the client's description of the mother — " muscular," " pregnant." The first suggests masculinity and the second suggests only a child-bearing function (if the mother does use her milk after the birth of the child it will go to the newborn child and not the older figure). Consequently, it is suggested that in his relationship with his mother, the client's dependent needs, need for love and affection from her, were frustrated. This may stem either from her " coldness " or the appearance of another sibling. His frustration in this regard may be the reason for leaving the situation.

Uh, she'll leave directly. 45″

The heroine finally leaves the farm. Note that in contrast to the story to Picture #1, the leaving does occur in the story. Because the figure in Picture #2 is older than the one in Picture #1, it is suggested that the client may have been able to detach himself physically from his parents, but to learn whether he was able to break emotional ties it will be necessary to check the data that follow.

Summary Picture #2: The client's relationship with his parents is quite unsatisfying and frustrating. He regards himself as weaker than they and as having different interests. The mother appears to be regarded as a cold, masculine person with whom his dependent needs are frustrated. In getting out of his uncongenial environment he may select activities which are not pleasurable in and of themselves but because they get him out of difficult situations. He is also inclined to be impulsive and critical. Criticism which he cannot express toward older figures can be expressed toward inanimate objects.

TAT PROTOCOL

ANALYSIS AND INTERPRETATION

PICTURE #3

5″ (Sighs) This is, well, a boy of, uh, when I associated with him he was about five. He was teasing his brother. I told him, uh, to stop it. He picked up his brother, and I shouted at him and he cried in his chair for quite a while.

It was sad that I'd withdrawn my love.

The entire story here is rather unusual. One of the factors that makes it so is the almost complete lack of distance that exists between the storyteller and the story. The client states that it is autobiographical; whether it is so or not is another matter, but its content can be analyzed.

A conflict situation between two brothers is described and the client intervened. The client "shouted" at the teaser and this he associates with withdrawal of "love." Thus aggression or criticism is regarded as evidence for the lack of love. Furthermore, his statement has an intrapunitive quality and this may also serve as an inhibiting factor.

One of the specific aspects of this story which is most unusual is the client's use of the term "love" in characterizing the relationship between himself and the boy. The boy was five years old; the age of the client at the time of the incident is not known but from the content of the story it is assumed that he probably was older. Why is it that he, the client, is so aware of the withdrawal of love? It is suggested that his low threshold or sensitivity in this regard is a function of the deprivation he experienced within his own family. In other words, he loves someone else as he himself would have wanted to be loved. The fact that the frustrated need is active and with a male suggests the possibility that the client may have strong homosexual tendencies if he has not had homosexual experiences.

I think he expected that, uh
. . . he thought I expected
him to sulk in the chair.   47″

Here the client is capable of taking another person's point of view — capable of
understanding   another's   motivation.
But note that the implication of this
statement is that the boy did not sulk
because he felt badly about what he had
done but because he thought it was expected of him and probably was a means
of restoring or maintaining the relationship with the client.   This conforming
behavior is similar to the client's behavior in relation to his parents as described
above.   Thus, his capacity to understand
others is a function of his own experiences.

Summary Picture #3: The client is very sensitive to withdrawal of love
and acceptance.   This is related to his own deprivation in this regard.
Verbal aggression or criticism is associated by the client with loss of love
and this may not only affect his relationships with others but also inhibit
this behavior on his part.   When and if he does express such behavior it
makes him feel badly, especially if it is expressed to a weaker person with
whom he can identify.   It is also suggested that the client may experience strong homosexual tendencies.

TAT PROTOCOL

ANALYSIS AND INTERPRETATION

PICTURE #4

2″   Good heavens!   This is
a scene from a movie in Hollywood.   Uh, the woman is,
uh, mistreating the man.

Most frequently in stories told to this
picture, if there is any " mistreating " it
is usually on the part of the male.   But
here the reverse is true; the man is being mistreated.   Consequently, it is suggested that the reversal of role in the
story thus far is support for the idea implied above that the client may have difficulty in assuming a masculine role.
Furthermore, the " mistreating " which
occurs here is associated with the interference of his own desires.

At the state of his eyes are
fixed on, uh, the good thing
off in the future such as the
picture in the background of

The structure here is quite similar to the
structure in Picture #2.   Here again the
client goes off to a new situation as a result of a bad one.   It is as if the woman

the woman in the filmy underclothing. Uh, this represents his ideal and he's about to go off and, uh, try to achieve it. 31″

in the future becomes his ideal only as a result of inadequate relationships in the present. Note that strong need sex is associated with the woman in the background and it does not necessarily involve a real emotional relationship but satisfaction of sexual needs. Thus no feeling of responsibility is involved.

Summary Picture #4: The client feels mistreated by women and this seems to be related to his feeling that they interfere with his desires. He seeks release for sexual tensions rather than a relationship.

TAT PROTOCOL

ANALYSIS AND INTERPRETATION

PICTURE #5

6″ Uh, here is a mother spying

Again the mother is assigned a negative, dominating role, and the fact that she is " spying " suggests suspiciousness and feelings of guilt on the client's part. In view of what follows the guilt appears to be associated with sexual behavior.

on her two children who are sitting in front of the fire smooching.

At this point in the story the client describes the individuals in front of the fire as the mother's children. Therefore they are siblings. But as the story continues it turns out that they are not siblings but a young couple. However, since he did refer to them as siblings, it is suggested that one of the factors that may interfere with his ability to adjust adequately in a heterosexual situation is possible incestuous tendencies.

She has suspected it all along because the noise of the smooching has filtered out through the woodwork.

Note the exaggeration of the intensity of the sexual play. Such intensity may well betray some underlying feelings of inadequacy or problems in the sexual areas. Just as in the previous story where the hero goes off to a sexual object while a woman with whom a more mature sexual adjustment could possibly be established is rejected, so here too the emphasis is on sex play itself but not on sex and a relationship. The factors here are dynamically related to his interaction with his mother.

Uh, she is, uh, judging from her bland expression that she's, uh, uh, feeling very conflicting emotions; she thinks it's a good thing, and she's probably jealous. Uh, she wants her daughter to get married — this is the daughter's mother — uh, but conventionality will win out in the end and she will interrupt. 42″

In addition to previous characteristics of the mother, she is now described as jealous and conventional.

Summary Picture #5: The client regards his mother as envious and conventional. His heterosexual activity is exaggerated and belies problems in this area. There is also evidence for feelings of guilt with regard to sex.

TAT Protocol

Analysis and Interpretation

Picture #6

4″ (Sighs) Here is another Hollywood situation where, uh, the old mother is, uh, reprimanding her son (words lost)

Conflict between the mother and son, with the mother taking the dominant role.

Some, uh, lack of love or affection was shown when he was out motorcycling, assuming that's a leather jacket he has on.

One of the problems in analyzing this sentence is that there is no subject or object in the first part of the sentence. The client says " lack of love or affection was shown " but by whom and for whom? Did his mother show lack of love because he was out motorcycling or did he show the lack of love toward her by going off? It is impossible to answer these questions from the material available but whatever the reason it should be noted that the relationship is characterized by lack of love.

Another aspect of the story which should be attended to is the thought process. Several factors are referred to in the segment at the left but they are not logically related. Such behavior is most apparent in stories to pictures that stimulate problem areas.

The activity he engages in, motorcycling, is worthy of further interpretation because this may lead us to an understanding of the conditions under which there is a lack of love. Motorcycling is an independent, solitary activity which may reflect a desire for freedom and a devil-may-care attitude. If this is so then it is suggested that the client does not receive the love he desires because he goes contrary to his mother's wishes, or being free will result in lack of love, or because of lack of love he may indulge in activities of which his mother does not approve. It should also be indicated that motorcycling and the leather jacket are rarely found in TAT stories to this picture.

He is feeling, uh, rebellious, cocksure and, uh, she is feeling, uh, shy and long-suffering.

Two diametrically opposed attitudes by the mother and son. Note the difference between this and the story to Picture #1, representing again differences in stages of development. There are additional characteristics of the mother revealed here — " shy and long-suffering " — which may be descriptive of her technique of controlling her son. Note also that the son is rebellious and excessively self-confident.

And, uh, things will go on just as they always have done. 43″

The conflict remains unresolved.

Summary Picture #6: There is unresolved conflict with the mother. The client feels reprimanded for engaging in independent and devil-may-care activities which are expressions of his hostility toward the mother. Such behavior is related to lack of love. The client regards himself here as rebellious and excessively self-confident and the mother as shy and long-suffering.

TAT Protocol   Analysis and Interpretation

Picture #7

3″ Here is Dr. Allen Roy Dafoe talking to, uh, Mr. Dionne. And he's, uh, explaining to him about the seriousness of life. And, uh, Mr. Dionne is, uh, really feeling how, uh, life is indeed grim in spite of all the money he's made off of his children. This sort of talk will go on, uh . . . 32″

Needless to say, it is quite unusual to have the figures in this picture referred to as Dr. Dafoe and Mr. Dionne, the father of the quintuplets. The question arises as to why he has selected these two persons. In the light of the material gathered thus far, it is apparent that the client has a problem concerning his masculinity. It is suggested that Mr. Dionne may represent for him an example of masculine potency. But note that Mr. Dionne is depreciated in this story — he is having " the seriousness of life " explained to him. Consequently, the client is depreciating that which Mr. Dionne stands for. Because of the data obtained previously regarding the client's intellectual interests and because the client implies that Mr. Dionne is not too wise, it is suggested that he may compensate for his own felt inadequacy as a male by achieving superior status intellectually, and thereby feel superior to other men. However, he is not completely satisfied with the intellectual superiority because the sexual problems are too pressing. Thus, it is suggested that he was trying to prove himself in Story 4 and in Story 6. (In the former he was going off to a sex object and in the latter he was quite masculine in his motorcycle driving — these activities might be regarded as protests against his feeling that he is not quite a male.) The client is therefore in conflict because the value system of the intellectual and the value system that is involved in proving his masculinity are likely to be in conflict — especially since the sexual contacts do not necessarily provide him with the love he desires.

Finally, it should be noted that the relationship between Mr. Dionne and his children is not one of warmth. It is a money-making proposition. The client, it is therefore suggested, does not regard father-child relationships as close, warm relationships.

Summary Picture #7: The client depreciates masculine men and attempts to compensate for this by attaining intellectual superiority. His sexual behavior may be a means of proving himself sexually and need not necessarily involve a differentiated relationship. The roles he desires to play are conflicting. He does not regard father-child relationships as characterized by warmth.

TAT PROTOCOL

ANALYSIS AND INTERPRETATION

PICTURE #8

5″ Here is a shy, uh, introverted boy dreaming of violence.

The client describes here the discrepancy between the external façade and the internal activity. Intense aggression is covered up by a shy exterior. It is likely that the client has himself become aware of the Jekyll-Hyde aspects of his own personality and this conflict has turned him to therapy.

Perhaps he's reading from Joseph Conrad. Uh, homosexual tendencies, uh, represented in his dream by the, uh, the knife, the gun, and the violence he is seeing anywhere. The man is, uh (words lost)

Beneath the shy façade there is not only aggression but homosexual tendencies (bearing out the hypothesis suggested in this regard above), and possible concern with castration (knife). It should be indicated that the homosexuality occurs on the level of ideas but not in action. Unfortunately, due to the fact that words were lost, it is impossible to evaluate further the significance of the foregoing material.

Uh, nothing will come of this and he'll be a mediocre accountant. 34″

The boy's vocational choice seems to be out of place here but it may well have followed logically from the words that were lost. It is interesting to note that the boy becomes only a mediocre accountant; this is in marked contrast to the intellectual interests that the client manifests in talking about Conrad and others in the course of his protocol. This suggests that the confusing emotional problems which the client is experiencing may be of such intensity that he is unable to make full use of his knowledge and potentiality.

Furthermore, it should be noted that this is the second time an occupation is mentioned by the client. The first occurred in the first story when he referred to physics. Both of these occupations place a minimum of emphasis on interpersonal contact. In view of the story to this picture, it is possible to understand the reason for such choice — being close to people might involve feelings of aggression and homosexuality and these are too disturbing to him; therefore he is likely to forego such activities. However, previous stories indicated that he has a strong desire for affection and love and he is a sensitive person — these may be the forces that may push him towards people and it is likely that as he becomes more integrated he may well change his occupation.

Summary Picture #8: The client is aware of his own lack of integration in that he presents a façade of a shy person but beneath it are strong feelings of aggression, homosexual tendencies, and possible castration fears. These problems interfere with his capacity to make the most effective use of his abilities. He is inclined to avoid people as a means of controlling his feelings, yet the desire for contact is strong.

TAT Protocol	Analysis and Interpretation
Picture #9	
3″ Here's an indeterminate number of bums sleeping in, uh, in the jungle. Uh (words lost) ideas. They're, uh, sleeping and not thinking very much.	This is the second story in which the client depreciates men. Note also that one of the factors involved in his depreciation is that they are not " thinking."

It would be nice to imagine that they were feeling in communion with nature. But I think that's probably a romantic notion.

In this comment to the picture, the client reflects his own sensitivity. Furthermore, it should also be noted that although he may not be in communion with people, as indicated by the previous material, he is likely to be in communion with nature, possibly because of the greater freedom involved here than with people.

They will, uh, jump up probably and catch the next freight.   38″

The passivity at the start is followed by activity. It is therefore suggested that the client may be an energetic person when he engages in task-oriented activities.

Summary Picture #9: The client depreciates other men because they are not thinking individuals as he is, nor are they as sensitive as he. He is more capable of expressing his feelings in an environment that does not directly involve people than one which does. The client probably engages in task-oriented activities energetically.

TAT PROTOCOL

ANALYSIS AND INTERPRETATION

PICTURE #10

14″ Here's a man and a woman . . . probably older.

Here a relationship between a man and a woman who is older than himself is described. The fact that the woman is older than he suggests that ties to the mother are strong.

She's leaning on his breast

Although it is not erroneous to refer to a man's chest as his breast, it is interesting that this is the word that was chosen. The breast is feminine and it is suggested that the client's statement reflects his feminine identification. Furthermore, the breast is a giving organ and therefore it is suggested that he may regard himself as a giving individual. Note that he does " give " to the woman later. The woman is later described as " helpless." Thus, having himself experienced weakness as indicated in the above material, it is likely that he is able to give to weaker people.

as though she's bought a new hat.

On the face of it, this statement does not follow logically from the previous sentence. But there is sufficient data in the previous material to help in interpreting. In the story to Picture #3 the boy sulked because he was expected to, and in Picture #8 the hero appeared to be a Jekyll-Hyde personality. In other words, one's actions need not be directly related to one's feelings. In this story, therefore, it appears that the initial closeness described is not instigated out of affection but has other purposes. In other words, people have ulterior purposes when they get close.

They had a violent quarrel

A relationship between male and female is not without conflict.

and, uh, now they're making up. She is thinking about, uh, very little except she's glad she has the hat and that he made up.

The female is characterized as a sort of egocentric individual. She thinks of her own needs — the hat and the fact that he made up. The latter statement also suggests that she is the dominant person in the relationship.

And he is feeling protective and thinking that his wife is a, uh, helpless creature and doesn't know how to handle money. And (words lost) 53″

The man, on the other hand, assumes a warm, sympathetic, kindly attitude. Despite the fact that he believes that she was in error he apparently felt protective toward her.

Note that even after the two people make up, they are not in communion with each other. The woman thinks about herself and the man thinks about his feelings and a negative characteristic of the wife's, which he apparently does not seem to mind.

Summary Picture #10: The analysis of this story suggests that the client has strong ties to his mother and feminine identification. Women whom he regards as helpless he protects. He apparently can give warmth to weaker people. It is also suggested that close relationships may involve ulterior ends for him. And finally, that although he is displeased by a woman's behavior he is apt to give in to her desires.

TAT Protocol

ANALYSIS AND INTERPRETATION

PICTURE #11

2″ This is a major catastrophe in which, uh, uh, two ants are battling over a, uh, chasm. Uh, monsters are gleaming out of the fog like a picture of Bosch. Uh, the bridge is about to collapse, the cliff will fall down; everything will dissolve in dust. 29″

A picture of utter destruction starting with a conflict between two minor beings (the ants) who are unaware of the impending disaster. Evidence of violent, hostile tendencies and depression are, therefore, apparent.

In view of the material presented previously, it is also suggested that the story to this picture is a representation of the impending doom that the client is experiencing — he is afraid that the inner material will break through and he will disintegrate.

Note also the client's artistic interests. Bosch is not a commonly referred-to artist. This should be added to his literary interests in Story 8.

Summary Picture #11: The client is anxious about the possibility that internal feelings and needs may break through and that he faces disintegration. Intense hostile feelings and depression are indicated. The client is interested in art as well as literature.

TAT Protocol

ANALYSIS AND INTERPRETATION

PICTURE #12

2″ This is from a story by André Gide where, uh, uh, his confessions . . . where, uh, he describes . . . André, uh, describes Oscar Wilde as leaning over a boy, uh, with whom he is having sexual relations like a great bat.

Although the story is cited as having a source in literature, it does not detract from its significance, especially since there is previous evidence to suggest that homosexuality is a problem for the client. Citing stories from books may well be a defensive reaction — it places the content in another setting and therefore the client does not personalize it. The types of books the client cites are not only an indication of his literary tastes but also of his superior intellectual capacity.

The boy was, uh, different and he was repulsed; Wilde was lustful. 31″

Although the first part of the story suggests that homosexual relations did occur, here it is denied. In view of the previous material in which the client's intellectual interests were indicated and in which his strong sexual needs were also indicated, it is suggested that the client probably identified with Wilde. The fact that Wilde is repulsed in the story suggests that the client may feel that he has inadequate control over his homosexual desires.

It was pointed out elsewhere in the manual that stories to this picture may well yield significant data with regard to the therapy. In this case it is suggested that a homosexual attraction between the client and a male therapist is going to be a problem that may interfere with the therapeutic process. Furthermore, in view of the client's intellectual capacity, it is suggested that one of the major defenses of the client will be his tendency to intellectualize.

Summary Picture #12: The client has difficulty in controlling his homosexual desires. This will also pose a significant problem in treatment with a male therapist. One of the client's defenses that may also interfere with therapy is his tendency to intellectualize.

TAT PROTOCOL

ANALYSIS AND INTERPRETATION

PICTURE #13

8″ Uh, (pause: 5″) this man is filled with remorse at the horrible act he has just committed. Uh, namely, sleeping with this woman who is, uh, apparently dead.

The card that is most frankly heterosexual results in the longest reaction time. The reason for the long reaction time is readily apparent in the content of the story, which refers to necrophilia. It should be noted that the conditions under which heterosexual relations take place are those in which the female is nonthreatening. In the story to Picture #10 the client was close to a woman who was " helpless " and here the client has intercourse with a dead woman. In other stories, where the woman is alive and assertive, the relationship is inadequate. Considering these facts, it is suggested that one of his problems in heterosexual relationships is fear of castration. Stated differently, this is fear of losing his freedom.

No emotion probably. Maybe he's just wiping his eyes . . . I don't know. (sighs)

The statement that there is no emotion is in contradiction to the " remorse " or guilt spoken of previously and the client's own sigh. It is as if the client were trying to conceal the emotion that was stimulated, and reflects his difficulty in dealing with these feelings and tendency to deny them.

He'll walk away and, uh, give himself up to the police, or the FBI. 34"

Note that only two people were involved in the situation described — the man and the woman. Since the woman was dead there is no possibility that he would have been discovered. Yet the hero gives himself up to the police or FBI (and so increases the magnitude of the offense). His doing so, it is suggested, is a reflection of the intense guilt that the client experiences and his strong desire for punishment. In other words, he wants to be found out with regard to his sexual behavior in order to be punished for it. It is rather interesting that similar behavior occurred in Picture #5. There, too, the young people " smooch " so loudly that the noise " filtered out through the woodwork " and they were discovered by the mother.

The stories obtained thus far indicate heterosexual desires (Picture #4), homosexual desires (Pictures #8 and #12), and necrophilic desires here. The sexual object does not seem to be of primary concern to the client. The drive is intense and not integrated on a mature level.

Summary Picture #13: The client feels safest in establishing heterosexual contact with nonthreatening females and this is related to his castration fears. The sexual object is not important for him but the drive is strong and poorly integrated. He has strong guilt feelings regarding his sexual behavior and although he denies these he seeks punishment, which would be one way of alleviating the guilt.

TAT Protocol	Analysis and Interpretation

PICTURE #14

2″ Uh, this is a boy, uh, who knew (words lost) of a, uh, future escape from this black hole in which he finds himself. The lighting is very poor such as the library at the University. He's looking out the window where he sees the ideal future and stuff like that.

The client is apparently aware of the difficulties he is in. It is a favorable prognostic indication that he can see an " ideal future " — there is some hope for getting out of his difficulties. However, note that he does not do anything to achieve it and he may not be able to without therapy. Another question is whether the future he thinks of is so " ideal " that he may not be able to attain it.

The association regarding the University library in the midst of the story suggests that he may seek to escape from the " black hole " through intellectual enlightenment. Relating this to therapy suggests that he may approach it in a very intellectual fashion.

It's not very emotional now; I'll make up an emotional story. (Voice changes — deepens.) Uh, he's, uh, sitting in this dark room, uh, moaning about, uh, the fact that he axed his mother, and is about to jump out of the window. 41″

Two stories to the same picture are often related in some way. In this instance it is suggested that one aspect of the " black hole " referred to above is his aggressive feeling toward his mother.

The fact that the hero " axes " (or castrates) the mother, it is suggested, is the client's desire to do to the mother what he feels she has done to him by interfering with his freedom. Note that expressed aggression is followed by intra-aggressive behavior — suicide.

In view of the fact that the dynamics and content of this case are so similar to that obtained in the previous case and in view of the fact that the content of this client's stories appears so pathological, yet unlike the previous case this client is not hospitalized nor does he appear as disturbed, several comments are in order. First, the reader may be aware that I have made a conscious effort in these cases to avoid assigning to any of the cases discussed in the manual any nosological category, but have rather concentrated on the dynamics or ego-structure in each case. Therefore, I shall not differentiate between these two cases in terms of nosological categories.

In the previous case the client's needs were so intense that they interfered with his capacity to differentiate reality from irreality. It was as if the drives had overpowered the ego and the ego was fighting a losing battle. The drives that were troubling this patient were felt as part of the self, albeit not completely.

The protocol of the client discussed here, and especially the last segment presented, reveals significant differences from the previous case. This client's thought processes may not always be very logical, especially when he is dealing with affect-laden material, but they are not as confused or as autistic as that found in the previous case. Also, note that although the dynamics here are similar to those told by S. Z., they are woven into a story and this reflects the client's control. Furthermore, in the last segment quoted note how the client behaves — he first comments that his first story was not very emotional and then his voice changes. It is as if he were changing his role and is fully aware of doing so. In this fashion he increases the psychological distance between the material discussed and himself, and indicates that he has some defense against it and that he regards it as ego-alien. To be sure, the material referred to may still be anxiety-provoking, but he still has defenses against it, unlike S. Z. His other defenses were also pointed out previously.

Another important difference between the two cases is that S. Z. gave direct expression to the content of his problems in the first ten stories while this client, with the exception of the story to Picture #8, did not yield transparent stories until the second half of the test, when the pictures are also more ambiguous. Finally, in view of the client's knowledge of literature, he appears more sophisticated than S. Z. and he may therefore believe that psychologists deal with this kind of material and is less concerned about revealing it than one who is ignorant of such matters.

Summary Picture #14: The client is aware of the difficulties in which he finds himself and here one of the major problems is the aggression he feels toward his mother. Expressing such aggression results in intra-aggressive behavior. He is, however, hopeful that he can resolve his dilemma.

TAT Protocol	Analysis and Interpretation

PICTURE #15

5″ This is a Poe character. Uh, he's whittled his emotions of communing with the dead, uh, to a fine inch.

The emotional experience described here is quite intense. The experience has a self-punitive character about it. It occurs in a situation where the hero apparently refuses to accept reality, for he cannot commune with the dead. Yet the desire to do so is strong.

He has retired to the cemetery to masturbate . . . over the grave of his beloved . . . and which he is doing right now. (laughs) 36″

The reason it is so strong is that he lost a loved one. In view of the material presented previously, it is suggested that the beloved one is his mother whom he realizes he cannot have.

Masturbation, an additional sexual activity not mentioned heretofore, seems to serve several functions here. It is a means of discharging the tensions that have been accumulating as a result of undischarged emotion, it is a means of getting closer to " his beloved," it is a means of expressing disrespect or hostility, and it may also reflect a pseudosexual freedom.

Summary Picture #15: The client cannot break his ties to his mother and he feels hostile toward her. Masturbatory activity is a means of getting release from emotional tension for the client.

TAT PROTOCOL   ANALYSIS AND INTERPRETATION

PICTURE #16

9″ Well, I can see my own reflection. See, uh, there's a tempestuous storm. A ship is being, uh, torn apart, uh, by the waves. It's in pursuit of, uh, Moby Dick, the white whale. Ahab is on the quarter deck and presentation of the American (words lost). 32″

Although the client's first sentence indicates that he is being autobiographical, note that he does so by means of an allegory, thus indicating that conceptual and abstract ability is still good.

Note that the ship is tossed about by the storm. This is interpreted as reflecting the intensity of his problems and that he does not feel that he has control over them. Nevertheless, there is direction; he is after something. But the whale is unattainable. Just what the whale represents for him it is difficult to say. It may be reunion with a loved one, as in the story to Picture #15, it may be the ideal future referred to in Picture #14, or something else.

Summary Picture #16: The client feels beset by forces over which he does not have complete control, yet he has a sense of direction. Just what his goal is, is not clear.

TAT PROTOCOL   ANALYSIS AND INTERPRETATION

PICTURE #17

5″ A drawing by, uh, Daumier, I guess. This is a su-

Once again the client is critical of men. Here, specifically, he is critical of a male

percilious or rather fatuous clown who is climbing up the rope so that his love will admire him.

who demonstrates his muscular superiority, and note that in so doing the man gains the admiration of the woman. The extent of his protestation and criticism suggests that he may indeed be envious of the male who is more masculine than he. Furthermore, note that although the male is muscular he is stupid and the client, it is inferred from his references to art and literature, regards himself as smart. Thus he makes up for his feeling of physical inferiority by intellectual superiority. However, intellectual achievement is apparently not completely satisfactory — no story has yet been told in which the hero gains love and admiration, factors which the client desires, as a result of his knowledge.

He's demonstrating his muscles.

The emphasis on the physical body of the figure in the picture reveals certain narcissistic tendencies.

While his love who is sitting down in the, uh, in the chair over to the right, uh, looks admiring up, he is thrusting out his jaw. Looking effective. 34″

Note how the client specifies the precise position of "his love." It isn't simply that she is sitting down below but she is in a specific position. Such behavior as well as the naming of the pictures suggests that the client has strong need for control and structure.

Summary Picture #17: The client is very critical and envious of men who are muscular. He compensates for his feeling of physical inferiority by achieving intellectual superiority but such behavior does not lead to the love and admiration he desires. Narcissistic tendencies and desire for control and structure were also indicated.

TAT PROTOCOL

ANALYSIS AND INTERPRETATION

PICTURE #18

7″ This is Edmund Wilson or Billy Graham who's being clutched from behind by a monster out of the cellar. Uh, perhaps the, uh, ghost of the Effingham's-Drooping-

The story involves an attack from the rear which culminates with the hero's being eaten "starting with the nose." The "nose" is regarded as a displacement upward and it is suggested that the story reflects fear of oral aggression and

ham's from Little Abner, which will pull him backwards into the cellar and there eat him starting with the nose. 30"

castration. Since the "monster" comes up from the cellar it is suggested that feelings and attitudes which were previously unconscious are coming to the fore — evidence for which is available in the stories analyzed previously.

Summary Picture #18: The client is anxious about oral aggression and castration. Feelings and attitudes that were previously unconscious are now coming into consciousness.

TAT PROTOCOL

ANALYSIS AND INTERPRETATION

PICTURE #19

3" Ghosts arising on a, uh, on a winter wind. (Pause: 5") (Sigh) There seem to be some characters inside the windows which I can't make out . . . who think they're warm and cozy, but they don't realize that the, uh, house is about to blow down. 25"

The people in the house "think they're warm and cozy" but the external environment is hostile. Furthermore, it is superior to the house and will destroy it. Thus the serenity and calm which one may experience is only temporary for there are always forces working against it. Even the people in the house are not certain that they are warm and cozy, they only "think" they are. (Compare this story with that told to Picture #16, where the client feels battered around.) The client appears to be the sort of individual who cannot accept moments of security; he feels that they are too temporary and that some force will come up and upset him. Thus both pessimism and aggression are reflected here.

Picture #19 is one of the more unstructured TAT cards. Note that the client has some difficulty in telling a story to it. This, it is suggested, is consistent with the statement made previously (Picture #17) that the client prefers structured situations. Also note his attention to "minor details" ("characters inside the windows"). Such compulsiveness or need for control is dynamically related to the fact that without it all that which troubles him may break through and be more catastrophic than it is now.

Summary Picture #19: The client sees environmental forces as hostile and his moments of security are only temporary, for he anticipates destruction. Compulsiveness and need for structure were again indicated.

TAT PROTOCOL	ANALYSIS AND INTERPRETATION
PICTURE #20	
11″ Uh, a man under a street light in a, uh, big city. Uh, he's had a few drinks. He's out of money. (Pause: 5″) He's feeling gloomy. He's just, uh, relapsed, uh, from Alcoholics Anonymous and that's very gloomy. 41″	In addition to the depressed feelings of loneliness there is also evidence here for the client's oral-dependent needs (alcohol) and evidence for his inability to effect adequate control (his relapse) which may result from the excessive frustration that he experiences.

Summary Picture #20: The client experiences feelings of depression and loneliness; these are related to his frustrated oral-dependent needs. These needs are rather strong and he is unable to deal with them adequately.

Final TAT Summary

Mr. Beri is a man of superior intellectual capacity and interests who is unable to make full use of his abilities and potentialities because of severe problems in the sexual area. His problems are so intense as to threaten his capacity to control his drives, allay his anxiety, and alleviate his guilt.

The client has diffuse sexual drives for which he seeks satisfaction. The sex object is of relatively little moment to him and the sexual aims are various. Masturbation, homosexuality, heterosexual behavior, incestuous wishes, and necrophilic fantasies are all manifestations of his immature sexual development. At times his sexual behavior is designed to relieve emotional tension, while on other occasions its purpose is to demonstrate and prove masculinity to himself, or express his aggression, or achieve a close relationship where he can gain satisfaction for his need for love and acceptance. The primary pleasure is quite narcissistic and there is little, if any, evidence at the present time for the capacity to establish a differentiated relationship in which the needs of others are considered. The client experiences a good deal of guilt and anxiety with regard to his sexual impulses. Indeed his guilt is so intense at times that he seeks punishment or outside aid in an effort to help him effect more adequate control.

Mr. Beri has strong needs for love and affection but these have been and still are frustrated. One of the reasons for his frustration in this regard is that to attain satisfaction for his needs would possibly require at times assuming a subordinate position, while at other times it may involve responsibility and the necessity to satisfy the other person's needs. None of these is he able to accomplish with equanimity. To assume a subordinate position makes him feel that he may be sacrificing his independence and this, coupled with a history in which his personality was dominated by authority figures, stimulates feelings of inadequacy and hostility. Furthermore, he is too narcissistic to satisfy the other person's needs and his desire for autonomy is too strong to permit him to assume responsibility without undue tension. There are two situations in which he is more free in expressing his sensitive feelings. One such situation is that in which he can interact with impersonal objects — such as communion with nature or in his literary and artistic interests. Another situation is one in which he interacts with a weaker person. Here he is capable of giving warmth and the psychological basis for this behavior is his identification with the weaker person. In other words, he loves the weaker person as he himself would have wanted to be loved.

Aggression is another need with which the client has difficulty. If aggression is expressed toward him, and this may not be intense aggression but only criticism, he equates it with the loss of love. This equation still holds when he expresses negative feelings to weaker individuals and consequently he inhibits himself in this regard and probably also in relationships with superior adult figures whom he respects and whose approbation he desires. This does not mean to say that he does not express criticism, for he does with peers and against strong individuals. Here he can be sarcastic and depreciatory, using his intellectual capacity and knowledge as a means of demonstrating his superiority over these others.

Mr. Beri is inclined to avoid social contact, for social contact only aggravates the problems touched upon above. Furthermore, his critical attitude does not foster good relationships unless others are as quick and as bright as he. He does not permit his warmer feelings to come out in social situations.

With men he depreciates their masculinity and seeks satisfaction in demonstrating his superiority in intellectual matters. This is not completely satisfying, for he is insecure in sexual identification and rather envious of masculine males who can also be more attractive than he to women. He may also seek to exaggerate his sexual capacity as a means to gain masculine status but this too is unsatisfactory for him. His feminine identification or inadequate sex role identification, in addition to sexual problems indicated previously, is another factor in his inability to establish adequate heterosexual relationships. He depreciates the female and at best he can establish relationships with nonthreatening females, or women who seek from him protection. But here the relationship is not without conflict, for his autonomous needs may soon come to the fore to disrupt the relationship.

For Mr. Beri, parent-child relationships are characterized as lacking in warmth. His mother appears to have played a more dominant role than his father. The mother is regarded as a cold, dominating woman with masculine attributes, who was quite conventional in her attitude. She is regarded as having interfered with the client's capacity to establish his own independence, and as a person who did not sufficiently satisfy his desire for love and affection. He is quite hostile toward her and even now his rebellious attitude to authority stems from his hostility to the domineering attitude of his mother, who did not sufficiently consider her son's needs. Although he had desires of his own, his tendency was to conform to the demands of his parents and still remain hostile. He sought to effect compromises in which neither their needs nor his own would be completely satisfied. Thus it was early in life that the pattern was established in which he did not make full use of his abilities as a means of dealing with his problems. He did not seem to go into a new situation because of the intrinsic satisfaction it had to offer but because it would get him away from the uncongenial, restricting environment at home. At the present time the client is still tied psychologically to his mother and this is complicated by his sexual drive to her.

The client's thought processes are quick. Indeed, thoughts and associations occur very rapidly to him, almost more quickly than he can verbalize them. This may at times be manifest in impulsive behavior and in confused communication. The pressure on himself is often greater than his capacity to consider whether or not he is communicating with others. The client does better in structured than in unstructured situations. The latter put more stress on his inner resources and since unresolved problems are brought to the fore he has to attend to the details in the environment to seek out the controls that are existent in it.

In addition to the compulsiveness implied above, which serves as a defense mechanism, the client also intellectualizes a good deal about his problems and thus divests them of any affect. He tries to dissociate himself from his problem areas and his self is like a house divided. He himself is aware of the lack of integration that is involved here and also of the Jekyll-Hyde characteristics that he may present socially.

The client regards himself as a superior person with a good deal of ability. He would like to think of himself as quite rebellious and extremely self-confident and although he realizes his shortcomings in this area, he cannot accept them. His tendency at the present time is to be an island unto himself, coming out of his shell to seek narcissistic pleasure. However, because his attitude and behavior may be in conflict with his intellectualized values and because of the guilt and tension he experiences in his present status, he desires help.

PART II: THE SAME CLIENT AFTER THERAPY

TAT PROTOCOL   ANALYSIS AND INTERPRETATION

PICTURE #1

5″ Uh, this is a potential Albert Schneider whose parents have driven him very hard, uh, to learn the violin, and he has rebelled against it.

The fact that the client identifies the boy as " a potential Albert Schneider " reflects the client's interest in music, but in terms of his personality it also suggests that he regards himself as having great potentiality. Contrasting this potentiality with the conclusion of the story reflects the extent to which the client will go to defy authority — he will not satisfy the demands of authority figures nor will he actualize his own abilities.

The story thus far is similar to the client's story the first time he saw this picture. It involves press dominance. But one difference is also to be noted, namely, here the boy " rebelled," albeit unsuccessfully, while before therapy the boy only " wonders " how he is going to get out of his predicament but rebellion is not mentioned directly.

Uh, this is hard. At the moment he has very mixed feelings about the, uh, the, uh . . . oh hell, the symbol of the violin, the female symbol. This is trouble with sexual feelings about his parents.

Although the client speaks of " sexual feelings about his parents," it is suggested that he really means his mother, since he refers to the violin as a female symbol.

Not once throughout the whole protocol before therapy did the client refer to sexual feelings about his parents directly. In the content of the stories in which such interpretations were made, the client referred to a " loved one " or used some other term from which his attitude to his mother could be inferred. Here, however, the client makes direct reference to his goal object. It is likely that he has learned this during the course of therapy. Such information is disturbing and is not as yet integrated, for in the story his association regarding his sexual feelings interferes with and disrupts the development of the story. This is an example of what is meant when it is said that during the course of therapy a person may become more disturbed in certain respects before he gets well. Finally, although the criteria for a successful therapy are not well defined as yet, it is apparent, if only from the data obtained thus far, that the client has not as yet dealt successfully with his problems and that the therapy is incomplete. This statement is not based solely on the content of his association, for it often occurs that after therapy a person may tell stories to the pictures which refer to " deep " material — sexual attitudes, etc. It is also based on the fact that the thought interfered with the development of the theme.

His mother was very permissive, while his father wanted to drive him, which isn't the case in my own life.

The autobiographical material here indicates that the client's mother was dominant and his father permissive. This contrast in parental roles is one of the significant factors in his own sex role identification.

Uh, and he will compromise in this case by doing very poorly. Uh, that's about it. 1' 00"

As pointed out above, the client does not resolve his problem by gaining satisfaction. He fulfills neither his parents' desires nor his own. Hostility is expressed indirectly.

Summary Picture #1: The client regards himself as a person who has great potentialities but who will not actualize them because of hostile reaction to his mother's dominance and his sexual feelings toward her. His hostility is not expressed directly.

TAT PROTOCOL

ANALYSIS AND INTERPRETATION

PICTURE #2

6" Hmm . . . this is my wife, Mary, who is, uh, leav-

As in other stories where the client refers to what may have been a real life sit-ing her family who are nothing like this. Uh, they wanted to keep her down on the farm, uh (words lost) proper tradition, and applied much more pressure than these people look like their . . . would have . . . to do so. However, she's leaving with mixed feelings, uh, of guilt and leaving the tradition in which . . . of which she took so much. Uh, however Mary left and was successful in breaking away, this girl left them and was successful in breaking away. 1' 03"

uation or a story from literature, so here the basis for the interpretation that follows is that that which the client has selected to talk about has resonated with a specific aspect of his own behavior, personality or history, and therefore it is meaningful. Thus in this story the client refers to his wife's relationship with her parents and describes a situation that is consistent with his own life as reflected in the story to Picture #1. Thus parental dominance plus ambivalent feelings at breaking ties with them is the theme. The last sentence in the story indicates that he regards his wife as being more successful in breaking ties with parents than he is. The fact that she was able to do so and not he suggests personality differences between the two — his wife was stronger in this regard than he.

Summary Picture #2: The client has very mixed feelings in breaking ties with his parents, who again appear dominant. His wife was probably stronger in this regard than he.

TAT PROTOCOL

ANALYSIS AND INTERPRETATION

PICTURE #3

3" This is a boy downstairs. Uh, his parents treat him in a very ambivalent fashion; love him, hate him. Uh, there seems to be a . . . scissors on the floor. Let's see, uh (pause), uh, he has been wanting to have a pair of cowboy boots, uh, which his parents have refused to give him. Uh, and he is thinking now that if he had the cowboy boots, he would just cut them up with the scissors; that he doesn't want them anyhow, uh, which is

Not only are parents domineering and want their own way, as indicated in previous stories, but they are also inconsistent in their attitudes toward him. The fluctuations of love and hate are not an adequate foundation for the establishment of feelings of security necessary for the development of good ego-structure.

Another interesting datum here is the cowboy boots. For the young boy cowboy boots are the means of signifying his masculine identity. Note that he had a desire for them and that this was denied him by his parents. Comparing this with the story to Picture #1, where the

to say he wants to hurt his parents. Pretty soon, he will go outside and play without having resolved his, uh, feeling of hostility.   1′ 03″

parents demanded that he learn to play the violin, it is suggested that the parents were not sensitive to his desires and that they may have fostered his less masculine interests.

Finally, note how the aggression is dealt with. The aggression occurs on a fantasy level and is directed toward an inanimate object. He hurts himself as well as his parents. He is spiteful but the conflict remains unresolved.

Summary Picture #3: The client regards his parents as being inconsistent in their attitudes towards him. They did not foster his masculine interests. The client expresses aggression on a wishful level in this story. If his desires are not fulfilled he is ready to hurt himself as well as others. His conflict with his parents remains unresolved.

TAT PROTOCOL	ANALYSIS AND INTERPRETATION

PICTURE #4

3″   This is a — a true story. Uh, there is a woman in the background, evidently an illustration . . . lower class household. He has wanted to break away from her and go in search of (pause) sexual adventure, uh, he wants to engage in the Trans-Arabian oil race where he thinks that the, uh, the girls will be very cute . . . not in the sense of any language at all. His wife holding him down from these high adventures and, uh, she wants to hold him there for she wants to have a baby and, uh, put up new curtains, tear down the old pictures and have the executive type husband. He will probably stick around, uh, again without solving his conflict.   1′ 05″

The fact that the client's first response is to the picture in the background suggests high need sex. This is borne out by the content of the material that follows. In contrast to the pre-therapy story to this picture, this story indicates that he has more control over his sexual drives but sufficient change has not occurred in this regard so that he can establish his marital relationship without conflict. His wife's values are in conflict with his own. Her values are oriented to stability, while his are oriented to freedom and irresponsibility. In his positive cathexis for freedom it is as if he were trying to make up in the present what was denied him in the past by his parents. The fact that he does stay with the wife suggests the possibility that he may see something positive about her values.

Summary Picture #4: The client's strong need for diffuse sexuality and lack of responsibility is in conflict with his wife's desire for greater stability. In contrast to the pre-therapy story there is evidence for more control over sexual needs but these are not sufficiently integrated as yet to make for a completely satisfactory marital relationship.

| TAT PROTOCOL | ANALYSIS AND INTERPRETATION |

PICTURE #5

2″ This reminds me of a shocked episode. (Words lost) it's different. It was told to me by a friend. Uh . . . perhaps I'll make up a different story . . . not tell that one. Uh, boy and girl are necking in the, uh, at the fireplace. Uh, and the mother looks in the door, uh, with very mixed feelings of jealous, uh, moral disapproval, excitement . . . and a *Reader's Digest* feeling that, uh, well, uh, young people (words lost) and all that. Uh, I'm making it so complex that I'm going to immobilize her . . . won't be able to give the outcome. Uh, she'll quietly shut the door and go away. Still a *Reader's Digest* outcome. 1′ 20″

The heterosexual behavior is disapproved of by the mother and yet it excites her. Her excitement and jealousy suggest that the client probably wishes to make her jealous and that this is a reflection of the client's sexual ties to his mother. This is coupled with his hostility toward her, for he is " making it so complex " as to immobilize her. At the same time, however, he immobilizes himself and suggests that he won't be able to give an outcome. This suggests that the theme of this story — heterosexual behavior and reaction to the mother — have stimulated a good deal of tension in the client.

There are some interesting contrasts between this and the pre-therapy story. In the pre-therapy story reference is made to siblings. This does not appear here. The former intense sexual behavior which " filtered out through the woodwork " is now toned down. More hostility is expressed toward the mother than previously and finally the mother does not spy on or interrupt the sexual activity but permits it to continue. All this suggests that the client has made some progress in being able to establish more adequate heterosexual relationships.

The activity described in this story occurs between a " boy and girl." In order to gauge how much progress the client has made in his heterosexual adjustment it will be necessary to attend to the content of his stories, when the characters involved are more mature individuals, and to note their sexual behavior.

Summary Picture #5: Although the client still experiences some difficulty in heterosexual activity as a result of his relationship with his mother, he has made some progress in this regard.

TAT PROTOCOL   ANALYSIS AND INTERPRETATION

PICTURE #6

6″ The old mother is, uh, giving her son good advice on, uh, what he ought to do in his job. She thinks that he again, wants to break away and she's holding him there. He is, uh, gotten a good job as a garage mechanic and is working his way up in the world, and she feels he ought to stay with this.

Again the mother assumes the dominant role. The son is not asking for advice but is being given advice. Furthermore, she is now trying to hold on to him and he manifests a strong desire to fulfill his own needs. In this story his own needs are in the area of achievement. It is interesting to note that he speaks of her advice as " good " advice. This is consistent with the story to Picture #2 in which the client spoke of the girl's leaving the tradition " of which she took so much." Both of these data suggest that the client may be more capable now than he was during the pre-therapy record of distinguishing between the " good and bad " in his relationship with his mother. He may still feel, however, that if he accepts the fact that there was anything good at all in the relationship, then this may suggest to him that he is becoming too submissive to her and giving up some of his independence. This may arouse negative feelings in him.

The relationship described here is very similar to that described in the story to Picture #4. This suggests that one of the factors affecting his marital relationship is that there are too many factors in this relationship which are similar to that which he encountered with his mother.

However, he wants to go out and play the races. Uh, and she is pointing out to him that he ought to do the proper thing and stay around the home, and, uh, he appears cross at this advice.

Again there is conflict between that which the mother regards as proper and his own desire for more or less responsible activities.

Uh (pause: 5″), he'll go off to the saloon and have a beer. (pause: 5″) Maybe this fellow will go off to the races after all. 1′ 00″

Two conclusions are found for this story. The first is the client's typical " compromise solution " in which he foregoes his own pleasure and at the same time does not accept the mother's views. It is interesting to note that the activity in the first conclusion is an oral one. Dynamically, this is related to the frustrated dependence needs that were manifest in the content of the story discussed previously.

The second conclusion is one in which the client fulfills his own desires. But note the structure of the last sentence. It is preceded by " maybe," and it occurs in the future tense " will go," and it is in the nature of a comment, " this fellow," in contrast to the " he " discussed previously. This suggests that while the compromise solution may still be typical of him, there is a growing need for independence which is yet to be attained.

It should be noted that in contrast to the pre-therapy story, a conclusion to the story is presented here, suggesting an element of decision.

Summary Picture #6: Conflict with the mother is indicated again. While this conflict is not adequately resolved, the client's story indicates a growing need for independence from her.

TAT PROTOCOL

ANALYSIS AND INTERPRETATION

PICTURE #7

3″ This is the old family doctor and he is worried

In contrast to male-female relationships described above, the relationship with

about the young medical student. Uh, he is saying to him, son, uh, there's been a lot of loose talk about socialized medicine, uh, and, uh, I hope you're not . . . not going to be taken in with this; it will destroy the client-patient relationship and so forth.

The son is drinking all this in;

an older male is more positive here. This is consistent with the client's autobiographical comment to Picture #1. But note that in the stories told here and previously, the other figures initiate the activity and not the person with whom the client identifies. This is consistent with the previous interpretations regarding his passivity in relationships with older persons.

The metaphorical description of the son's activity reflects the client's oral-incorporative tendencies. Combining this with the oral frustration ascribed to the client previously, it is suggested that he satisfies his needs through the more socialized channels of education and profession.

he's looking seriously into the future and wondering how soon he, too, can get, uh, copies of William Osler's *Physician* to distribute to his patients. Uh, continuing his fight, which he will do. 48″

In contrast to previous stories in which the dominant role is played by the woman and in which the client resolves the situation by having the hero effect a "spiteful compromise," here the client considers a goal that is more in keeping with his abilities and potentialities — as is inferred from his intellectual interests. This is also one of the few stories in which the client evinces a strong need for professional achievement unencumbered with the intensity of his own problems. It should also be noted that the hero in this story is following the profession of the older man. This is interpreted as reflecting masculine identification and the fact that he now feels more capable of assuming a mature masculine role for himself. (Note the contrast between this and the pre-therapy story to this picture.)

Summary Picture #7: The client manifests here a capacity for masculine role identification — a role which is still to be more completely integrated. Need for professional achievement as a sublimated means of satisfying his oral incorporative tendencies is also indicated.

TAT Protocol

Analysis and Interpretation

Picture #8

3″ Homosexual boy has been reading . . . homosexually inclined boy . . . has been reading *Treasure Island.*

The difference between the characterizations of the boy, "homosexual" and "homosexually inclined," is interesting. It may reflect a change that is consistent with the client's new behavior and/or his attitudes toward himself. The perception is that he is not homosexual (i.e., acting out such behavior) but only so inclined.

This also looks like a — an operation under difficult conditions. Uh, perhaps for appendicitis or something. (Pause: 7″) He, uh, (Pause: 6″) he has been reading *Treasure Island.*

The lengthy pauses in this story indicate blocking that may well have been stimulated by the content that follows.

He thinks about various gory details, how he will stick knives into people, shoot them. He is both . . . the Negro, he is lying on his back and the man cutting. The figure holding the light is, uh, myself observing this picture.

The client is both the aggressor and the recipient of the aggression in this story, thereby indicating strong sado-masochistic attitudes. But note the structure of the story: the figure in the foreground is thinking about the activity and the figure in the background with whom he identifies directly is an observer. The client therefore appears to detach himself from his own feelings and attitudes — it is as if he were two individuals with one part feeling sadistic and masochistic and the other merely observing, recounting, or intellectualizing about the process.

Note that the Negro in the story assumes a passive role — he is being operated upon. In view of the previous stories (especially Picture #4, in which the client manifests a social class consciousness, it is suggested that the Negro, representing lower status, is a rejected part of himself and that the client cathects more positively the more aggressive role but he may not as yet be able to attain it. The fact that he does cathect this role is borne out by his last sentence in the story.

Uh, although he looks awfully calm for such — such thoughts, he's deriving his satisfaction from brutality and such.

The Jekyll-Hyde attitude portrayed here is similar to that which was obtained to this picture during the pre-therapy protocol.

Uh, he will go out and, uh, see if he can find a small playmate whose arm he will twist till she screams. 1′ 29″

The aggression is displaced toward a subordinate and inferior person — "small playmate." But note also that the object for the aggression is a girl.

Comparing the post-therapy story with the pre-therapy one, the client appears to be somewhat more capable in dealing with aggressive themes in the former than in the latter.

Summary Picture #8: The client is involved with sado-masochistic thoughts. He assumes a detached attitude with regard to these thoughts and attempts to deal with them by isolating them. In dealing with his aggression he is more likely to displace it to subordinate persons rather than his equals, who might reciprocate. With regard to homosexuality, he has inclinations in this area but is less likely to act them out than previously. He has a more positive cathexis for an active than a passive role but is not as yet capable of completely achieving this status.

TAT PROTOCOL

ANALYSIS AND INTERPRETATION

PICTURE #9

3″ These comfortable men have been working on the railroad out west in the fields. Uh, at the noon break, they take a nap. (Pause: 5″) They're content with their lot. The sun is warm. Presently the foreman will come and send them back to work. 35″

The passivity of the men is interrupted by the active role assumed by the foreman. Thus the structure of this story is similar to several of those told previously in which the hero is prodded on by others, indicating that motivation for energetic activity is not internalized but is dependent on stimulation from outside.

There is less hostility expressed toward the figures in this picture than there was expressed in the pre-therapy record.

Summary Picture #9: Motivation for energetic activity is not internalized but is dependent upon external stimulation.

TAT Protocol	Analysis and Interpretation

PICTURE #10

4″ Aged couple, like my parents, by Courbet, I guess it is . . . a modern artist. His pictures are nothing like this. Uh, after a long and happy life, uh, long and happy therapeutic session, uh, regard to myself . . . uh, they're considering how their children have grown up and gone away.

In contrast to the client's story to Picture #6 in the pre-therapy protocol, here the parents realize that their children have grown up and gone away. This reflects a growing independence from the parents which the client himself appears to believe is directly related to his therapeutic experiences.

They're getting old and will die. (Pause: 8″) These, uh, sentimental thoughts are attracting them together. (Pause: 6″) Pretty soon they'll go to bed and, uh, renew futile attempts to have intercourse. 1′ 13″

The positive feelings expressed at the beginning of this story are followed by hostile and disparaging remarks. (Note that the disparagement occurs in the sexual area.) It is as if the client cannot tolerate for too long the expression of positive affect toward his parents.

Summary Picture #10: The client shows a growing tendency to establish himself independently of his parents. He is, however, still quite ambivalent about them.

TAT Protocol	Analysis and Interpretation

PICTURE #11

6″ (Sighs) A horror scene from, uh . . . some mythology, or pictures by Klee where, uh, the lone traveler has, uh, been trying to reach Shangri-La. Perhaps pilgrims . . . Bunyan's *Pilgrim's Progress.* It's a tragically strange monster, wild, and his (words lost) forlorn. He is not running away in fear of his life, but

The client operates alone in an effort to achieve what is an unrealistic goal.

From what is available here, it is significant that the client is not running away from something but toward a goal. This is one of the few stories in which he is goal-oriented and optimistic, and quite a contrast with the pre-therapy story to this picture. The fact that he does not fear the monster suggests that he feels more in control of his instinctual drive

forward, and he will have an eventual good outcome. 50″

and this is consistent with the content of the data interpreted previously.

Summary Picture #11: The client feels more in control of his instinctual drive. He is goal-oriented and although his goals may be unrealistic, he is optimistic.

TAT PROTOCOL

ANALYSIS AND INTERPRETATION

PICTURE #12

3″ A dianetics therapy session. Where, uh, the, uh, therapist has, uh, hypnotized the boy on the bed . . . seems to be exerting some sort of malign influence over him; in fact, he seems to be on the point of entering the bed, perhaps with homosexual intent. (Pause: 9″) Perhaps the boy is dead. A certain uncertainty about this picture. (Pause: 7″) Thus a Svengali situation in which the man will have, uh, sexual intercourse with him . . . certainly a malign influence. Perhaps because of his hunched back. Perhaps also a friendly figure, maybe he's drawing forth or evoking or . . . a pleasant dream. 1′ 37″

In calling the therapy "dianetics therapy" and in referring to the therapist as a homosexual the client depreciates both. In the latter instance he is also projecting his own feelings. The depreciation is consistent with the client's usual pattern, in which frustration leads to aggression, and suggests that the client-therapist relationship is not yet resolved. This plus the material obtained from previous interpretations suggests that the therapy is incomplete.

Note that in the pre-therapy story to this picture, the older figure was described at one point as having a homosexual relationship with the boy. Here, however, there is intent or the relationship occurs in the future. This suggests that the client's control over his problems in this area may be better than previously.

Summary Picture #12: The client tends to depreciate the therapy and to have ambivalent attitudes toward the therapist. This suggests that the relationship between client and therapist is not yet resolved and that the therapy is incomplete in this respect.

TAT PROTOCOL

ANALYSIS AND INTERPRETATION

PICTURE #13

6″ The man is, uh . . . arisen from sleeping with a

Intercourse with a prostitute stimulates feelings of disgust. It should be noted

prostitute. Uh, sleepy . . . will go about his business, also feeling disgust at his act.

that heterosexual activity occurs when the female is depreciated.

(Words lost) I guess, but a man has not lived unless he's walked across the sand or something, feeling disgust in his soul at his action or some such thing.

This is an attempt to rationalize his behavior. Also, considering the material obtained in this and the pre-therapy protocol, it may be the client's attempt to integrate his sexual attitudes so that he is not beset with guilt feelings that may hamper his capacity to establish a new way of life.

She is content and at peace with the world. Full of seed. 58″

The contrast between the woman's behavior and the male's again indicates the inferior status assigned to her.

Comparing this story with the pre-therapy story, there is again some evidence for progress but the client is still not too well adjusted with regard to heterosexual behavior.

Summary Picture #13: The client manifests annoyance with his sexual behavior and there is evidence to suggest that he is attempting to integrate his previous behavior, of which he is not proud, in order to effect a more adequate adjustment. The female in heterosexual activity has for him inferior status to the male.

TAT PROTOCOL

ANALYSIS AND INTERPRETATION

PICTURE #14

2″ This is, uh, I remember this especially from, uh, the conflict about whether he was going to jump out . . . uh, being gloomy about his failures to, uh, succeed in medical school, or is looking forward to a bright future in the early morning light. And is, uh (Pause: 8″), resolving to arise and meet the new day with redoubled efforts. (Pause: 8″) Feeling of . . . " peaceful sleep and sweet dreams " . . . some

The client recalls his pre-therapy story to this picture and then develops a new theme. This theme indicates that the client is less tense, less intrapunitive, and more hopeful about the future.

quotation. The feeling of being calm . . . I don't think now he's jumping out as much as last time I took the test . . . he's looking forward . . . the time I took the test in school . . . when I was starting school. 1′ 10″

Summary Picture #14: The client is less tense, less intrapunitive, and more hopeful about the future than he was before therapy.

TAT Protocol	Analysis and Interpretation

Picture #15

5″ A morbid character much fixed on death. His wife has died . . . all the people he has cheated. All his friends and enemies, and he returns in advanced age to pray at their graves. Either that or he cheated his wife in life . . . I mean, from what I just said doesn't, doesn't . . . he's not successful in praying though. Like the king in *Hamlet,* his hands point down, his thoughts remain below. He looks a little as though he's masturbating. A field of broken stones . . . he'll return to just whatever he was doing before, eking out his old life without this changing, as one of his activities, that is . . . no change. 1′ 24″

The client feels guilty about his attitude toward his wife and others, and although he strives for prayer and possibly forgiveness he cannot bring himself to do so. Note that when he is frustrated he resorts to masturbation just as in the pretherapy story to this picture: after the Poe character had whittled his emotions he retires to the cemetery to masturbate. Masturbation seems to provide him with relief from tension.

This story does not end as hopefully as the story to Picture #14 in this protocol. The difference between the two stories lies in the fact that in the former the client discussed a single person's behavior while here he discusses an interpersonal situation. Thus it appears that attitudes toward the self have changed more than interpersonal relationships. However, since the former is theoretically a precursor to the latter, it is likely that more change in interpersonal behavior will also occur.

Summary Picture #15: The client feels guilty about his relationships with others but when it comes to expressing himself and possibly to absolve himself of his guilt, he encounters difficulty. It is likely that progress will still be made in this area. Finally, the client may masturbate as a means of relieving tension that arises from frustration.

TAT PROTOCOL

ANALYSIS AND INTERPRETATION

PICTURE #16

22″   A tree with a — a bird house, and a small boy below it. Uh, Peter woke up in the morning feeling that this was going to be a good day. He went out . . . this turns into a children's story, such as I might tell my daughter, uh . . . he went out into the fields and saw the birds, uh, ran across, picked flowers, and is now resting below one of the cork trees. He'll grow up . . . that is to say . . . and be a boy sexually potent; now he's, uh, asexual and enjoying a trivial, uh, and solitary communion with nature. There's the problem we have of what he'll do next. 1′ 36″

In line with the previous data, this story again suggests that the client has not yet established a mature sexual role. There is hope that he will do so but there are still problems to be overcome in this regard.

Summary Picture #16: The client has not yet established a mature sexual role. He is hopeful that he will be able to do so although there are problems still to be overcome in this area.

TAT PROTOCOL

ANALYSIS AND INTERPRETATION

PICTURE #17

2″   This is a Daumier, of a man climbing a rope. Uh, the acrobat is enjoying the adulation of the crowd as he climbs up the rope, hand over hand. Uh, a rather supercilious expression. Much — much muscular power; he'll climb up and leap around from trapeze to trapeze to roars of applause. I feel some contempt for this sort of popular entertainment similar to the photo-

What the client objects to in this story is not the pleasure that one may get himself from the activity but the exhibitionistic character of the activity. It seems as if he feels that gratification from an activity itself is all right but "showing off" is not. In view of the previous data that reflected interpersonal difficulties and need recognition, it is suggested that the criticism here is based on envy. His manner of telling stories and the intense criticism here suggest that the client's exhibitionistic tendencies are stronger than he is willing to accept.

graph of a contortionistic background of Metropolitan Opera House, or something like that. (Words lost) pleasure in the, uh, physical . . . it's like stretching, the physical activity of climbing up the rope. Stretching out, using the muscles and so forth. Which he feels, too, but with this guy it's principally the adulation of the crowd. 1' 22"

Finally, it may also be said that the client is energetic, as inferred from the hero's energy level in the picture, and that he is contemptuous of popular activities, and thus indicates a snobbish attitude and feeling of superiority.

Summary Picture #17: The client is critical of those who get gratification from exhibitionistic activities. He has difficulty in accepting his own exhibitionistic behavior and at the same time has an attitude of superiority and snobbishness toward others.

TAT PROTOCOL

ANALYSIS AND INTERPRETATION

PICTURE #18

5" I think a little too long. There are three hands in here, something like Charles Addams cartoon. Uh, none of them . . . there are four . . . none of them seem to be his. Five . . . counting his two. (Pause: 5") A mythical situation where, uh, because of his bland expression, uh (Pause: 5") he hasn't been knocked out, but it is potentially a violent situation but I prefer to make it mythical in that, uh (Pause: 6") Also a very peculiar belt line, it's a . . . perhaps pregnant or something. His pants are pulled down. He's been walking along the street, and ruffians have crept up behind him,

This is the longest story the client has told to any of the TAT pictures. The length of the story, the attention to detail which seems to interfere with the development of the story, and the general lack of coherence reflect the client's tension and uneasiness. The content of the story reflects the transitional stage in which the client finds himself. On the one hand there is a problem in sex role identification (the man is seen as possibly being pregnant) and fear of attack on his masculinity (being rolled) and on the other hand there is a struggle to go forward. The conflict is intense and the client is fatigued and unable to resolve the situation at the end.

Note that the client attempts to tone down the violence of the story by referring to it as a " mythical situation " and thus controlling the anxiety stirred in

hit him over the head, and are pulling him backwards into a dark doorway to roll him. Mythically, uh, he's feeling a Wagnerian *Weltschmerz* . . . uh, the forces pulling him back, and the struggle forward is, uh, too, too much for this frail, uh, whatever it is. And this feeling . . . it's all too much an esthetic sensation; he feels forces in varying directions. That in this case haven't interrupted a march . . . an esthetic emotion to overcome . . . in spite of the violence of the picture, it — this — this fantasy of the esthetic expression . . . perhaps from the expression on his face . . . contradicted by . . . I feel it contradicted by the hands on the . . . pulling in all directions. I prefer to make (words lost), that is in French, lackadaisical or slothful, perhaps, giving in to the forces of the world perhaps. And this interpretation (Pause: 7″) this — this view doesn't take the story in, you know, what will happen next. What . . . will he come out of it, go about his business (words lost). Doesn't have anything to do with the story. But the situation of being (French word lost) lackadaisical (French word lost) French word, you know, meaning a, oh, something like fucked out. 3′ 42″

him. Furthermore, note how he intellectualizes his conflict.

Summary Picture #18: The client is in a stage of transition. He still has problems referring to sex role identification and fear of losing his masculinity. Although he gives evidence of striving to go forward to overcome his difficulties, the struggle is intense and it leaves him fatigued.

TAT Protocol	Analysis and Interpretation

PICTURE #19

5″ Could be a contemporary American painting. Snow scene of — of fairy ghosts and, uh, wild clouds . . . symbolized for the small child . . . roaring outside . . . dangers of the outside world as compared to the scene inside, which in the picture as I . . . is very warm, vivid with ruddy light (word lost) in a way . . . whether it is or not, but ruddy light coming out of the window where he's very safe and sound inside the little house or self.

The outside environment is full of danger but the " self " feels secure, suggesting that the client has a feeling of security. This is in contrast to the pretherapy story told to this picture.

Uh (Pause: 6″), uh, she's protected against . . .

Although the story starts with a reference to a boy, here the client refers to "she," suggesting again a problem in sex role identification.

especially as a child against all the wild dangers of the world, which are exaggerated, probably too much, for esthetic purposes.

The client apparently feels that he may have exaggerated the dangers from the environment. This, coupled with the security mentioned previously, is a good prognostic sign for further development.

The boy has, uh, (words lost) he's been popping corn at the fireplace and he hears the shriek of the wind and looks out, and feels how warm and safe he is, uh, in his mother's bosom, uh . . . (words lost), that is to say

Note that the security referred to above which initially seemed to be within the self now stems from a close relationship with an older figure on whom he is dependent. It should also be noted that the mother is rejected and the father is substituted. The boy is close to the father's bosom — thus it is a male with

his father's bosom. And, uh, will eat the popcorn. (No time indicated)

feminine characteristics. This is interesting in that the client's therapist was a male. It therefore suggests that he now feels secure as a result of a relationship with a male who had " feminine " characteristics (probably referring to his capacity to accept and give warmth to the client) and it is also consistent with the fact that the client's major difficulty was with his mother and thus he transferred his relationship with her onto the therapist.

The reference to the eating of the popcorn, reflecting once again oral dependent needs, the dependency on the older male figure, and the fact that the whole story revolves about a child, reflects the client's immature ego state.

Summary Picture #19: The client still perceives his environment as hazardous but considers the possibility that it is not as dangerous as he thinks. Although he feels more secure now than he did when he told his pre-therapy stories, it is apparent that his security is a function of a dependent relationship he assumed with his therapist. He probably sought to gain from the therapist satisfaction for needs that were frustrated in his relationship with his mother. The client's problem in sex role identification and evidence for his immature ego state were also indicated.

TAT PROTOCOL

ANALYSIS AND INTERPRETATION

PICTURE #20:

9″ The man of those days came out of the bar where he has been drinking with his friends, drunk and melancholy, uh, leans against the light post (Pause: 5″), drunken stupor of cerebral anoxia, uh, considers that everybody hates him, uh, on the other hand, everybody likes him. If someone comes along and he will, uh, bud-

The client is uncertain how he stands with others. He does not know if he is accepted or rejected by them. Yet he desires a relationship, but note that it is a dependent one. His inadequate social relationships result in depression.

dy-buddy up to them in
hopes of getting home. 58″

Summary Picture #20: The client is uncertain of his relationships with
others. His inadequacy in this regard results in depression. Dependent
needs are strong.

Final TAT Summary

A comparative analysis of Mr. Beri's pre- and post-therapy TAT protocols indicates that he has made progress but he still has quite a way to
go to attain more complete personality integration and greater security.
He is in a state of transition in which there is a growing desire to give
up old habit patterns and to develop new ones. There is an intense struggle going on in this regard but underlying it is a sense of direction and
greater security than he experienced previously. His ego state at the
present time may well be described as immature and literally characterized as " young." It is a serious question whether he will be able to continue his progress without additional aid.

With regard to his sexual behavior, his needs do not appear to be as
diffuse as suggested by the pre-therapy record. Although homosexuality,
homoeroticism, incestuous wishes, and heterosexual relationships are still
problems for him, they are less intense than previously. He appears to
have more awareness of his feelings in this area and less guilt about expressing them (although he is not completely untroubled by his guilt).
He also has greater capacity to control his sexual drives but the control
is not always effective. Although there is still evidence for problems in
sex role identification, the client does show a growing capacity for masculine role identification. Some progress is also evident in heterosexual
relationships. The intense drive to prove his masculinity noted in the
pre-therapy protocol is less intense now and there is a diminishing fear
with regard to female sex partners. However, consistent with his pre-
therapy record, women are still depreciated in the sex act.

The client also shows a little more freedom in expressing aggression
toward authority figures and in asserting himself with respect to them.
But there are still problems in this area. His aggression is still largely
directed to inanimate objects or inferior persons and he gives evidence
of sado-masochistic tendencies.

The client feels guilty and irritated with himself for the nature of his
interpersonal relationships. Although he desires to atone for his guilt
and to effect more adequate relationships, he does not feel completely secure to do so as yet. He feels more at ease in solitary activities than in interpersonal situations. Although he has the desire for contact with others he is uncertain as to how he stands with them — whether he is
accepted or rejected by them. This results in feelings of depression and

the intensification of his frustrated needs for a dependent relationship. One of the factors that still contributes to his inadequate interpersonal relationships is his snobbishness and feeling of intellectual superiority. He still depreciates others who are capable of doing what he cannot do and he has difficulty in admitting to his own exhibitionistic needs.

While during the pre-therapy record he regarded his parents, and especially his mother, as domineering persons, and while this is still a predominant theme here, he now also regards them as being inconsistent in their attitudes toward him. His feelings toward them are quite ambivalent. Although he can see positive aspects of their relationship he depreciates them. He still is concerned with incestuous wishes toward his mother but there is a growing tendency to break his ties with her and to attain a more autonomous role.

In his relationship with his wife, the sexual problems referred to above may still interfere with an adequate relationship. Although he still cathects his freedom, and although he still has negative reactions to her desire for stability, he is not as concerned with the possibility of being dominated and appears to be more capable now of assuming familial obligations and responsibilities than he was previously.

Professional goals and need achievement are more evident now than previously. This may well have resulted from the freeing of energy that was previously delegated to dealing with his problems. While previously he manifested the tendency to forego the satisfaction of his own needs if they were in conflict with others' and to effect a compromise that was not satisfactory to any of the parties concerned, and while such behavior is still apparent, he does show a greater desire now to achieve the satisfaction of his desires. In doing so, he has cathected persons who have achieved and who now serve as models for him. His goals may well be somewhat unrealistic and in this his acquisitive tendencies are apparent. Although he can apply himself energetically in task-oriented problems, his motivation in this regard is not completely internalized, for he still feels it as an external force that goads him on.

The client sees his present environment as less hazardous than previously, and there is a suggestion that he feels he may have exaggerated the seriousness of his problems prior to therapy. He feels less disturbed, although there is evidence that he is struggling to integrate what he may regard as a Jekyll-Hyde personality. His problems still tend to be unresolved, but he feels more secure and hopeful than in his pre-therapy protocol that he may still resolve them.

Although the client may verbalize depreciation for his therapeutic experience, this may well be regarded as a cover for his more positive attitude toward it. He has not completely resolved his feelings toward his therapist. His attitude toward the therapist is friendly on the one hand and hostile and homosexual on the other. It appears as if what progress the client has made may be attributed to his having assumed a relationship with his therapist in which he could get gratification for his previously frustrated relationship with his mother.   The security of this relationship may have provided the foundation for the client's capacity to resolve some of his difficulties.   While he appears to have entered therapy as a disturbed adult, the intensity of his anxiety has diminished somewhat but the state of his ego development is such at the present time that there is room for improvement before he can establish a mature sex role, differentiated interpersonal relationships, and autonomous and spontaneous behavior.

Notes from the Case Folder

The following is a summary of the contact with the client, prepared by the therapist.

Mr. Beri was married, in his early twenties, with two children.   He was a veteran.   He never presented any complaints.   His initial interview was delayed twenty minutes because his counselor had had some difficulty in terminating a preliminary interview with a man and his wife, both of whom were psychotic.   Mr. Beri spent most of the first interview in a silent rage which he finally expressed with great difficulty and with mild words belying his demeanor.   This frozen hostility of his was so characteristic of him that counselors and clients noticed it when he sat in the waiting room.

Mr. Beri's main concerns were domination-submission relationships with others, and in particular with his counselor.   He felt humiliated at being a client and was deeply resentful of his counselor, against whom he struggled to aggress but couldn't do so.   At one time he became ambitious to become a therapist, and one superior to his counselor.   His main fears, usually expressed indirectly, were of being seduced by his male counselor, coupled with a wish to be so seduced, and a fear that he would become actively schizophrenic.   In my opinion and his, a great deal of progress had been made when he terminated his counseling, although we both agreed he still had much further to go.   A follow-up interview about two years later indicated that he had continued to progress.

CHAPTER 13

AN ADULT MALE BEFORE AND AFTER PSYCHOANALYSIS

PART I: BEFORE PSYCHOANALYSIS

The Case of A. C.

Mr. A. C. is a 41-year-old married man, the father of four children. He is employed as a biologist. The pre-therapy protocol was obtained about six months before the patient entered treatment as part of a research program. At that time therapy was not being considered by the patient.

In the protocol that follows, reaction times are not indicated. For the first ten pictures, the patient told his stories to the examiner and for the remaining pictures the stories were handwritten by the patient himself.

Pictures #11, 15, 18, and 20 were omitted from the series presented here. They had not been administered to the patient because they were not appropriate to the research that was underway.

TAT PROTOCOL

ANALYSIS AND INTERPRETATION

PICTURE #1

Looks as if he had been out playing. His mother called him to practice on the violin. He's very disgusted. He'd much rather be out playing, but I would guess that his mother would insist that he play on his violin and that he would play, reluctantly, of course.

The hero's free play activity is interrupted by his mother. Although the desire for freedom is still present and he is irritated with the press imposed task, he does not express his irritation, and conforms to the mother's demands with reluctance. In view of the reluctance and desire for freedom expressed here, careful attention should be paid to the stories told to those pictures in which the male figure is older than the one depicted here, to determine whether the patient is capable of more autonomous behavior at the present time.

Note that the hero had been out playing and that he does play the violin; this suggests that the patient's energy level may be rather good.

Finally, although the patient refers to the third person in discussing the past

329

and the present, note that his style changes when he comes to discuss the future. Here he comments on the picture and his comment reflects some uncertainty with regard to the future.

Summary Picture #1: The patient's desire for free play activity was frustrated by his mother. He conformed reluctantly to her request but the desire for freedom was nevertheless present. There is evidence to suggest that the patient is uncertain about the future.

TAT PROTOCOL

ANALYSIS AND INTERPRETATION

PICTURE #2

I didn't notice the bulge there at first which may explain things —

The patient's comment here suggests that he may have developed a story and then he notices a detail which possibly altered this story. Since all this occurred before he verbalized his story, it suggests that the patient may be a cautious person who tries to be systematic and attempts to integrate all the details of situations with which he is confronted. However, he is not necessarily successful in this regard, for although the " bulge " may explain things, it does not figure in the story that is developed. Speaking of a " bulge " rather than of pregnancy suggests that the patient may have difficulty in speaking of sexual matters, or if he used this term to describe the physical status or attractiveness of the woman it may be an indication of some depreciation of the woman.

Well, it would appear as though the man in the picture had been cultivating, can't tell whether furrows or young plants in the field.

The man is engaged in activity, thus supporting the hypothesis that the patient is capable of energetic activity. Two activities are suggested for the man; this again reflects the patient's attention to detail but note that he does not decide between the alternatives. Since this detail is not essential for the development of the story, he is not sidetracked by it. Note, however, how the patient makes use of other details later in the story, especially when he says, " All you have to go by here is a gesture by the farmer." This statement suggests that the patient can build a story about a minor detail. In view of the above, it is suggested that the patient, in approaching a problem-solving situation, responds not so much in terms of its over-all aspects but in terms of its detail. The details have to be indicated, although they may not necessarily figure in his solution.

It would appear as though the young lady with books might have come along to talk to the farmer. Possibly on her way to school. It would appear as though the wife of the farmer feels pangs of jealousy and suggested that the young lady proceed on her way. The girl with the books I would guess is most unhappy and appears to be in love with the farmer. All you have to go by here is a gesture by the farmer.

The major activity in the story is carried on by the women. Although they are involved with the man and although the man does have some preferences, as he states later in his story, the patient does not have the man take an assertive role, a reflection of his own lack of assertiveness in interpersonal situations. Note, also, that while in the story to Picture #1 there was uncertainty with regard to the future, here there is uncertainty and lack of confidence with regard to interpersonal relationships, as is indicated by the frequency with which he qualifies his statements — " it would appear," " possibly," " I would guess."

The content of the story presented thus far suggests that the patient is experiencing difficulty in his marital relationship. The fact that the wife is regarded as jealous and the girl is in love with the farmer suggests that the patient is here emphasizing his sexual attractiveness. Because so much emphasis is placed on this it is suggested that the patient does not feel adequate sexually in his marital relationship.

He might be disgusted with the fact that his wife came out and I would say that the wife has a possessive attitude

The wife is described as a possessive person and although he is irritated with her behavior he does nothing to alter the situation.

toward her husband and that she planned to stay there until the girl is out of sight.

Let's see, you wanted to know what happens after that.

The patient makes this comment just before he is to develop an outcome. This again reflects his uncertainty as to the future.

Let's say the girl went on to school. After she's out of sight the wife went back to the house and the husband went back to work.

The wife is successful in preventing the development of a relationship. She is stronger than he.

(How do they feel afterward?)

The girl suffers in silence rather than take the fellow away from the wife. The wife appears to be quite self-confident. She felt she won a small victory over the younger girl. I don't know what to say about the farmer, hard to tell.

The only one who comes out of the situation with a feeling of success and satisfaction is the wife. Note also that while the patient describes the reactions of the girl and the wife, that he has difficulty in describing his own feelings and attitudes. Although previously he was able to build the story about the man's gesture, here he would like to see the man's face. This is an example of the fact that when the inner life and feelings are not well structured, more structure is desired in the environment. Only as a result of his feeling that demands are made upon him by the psychologist (and here it should be noted that he conforms to these demands rather than rejecting them) does he give some indication of how the man feels. His statement suggests that the need for love is frustrated. This results in feelings of hostility which are not explained.

Summary Picture #2: The patient responds to situations not in terms of their over-all aspects but in terms of the details that make them up. Some of these details are elaborated a good deal, while others which are also attended to do not necessarily play an important role in his approach. This patient also appears to be a cautious person who tries to be systematic but he is not too successful in this regard. The patient feels insecure in heterosexual situations. There is evidence to suggest marital difficulties. He sees his wife as a possessive and domineering woman, while he is more passive and less confident in his relationship with her. One of the factors involved here is his feeling of inadequacy in his sexual relationships. His need for love is frustrated. This leads to hostile feelings which are not expressed.

TAT Protocol	Analysis and Interpretation

PICTURE #3

Can't get my teeth into this one — Let me talk to give my impression. For some reason or other this object suggests a lethal weapon, can't say whether it's a gun or a knife.

The patient's delay, his inability to identify the revolver, and his initial comment, all support the hypothesis that the patient has difficulty in dealing with hostility.

Say this woman killed somebody with whatever this thing is and is now overcome with remorse. One possibility is to give herself up to the police or commit suicide.

The fact that the figure here has been identified as a woman suggests feminine identification. By feminine identification is meant the patient's tendency to be passive in social situations (as in Picture #2) and to be low in assertiveness. The fact that the patient identifies the figure as a woman here is interesting in another respect. Note that the patient has difficulty in expressing aggression, yet the person in the story does commit an aggressive act. The fact that she is a woman and therefore unlike himself increases the psychological distance between himself and the person he is talking about. Furthermore, he does not indicate the object of the aggression. This indicates that he attempts to make hostile feelings, which are no doubt troublesome for him, alien unto himself. The fact that the aggression does occur suggests that these feelings are intense.

Finally, it should be noted that the aggression expressed here is followed by guilt and the need for punishment, either from oneself or others.

Summary Picture #3: The patient has difficulty in dealing with his hostile feelings. He tries to regard them as ego-alien. Associated with these feelings are guilt and desire for punishment, either from himself or others. Evidence for feminine identification was also indicated.

TAT PROTOCOL

PICTURE #4

I would guess that some third party not shown in the picture has made a remark or done something which has caused the gentleman in the picture to become very irritated. I would guess that it was an action or remark that affected the man and not the woman. He proposes to retaliate

and the girl is trying to restrain him. Now you want to know what happens. She's going to talk him out of it.

ANALYSIS AND INTERPRETATION

The patient's style in telling the story to this picture is somewhat different from that which was characteristic of him in the previous stories. The style here is stilted and formal. He speaks of a " third party " who " has *made* a remark " " which has *caused* the gentleman . . ." " It was an action or remark that *affected* the man . . ." and finally " *He proposes* to retaliate." His characters lack spontaneity and so does the patient. He is involved with details in a rather rigid fashion.

Note also that although the hero is " irritated " he only " proposes " to take action but does not.

Since the lack of spontaneity, and rigidity, indicated above occur in the context of an aggressive theme, it is suggested that the functional significance of his rigidity is that it facilitates his control over his aggressive impulses. The implication is that if the controls were relaxed, then the hostility which he is unable to deal with adequately would come forth.

It is not uncommon in themes of the stories to this picture that the woman " talks the man out of it." However, in this case it should be noted that the behavior described is consistent with the perception of females as dominant persons in the previous stories. In view of his difficulty at the beginning of the story it might well be suspected that he welcomed her intervention.

Summary Picture #4: The patient is a rigid person who lacks spontaneity. The function of his rigidity is to control aggressive impulses. A woman again appears as a dominant figure and here he does not mind her intervention.

TAT PROTOCOL	ANALYSIS AND INTERPRETATION

PICTURE #5

Curious arrangement of furniture. —— This has a lot of possibilities. I think the horror story possibility has the greatest appeal.

The patient's first comment has to do with details. This is consistent in a personality structure which is characterized by rigidity.

Well, we'll assume that this is a big room. There has been a scream. The woman hearing the scream came to the door and looked in and she seems to be feeling the emotion of consternation and perhaps some horror, at least revulsion and disgust.

Note that although previous material has indicated that the patient has difficulty in expressing aggression, he is nevertheless attracted to aggressive themes. (The intensity of the aggression described here is rather unusual.) The desire to express aggression is therefore strong, but he cannot accept the fact that it may be he who is aggressive. (It is hypothesized that the patient has identified with the woman here, since previous stories indicated the patient's difficulties in dealing with aggressive themes. The dynamics of the identification are the same as that discussed in the analysis of the story to Picture #3.)

The patient's phrase "she seems to be feeling the emotion of consternation" is again a reflection of his lack of spontaneity and tendency to intellectualize.

I presume she will go into the living room, find a corpse on the floor with a stab wound or bullet hole. Probably a stab wound be-

Despite the heroine's consternation, fear, disgust, and revulsion, the patient has her go into the room. This plus the fact that there is a good deal of discussion of the manner in which the corpse was

cause she heard a scream, not necessarily because she could have heard a shot. Well, she found the corpse.

Now you want to know what happens then? She calls the police.

You want another story on the same picture? Let's assume that this woman is a mother who has a daughter. This daughter has a male suitor who has come to visit her and this woman dislikes the suitor and comes downstairs, opens the door, peeks in to see what is going on. Expression on her face indicates that she's disgusted with the gentleman, wishes there were some way of breaking off the relationship, but having observed that the two young people are behaving decorously, she shuts the door and goes about her business, still feeling displeased by the daughter's choice of a boy friend.

killed suggests not only that the subject tries to be precise and careful but also is a reflection of the strong attraction that aggression has for him.

The patient was not asked for another story but he desired to give one.

It is interesting to compare this story with the ones told previously that involved aggression. Note that here where no aggression is involved, the style is freer and much less rigid and stilted.

The content of the story suggests that the patient may have been brought up in an environment in which he learned that one means of avoiding his mother's wrath was not to indulge in sexual relations.

The fact that an aggressive theme and a theme in which a mother-figure interferes with heterosexual activity appear together, suggests that the intense aggressive feelings he experiences now may stem from the frustration he experienced in attempting to develop autonomous behavior. It also suggests that aggressive fantasies may be associated with his sexual behavior and this may be one of the factors affecting his marital adjustment.

Summary Picture #5: Although the patient has difficulty in expressing aggression himself, he is attracted to and takes pleasure in aggressive fantasies. He is obsessed with aggressive thoughts. His heterosexual behavior and activities were frowned upon at home. His aggressive thoughts at the present time may well stem from his frustrated need autonomy in early life and lack of experience in dealing with aggression. Furthermore, aggression is fused with sex and this, too, may interfere with his marital adjustment.

TAT Protocol

ANALYSIS AND INTERPRETATION

PICTURE #6

Well, it would appear that the man in the picture is a son who has perhaps committed a crime or done something of which he is ashamed. He has come home and told his mother about it.

The patient feels guilty and ashamed for what he has done. These feelings are associated with aggression or something else. He seeks aid.

Mother is displeased, depressed, and they're presently deciding or wondering what should be done about the situation. I would guess that the mother would recommend that the son do whatever could be done to rectify whatever wrong had been committed and to make the best of it.

No punishment or rejection takes place — but the patient must do something to rectify the wrong. Note that he does not initiate plans in this regard himself but needs the help of a mother-figure.

Summary Picture #6: The patient feels guilty about and ashamed of his behavior. He feels the need to rectify his wrongs but cannot develop plans of action in this regard without the aid of others.

TAT Protocol

ANALYSIS AND INTERPRETATION

PICTURE #7

This picture suggests a father and son talking together. The son apparently has gotten involved in a business deal and is presently in a complicated situation. The father is attempting to offer suggestions and advice, telling him how he can get out of the predicament he is in. The picture suggests to me that any solution that might be arrived at would not necessarily be strictly on the up and up.

Once again the hero is in trouble and once again he cannot extricate himself from a " complicated situation " but requires the advice of the father-figure. Thus far, in structure, the theme here is similar to that observed in the previous story. But one difference between the two stories is that in the previous one, where the mother was involved, this resulted in a rectification of the wrong that was committed, but here the father-figure shares dishonesty with the son, suggesting that the patient shares common feelings with his father and he does not regard either himself or his father as being as socialized as his mother.

(Can you tell me some more about this?)

The two faces suggest that father and son are two unscrupulous individuals and would not hesitate, shall we say, to stoop to dishonesty and to achieve their ends.

It is interesting to compare the data obtained thus far regarding the patient's parents. In this story the father is unscrupulous but the mother in Story 6 is more socialized. Furthermore, in Story 1 she was the one who insisted that the boy play the violin — the boy did not refer to "parents" — and in Story 5 she looked in to see how the girl was behaving. It is therefore suggested that the patient's conscience or superego development in terms of its socializing aspects resulted from his interaction with his mother. This may also explain the historical reason for his feminine identification, for she may have had more to do with him than his father.

One other observation is in order here. In the previous stories where the patient was dominated by the parental figures he did not get into difficulty. But in the stories to Pictures #6 and #7, where the hero has presumably initiated activity on his own, he ends up in difficulty and complications. This suggests that without external controls the subject may fear that he will release aggressive tendencies. The reason "fear" of such responses is indicated is that the aggression is most frequently followed by guilt. Furthermore, intellectual controls still seem to be quite good — good enough not to permit the aggressive needs to break through into asocial acts.

Summary Picture #7: The patient thinks more highly of his mother than he does of his father or himself. Asocial tendencies are manifest here, but in view of the preceding material it is unlikely that they will be manifest in asocial acts. It is apparent that when the patient initiates activity he fears that he may get into difficulty and therefore restricts himself and requires external controls. It was also suggested that his mother played a more significant role than his father in the development of his superego.

TAT PROTOCOL

ANALYSIS AND INTERPRETATION

PICTURE #8

This would appear to be the dream of a young boy. I'm a little hard put to it to say what went before. Let me go on. Apparently this young fellow has a strong yearning to be a surgeon. To me this picture, wait —— got a gun in the picture. That complicates it. First impression is that the boy had a yearning to be a surgeon. This describes the vision of surgeon doing an operation. This apparently is not intent with gun here. —— I find it hard to piece it all together. What you want is a story that will put everything together. (You may do anything you like.) I think the best thing is for me to ignore the gun. The boy grows up, goes to medical school and becomes a great surgeon.

The patient starts with a need achievement theme but is unable to develop it because of the interference of an aggressive object. Although he tries to ignore it he cannot (similar to the attraction to aggression in Picture #5).

Note how the thought process is interfered with when an unresolved need is stimulated. Also, note that the goal is surgery — an activity in which his own aggressive needs may be sublimated.

Finally, the patient feels as if he must conform to the request of the psychologist. He is not sufficiently self-confident even to discard the picture. He is not capable of making use of his own resources here and it seems as if he felt that there were correct or incorrect answers to the picture, for he is concerned with the "intent" of the picture. This would be consistent with the rigidity, probably based on too much external evaluation, that was referred to previously.

Summary Picture #8: Once again the patient shows difficulty in dealing with aggression. Here he is unable to utilize his own resources and his unresolved tensions interfere with his integrative capacity. Evidence for conforming behavior, probably a result of too much evaluation of his behavior by others, was also indicated. Sublimation may be one of his defense mechanisms.

TAT PROTOCOL

ANALYSIS AND INTERPRETATION

PICTURE #9

I get the impression that these are hoboes who for

In view of the patient's problems indicated above and in view of the tension

some reason or other have had a long hard trek and have begged, borrowed, or stolen some food. Their stomachs are full, also tired, lying down on grass and fallen asleep.

that these problems no doubt stimulate, it is suggested that the reference to hoboes here is a reflection of the patient's desire for a period of relaxation and no responsibility.

Note that the hoboes " have begged, borrowed, or stolen some food "; because of this emphasis on food here, it is suggested that his oral-dependent needs are being frustrated.

After having a rest they get up and go on hiking.

After some relaxation the activity is continued, but note that although it may be assumed from the fact that the figures here do get up from their rest that the patient is energetic, the energy is not used constructively.

Summary Picture #9: The patient's problems result in tensions for which he seeks relief in a state of relaxation and no responsibility. Although his energy level may be good, it is not channelized into goal-directed activities. Evidence for frustrated oral-dependent needs was also presented.

TAT PROTOCOL

ANALYSIS AND INTERPRETATION

PICTURE #10

I would guess that the man in the picture has been away for some time and has returned home. He is in the process of embracing his wife. Both of them feeling great pleasure in being reunited and proceed to sit down and talk over what happened on the man's trip.

The relationship between the patient and his wife has positive aspects — there is a feeling of warmth between them and they share his experiences. The patient's marital relationship seems more positive here than it was in the story to Picture #2. There is, however, a significant difference between the two stories. In Picture #2 the story started with the married couple together. Here they were separated for some time. Consequently, it is suggested that the tension with the wife may develop as a result of the routines of daily living. But when a change has occurred, such as a trip, the relationship is restimulated.

Summary Picture #10: There are positive aspects in the patient's relationship with his wife. The negative ones may result from the routine of daily life.

PICTURE #11   Omitted

TAT PROTOCOL   ANALYSIS AND INTERPRETATION

PICTURE #12

An older man has just caused a youth to go into a state of hypnotic sleep. The youth is completely confident that the older man means no harm. The hypnotist, however, has ulterior motives and intends to use his victim's deep slumber to permit kidnapping with a minimum of struggle and disturbance.

Analysis of the previous stories has indicated that the patient has intense feelings of hostility. The data from this story suggest that he may have difficulty in relaxing in the presence of others because he tends to project onto them his own intense needs.

This story and the others following it were handwritten by the patient. It is an example of the problems one faces at times with such a technique, for here inquiry would have been appropriate to determine the purpose of the kidnapping.

Summary Picture #12: The patient projects his aggressive feelings onto others and this interferes with his capacity to relax in social situations.

TAT PROTOCOL   ANALYSIS AND INTERPRETATION

PICTURE #13

A man has come to the apartment of his estranged wife. Upon receiving no answer to his knock, he breaks in and finds her dead — presumably suicide. The man is overcome with grief from which he will gradually recover and lead a normal life.

Hostility toward the wife is expressed in an indirect fashion. She commits suicide but he has had no direct part in her death. The juxtaposition of " estrangement " and " suicide " suggests the possibility that the former may have been a cause or stimulus for the latter; consequently, it is suggested that the hostility expressed toward her may be retribution for the lack of love or the lack of a relationship that he desires.

Summary Picture #13: The patient has rather intense feelings of hostility toward his wife. These feelings may well have been stimulated by a desire for retribution for the lack of a positive relationship.

TAT PROTOCOL

ANALYSIS AND INTERPRETATION

PICTURE #14

A young man has just gotten out of bed. The sun is just coming up. The coming day will be one of great importance in the young man's life. He feels rested and ready to meet the challenge that the day is expected to bring. His confidence will be justified and the outcome of the day's activities will be successful.

This story suggests an optimistic attitude and view toward life. It is associated with a positive feeling toward himself. Note, however, that the patient primarily describes the day and the hero's inner attitude; there is no elaboration on the concrete activities that he pursues to achieve success. This suggests that although the patient may be optimistic, the extent of the positive feeling described here is more on a fantasy level than a realistic level. It should also be noted that the hero is not directly involved in an interpersonal relationship here. This too may account for the positive feeling tone of this story and it also suggests that he may be able to work off some of his tensions in daily work activities.

Summary Picture #14: The patient has optimistic tendencies but the extent to which they are described here suggests that they may be more on a fantasy level than a realistic level. It is also suggested that solitary activities are less tension producing for the patient than interpersonal relationships and that work may serve as an outlet for his tension.

PICTURE #15   Omitted

TAT PROTOCOL

ANALYSIS AND INTERPRETATION

PICTURE #16

I see a four-year-old little girl running with a peculiar limp and a bright smile on her face. She is running away from a house and across a lawn to her swing. She has been recovering from a bad burn on her foot, and after some days of inactivity, has regained her freedom. She is overjoyed to

Since the patient is a father it may well be that the situation he describes here is one that he may have experienced or witnessed with respect to one of his own children. The rationale for interpreting the story to obtain information regarding the patient's own personality is that the event must have resonated with a significant aspect in the patient's personality, otherwise he would not have told it.

find that she can run again and eager to get on her swing once more.

The theme of the story is that a little girl overcomes an infirmity and begins to enjoy her freedom once again. It is suggested that this story is a manifestation of the patient's own desire to overcome his infirmity and to be free once again. The infirmity here may be his aggressive drives and the guilt feelings they engender or, interpreting the symbolic character of the foot, it may refer to his sexual inadequacy.

Summary Picture #16: He has the desire to overcome his problems and to feel free of them.

TAT PROTOCOL	ANALYSIS AND INTERPRETATION

PICTURE #17

There is a fire raging in the hotel at which our hero has been staying. Fortunately the fire is in the upper stories and he has been able to find enough rope to reach the ground. Having been disturbed from his sleep there has been no time to dress. He is finding that he can lower himself to safety.

On the basis of clinical experience, it is suggested that the fire here represents the patient's instinctual drives — aggressive and/or erotic. Note that the patient escapes from them. The fact that the fire occurs when the patient is asleep suggests that when ego-boundaries or controls are relaxed, as in sleep, aggressive tendencies come to the fore which the patient in the waking state tries to avoid. Safety is achieved by avoidance.

Summary Picture #17: The patient seeks to avoid coping with his instinctual drives. When ego-boundaries or controls are relaxed these come to the fore; consequently, he must be vigilant against them.

PICTURE #18 Omitted

TAT PROTOCOL	ANALYSIS AND INTERPRETATION

PICTURE #19

In spite of the ravages of a sleet storm, powerful winds, and high waves from the nearby sea, the house portrayed has remained intact.

Considering the house as the reflection of his own ego-state, it is suggested that this story represents the patient's feeling that he has the capacity and ego-strength to avoid the ravages of the outside world

The occupants are warm and snug inside and the normal activities of the household are being carried on. The inhabitants are grateful to have avoided the clutches of the storm.

successfully. Note that in this story, as in the preceding one, he is grateful for having *avoided* a catastrophe. He is not one to meet difficulties head on.

Summary Picture #19: The patient regards himself as being capable of withstanding the ravages of life's experiences, but it appears that he has done so primarily by avoiding situations rather than by dealing directly with them.

PICTURE #20 Omitted

Final TAT Summary

Mr. A. C. is a rigid person who lacks spontaneity. The function of his rigidity and control is to keep strong hostile and aggressive impulses in check. These impulses are, as it were, pressing for expression. He avoids dealing with them directly for fear of the consequences that might eventuate. Although he tries to regard the drive as ego-alien, the drive does not remain quiescent, for there is pleasure and some gratification to be achieved in expressing it. Yet to express it, and in this case even to have thoughts about it, results in intense feelings of guilt and shame and the need for punishment. Consequently, he must remain constantly vigilant against his aggressive impulses and divert energy that might be utilized for more constructive activity to controlling them.

In the sexual area he is insecure and uncertain of himself and he feels inadequate in terms of fulfilling the masculine role in heterosexual activity. Another complicating feature here is that sex is fused with aggression for him and this too interferes with his capacity to effect an adequate adjustment.

His social relationships are marked by his tendency to maintain his distance from others and to be impersonal, if not cold. He is more comfortable in solitary situations than in interpersonal ones. In the latter he is likely to be passive and controlled. The control in this situation is, once again, directed toward his aggression and it limits the expression of warmth and spontaneity. Furthermore, he is likely to project his own hostile impulses onto others and this becomes another reason for him to avoid them. He is not an independent or autonomous person. He does not take the initiative in situations, for this might mean relaxing his controls and the impulses might come through.

His approach to problem situations is not conceptual. He does not deal with the over-all aspects of a situation but rather restricts himself to details. Some of the other details he attends to do serve the purpose of facilitating the solution of a problem while others sidetrack him and become elaborated in terms of his own needs. If the task is such as to stimulate hostility, then he becomes quite ineffective — his attempts at being systematic and cautious are disrupted. In non-affect-laden situations, he has the opportunity of working off some of the tension which is generated by his aggression and his attempts to control it. Work activity serves as such an outlet for him.

The patient sees his relations with his parents as those in which a more dominant role was played by his mother than his father. It appears that she frustrated his need for autonomy and desire for freedom. Although he felt angry with her, he conformed to her requests and his hostility simmered unexpressed. She is also perceived as having frowned upon the expression of sexual behavior and in order to remain in her good graces he controlled his inclinations in this regard. His conscience seems to have been developed primarily as a result of his relationship with his mother. He regards his father as someone who is as badly off as he.

His marital relationship is not completely satisfactory. He regards his wife as possessive and domineering. He takes a passive role with her. Their sexual behavior may well be affected by his feelings of inadequacy and the fusion of sex and aggression mentioned above. Furthermore, his need for love and affection is apparently frustrated in his relationship with his wife — he does not feel completely accepted by her — and this arouses hostility in him which remains unexpressed. He fantasies that he might be more acceptable to others.

The patient regards his environment as troublesome and difficult. He has the strength to withstand it but he does not do much to cope with it directly. He is uncertain about the future, unable to rid himself of his guilt, and incapable of dealing with his impulses. Yet underlying this is the hope that with outside help he may be able to effect a more adequate adjustment.

PART II: THE SAME PATIENT AFTER THERAPY

The following protocol was obtained from the same patient two months after he had completed two and a half years of psychoanalysis. The patient wrote out his stories.

TAT PROTOCOL   ANALYSIS AND INTERPRETATION

PICTURE #1

The boy's mother has insisted that the boy practice on his violin. He wanted to play and is very angry at his mother.

The mother here imposes a task upon the boy. His reaction, because practicing the violin interferes with his desire for play, results in anger. Although the patient does not complete the story he started to tell, it may be inferred from what follows that he conformed to her request.

Usually he will comply with her wishes but occasionally finds excuses for avoiding practice.

His typical reaction is to conform to her desires but on occasion he can gain satisfaction for his own desires, thus indicating some measure of independence.

As he grows older he begins to appreciate the possibilities of the instrument and ultimately becomes proficient as a player and composer.

The patient has interiorized the mother's demands and is now self-motivated. Note that not only does the boy become proficient as a player but he also demonstrates some originality.

Comparing this TAT story with the pre-therapy story, it should be noted that here the patient was able to experience his anger and say so, while in the pre-therapy record the boy was " disgusted " and this was regarded as a reaction against expressing his anger. Note that the patient deals more adequately with the future and does develop an achievement theme here which did not appear in the pre-therapy protocol.

It is interesting to note that a broader time perspective (as manifest in his dealing with the future) and an achievement theme do occur in a story in which the patient can state that he is angry. It is as if the energy formerly required to repress and/or suppress hostile feelings can now be utilized for more constructive purposes.

It is also interesting to note that the hero in the post-therapy story carries out the mother's request, as did the hero in the pre-therapy record. Thus it appears that what the patient objected to was not the activity required of him but whether or not he felt that he had some freedom of choice.

Summary Picture #1: The patient reacts to press imposed task from the mother with anger. He feels more independent. In contrast to the pre-therapy protocol, the patient manifests here a broader time perspective, need achievement, more independence, and a greater capacity to recognize and verbalize his hostile feelings. It is not clear as yet whether he can direct his hostility toward individuals when the situation demands it. It is suggested that the energy formerly deployed to dealing with hostile, aggressive feelings is now available for more constructive activities.

TAT PROTOCOL	ANALYSIS AND INTERPRETATION
PICTURE #2	
The schoolgirl with the books has cast an envious glance at the pregnant farmer's wife at the right. The farmer in the center is oblivious of the interchange between the women. He and the horse attached to his plough have noticed a deer running across the valley at the left. He is gesturing and calling to his wife to look.	The relationship between the patient and his wife is a positive one but the fact that he utilizes it to evoke envy in the schoolgirl suggests that it may not be as happy as he desires. Note that the hero is " oblivious of the interchange between the women " but he is not completely passive for " he is gesturing " and calling to his wife to look.
The schoolgirl is quite melancholy.	Being isolated results in depression but togetherness as described above leads, implicitly, to happiness.
She grows up and finds herself a husband.	Each must have his own is the theme here. The girl does not interfere with the relationship between the husband and wife but must become more realistic. This may be consistent with the patient's desire to seek realistic solutions to his problems.
	In contrast to the pre-therapy story to this picture, the story here is better organized (but this organization may in large measure be due to the fact that he wrote the story that is presented here while he told the story to the psychologist in the pre-therapy session, and written protocols are almost always better

organized than dictated ones), he is capable of referring to sexual material ("pregnant farmer's wife" as against "bulge"), he is less concerned with details and less uncertain of himself, feelings of sexual inadequacy are not present, there is no expression of hostile feelings, and he is more active than previously.

Summary Picture #2: The relationship between the patient and his wife is positive, although possibly not as happy as he would like it to be. Being isolated is associated with depressive feelings and, finally, it was also suggested that he attempts to be realistic in solving his problems. In contrast to the previous record, the patient appears here to be more active, more certain of himself, less concerned with details, less anxious about his masculinity, and there is no expression of hostile feelings.

TAT Protocol

ANALYSIS AND INTERPRETATION

Picture #3

The girl has shot her lover in a fit of jealous rage.

The patient has intense feelings of jealousy and hostility which he attempts to make ego-alien. The object for his feelings is a loved one and it is likely that, because of the jealousy which is indicated, his need for love and acceptance is frustrated. This datum supports the hypothesis presented in the analysis of the story to Picture #2 that his marital relationship is not as happy as he would like it to be.

Identifying the figure as a woman suggests feminine identification.

She is now overwhelmed with sorrow. She will be forced to spend much of the rest of her life in prison expiating her crime.

The expression of aggression is followed by sorrow, the need for punishment — from which it is inferred that guilt exists.

Comparing the story developed here with the pre-therapy one, it is evident that the patient now has less difficulty in dealing with aggressive themes, and now an object for aggression is presented. In other respects both stories are the same.

Summary Picture #3: The patient has intense feelings of jealousy and rage which are directed to a loved object and which he tries to make ego-alien. These feelings are stirred in situations where he feels deprived of love and acceptance. Expression of aggression is followed by sorrow, guilt, and the need for punishment. Evidence for feminine identification was also presented. Comparing this story with the pre-therapy story suggests that the patient now has less difficulty in dealing with aggression and that now he has an object for it.

TAT Protocol

Analysis and Interpretation

Picture #4

The actor has seen something which arouses resentful aggression feelings within him (perhaps a girl of his choice walking off with another man).

The patient refers to the male as an actor. In calling the male an actor, two hypotheses are suggested: the patient has exhibitionistic tendencies, or he regards himself as an actor now in the sense that he is playing a new role — a role in which he may be trying to utilize what he has gained in therapy and to do so independent of his therapist. These two hypotheses are not incompatible, for he may be exhibitionistic in his new role — that is, trying to show others how he has changed.

Resentful aggressive feelings are aroused in him when he feels rejected.

The dancer senses his feeling and restrains him. He gradually cools down, he looks at the situation realistically and eventually finds himself another girl.

Control from another person is required at first and then he is able to effect control over his own feeling and behave in a constructive fashion in attaining a sexual object.

To look at a situation " realistically " is probably what he had been told during the course of his analysis — this term might well be considered a psychoanalytic cliché. The fact that the patient makes such specific mention of this behavior here suggests that he may have to remind himself to be realistic (consistent with the material presented above regarding the word " actor ") and that he may have difficulty controlling his feelings.

Although sex and aggression are mentioned here, aggression alone was the major aspect of the story in the pre-therapy protocol.

Summary Picture #4: Rejection in a heterosexual relationship results in feelings of aggression. Although he still may require some outside aid to simmer down, he has a greater capacity to control his feelings now than previously and to behave in a constructive fashion. It is suggested that he does not do so spontaneously but has to remind himself as to how he should behave now that he has completed his therapy. It is also suggested that he gets satisfaction in demonstrating his capacity to function in his new-found role. While need aggression was the major aspect of the pre-therapy story to this picture, he now presents press rejection, need aggression, and need sex.

TAT PROTOCOL

ANALYSIS AND INTERPRETATION

PICTURE #5

Mother wondered why it was so quiet and decided to have a look in the living room. She saw her daughter and her lover embracing one another. She felt shocked, embarrassed, envious and then feeling once again the joy she had experienced in similar situations in her youth, she quietly withdrew.

Just as there is a change in the interaction with the mother in the pre- and post-therapy stories told to Picture #1, so too is there a change to this picture. The mother is now more permissive and heterosexual behavior is more acceptable to her. Note that in the pre-therapy story the mother figure was not so approving and the behavior of the couple was decorous. Because the mother is more permissive here and because her behavior is a function of what she recalls of her past experience, it is suggested that the patient may now too be more permissive with others since he also has learned about himself.

The pre-therapy aggressive theme, which was rather unusual, does not appear here.

Summary Picture #5: Heterosexual behavior is now more permissible. It is also suggested that the patient may now be more permissive in his relationships with others as a result of his therapeutic experience. The pre-therapy aggressive theme to this picture does not appear here.

TAT PROTOCOL

ANALYSIS AND INTERPRETATION

PICTURE #6

He has decided that he must break away from his mother's apron strings and has decided to leave home and strike out for himself. He is finding it very difficult to explain his point of view to the mother who is taking it very hard. He is very reluctant to hurt his mother, but persists in carrying out his resolve.

The patient has become more assertive and desire for autonomy is strong. Although he is sensitive to the mother's feelings and although he finds it difficult to fulfill his desire, the desire is apparently strong enough so that he follows through.

The data obtained here are in contrast to the aggression, guilt, and desire for absolution that are the basis for the story told to this picture prior to therapy.

Summary Picture #6: The patient has a strong desire for autonomy and he seems more capable of assuming an assertive role. Although he may feel sensitive about hurting his mother, this does not stop him from achieving his goal.

TAT PROTOCOL

ANALYSIS AND INTERPRETATION

PICTURE #7

A son has encountered a particularly difficult problem and has sought counsel from his father. It would appear that the son's mind is made up, however, and he will act according to his previous plans in spite of words of caution

from his kindly father.

The patient starts by telling us that the hero has sought counsel from the older figure. Yet it appears that the striving for independent action is so strong that despite the fact that he seeks counsel he acts in terms of " previous plans " and " in spite of words of caution."

The word " kindly " here is unusual. " Kind " would have been more consistent with the patient's previous use of language. The emphasis implicit in this word plus the fact that it occurs as an afterthought suggests that the patient is making a deliberate attempt to see his father as kind. This may be related to the fact that during the course of therapy he may have learned the basis for his negative feelings toward his father, and has tried to change them but the new feelings are not quite integrated as yet.

The data obtained here are in contrast to the attitude expressed to the father in the pre-therapy story.

Summary Picture #7: The patient has a strong need for autonomy and desire for independent action. His wish in this regard may be so intense that he may not be cautious. The patient's attitude toward his father has changed but the new, more positive attitude is not completely integrated as yet.

TAT PROTOCOL	ANALYSIS AND INTERPRETATION

PICTURE #8

The boy has been experiencing some exceedingly hostile fantasies regarding his father.	The content of the story here is consistent with the interpretation that was made above regarding the " kindly father." The hostility occurs on a fantasy level.
	The patient, it is suggested, does not react spontaneously with regard to his hostile feelings — this may be due to the fact that they are either too intense or they are associated with guilt. Furthermore, the phrase " experiencing some exceedingly hostile fantasies " may also be regarded as an intellectual technique for dealing with his hostile feelings.
He feels guilty about this,	The fantasy of hostility is followed by guilt.
and tries to visualize a surgeon operating on his father.	This statement is a very interesting one. The patient starts with a hostile fantasy and feels guilty about it; nevertheless he makes a conscious effort or, if you wish, forces himself, to deal with this fantasy. This is a counterphobic reaction which is apparently designed to aid him in divesting the drives, aggression, of anxiety. Thus if he can conjure up the aggression,

visualize the situation in which it may occur, and experience it without intense anxiety, then he will have mastered it and be in control of his drive rather than be controlled by it. Describing the process in somewhat different terms, it may be said that the patient is still testing himself and exerting himself to find testing situations. This is consistent with the analysis of the previous stories in which the patient seems to be rather intense in his attempts to assert himself and manifest his independence.

It is apparent both from the content of the story and the analysis presented above that although the analytic sessions may be over, the therapeutic process and the new learning still continues.

He may ultimately identify himself with this imaginary surgeon and grow up to be a doctor.

Apparently the hostility is controlled and the patient is capable of sublimating it.

Note that the patient uses the term "identify" — a technical term which he probably learned in the analysis. This sentence here may well be a reflection of the strength the patient gathered as a result of having identified with his own therapist.

The material presented above is in contrast to the pre-therapy story to this picture, for there the appearance of the gun interfered with the thought process. The story here is also in contrast to the pre-therapy story to Picture #5. In the latter the patient seemed to have gotten some pleasure from the horror he witnessed. There was curiosity about the aggression and a positive valence involved in it, while here he masters his aggression.

Summary Picture #8: The therapeutic process is still continuing. The patient is trying very hard to master his aggressive feelings and to divest them of anxiety. He also shows a tendency to sublimate his aggression. This is in contrast to the pre-therapy story, where hostile thoughts interfered with the thought process.

TAT PROTOCOL	ANALYSIS AND INTERPRETATION

PICTURE #9

The day has been very hot and the boys decided to have a snooze. They are without a care in the world. Later they will get up, shave, get shined up and go out on their various dates.

The patient manifests the capacity to relax here. This is also followed by need sex.

The figures in the picture are described, however, as boys. This is rather unusual, for they are most often referred to as men by individuals of the patient's age. This suggests that he now regards himself as a younger person — no cares, freedom, and capacity to enjoy heterosexual behavior.

Note that the dependent needs manifest in the pre-therapy story are not manifest here.

Summary Picture #9: The patient manifests here need sex and the capacity to relax. It is also suggested that the patient regards himself as a younger person.

TAT PROTOCOL	ANALYSIS AND INTERPRETATION

PICTURE #10

A good supper, conversation, warm embrace, intercourse, deep sleep.

Judging from the content alone, it would appear that the patient has achieved an almost ideal state; a good number of needs are satisfied. There are factors, however, which indicate that this is not necessarily so. First, note that no people are mentioned. And secondly, note that the style of the " story " is very different from that which was characteristic of the previous stories. The story does not flow consistently and smoothly. Both of these items suggest that what the patient discusses here may be the type of relationship he desires, but it is not necessarily what he has already attained. If the patient had already attained this blissful state then people would have been mentioned and a rather well-developed story would have been produced. The foregoing material does not negate the possibility that his marital relationship may be good; it only suggests that it is not as good as described here.

Summary Picture #10: The patient's marital state is a positive one but he desires it to be more blissful than it is described.

PICTURE #11   Omitted

TAT PROTOCOL   ANALYSIS AND INTERPRETATION

PICTURE #12

A psychiatrist in treating his patient has encountered some unusual difficulties. He has persuaded the patient to submit to hypnosis. The patient is serenely confident of a successful outcome but the doctor is by no means certain and is somewhat anxious. Many months of treatment are necessary before satisfactory results are secured.

In view of the fact that the analysis of the previous stories indicated that the patient is making a concerted effort to establish a new role and patterns of behavior for himself, it is suggested that the therapeutic relationship described here refers to the patient's attempt at treating himself. He is aware of the fact that he still has some problems to deal with but he is uncertain, although hopeful, that he will be successful in his efforts.

The theme here is quite different from that presented in the pre-therapy story to this picture.

Summary Picture #12: The patient appears to be " treating " himself. He is aware of the fact that he has still to deal with some problems. Although he is uncertain about how effective he can be in this regard, he is hopeful.

TAT PROTOCOL   ANALYSIS AND INTERPRETATION

PICTURE #13

After a quiet evening of talking and reading, the hus-

The relationship with the wife is positive. Need sex is strong. However, beband is sleepy but not too tired to consummate his love for his wife. She is perhaps somewhat more than receptive.

cause it follows the "sleepy but not too tired" phrase, it is suggested once again that the patient may be pushing or urging himself on in this regard.

The reference to the wife's receptivity which is qualified by "perhaps" suggests that her sexual needs may not be as strong as his and reinforces the hypothesis suggested in the analysis of the story to Picture #10.

Note how different the relationship described here is from that described in the pre-therapy story in which estrangement and hostility figured.

Summary Picture #13: The patient's relationship with his wife is a positive one. He has strong sexual needs and he seems to be urging himself on to express them. His wife's needs in this respect may not be as strong as his.

TAT PROTOCOL

ANALYSIS AND INTERPRETATION

PICTURE #14

After a sound sleep — unmarred by dreams —

In the previous stories it was suggested that the patient was trying very hard to effect a new role for himself. This role was quite a "normal" one and because it was almost "too normal" it was suggested that the patient was still dealing with some unresolved problems. This was also the interpretation of the story to Picture #12. The segment is additional support for the hypothesis suggested above. The introduction to the story to this picture indicates that the patient regards a sound sleep as one unmarred by dreams. Or, putting it differently, that dreams may mar sleep. Since the patient was psychoanalyzed, he no doubt knows the significance of dreams in that they reflect the unconscious. Because of his concern in this regard, it is suggested that the patient is still dealing with his problems.

our hero arises refreshed, goes to the window, gulps in the fresh morning air, and looks forward with joy to the eventful day he has planned. The day turns out to be a particularly productive one.

The content of this segment is very similar to that obtained during the pre-therapy session. However, there are some significant differences. During the pre-therapy story the patient spoke of the hero's readiness to meet the challenge that the day is expected to bring. Here, however, he " looks forward with joy to the eventful day he has planned." This suggests that he is taking a more assertive approach to his work. Furthermore, while in the pre-therapy story he says that the hero's " confidence will be justified and the outcome will be successful," here he speaks of the day as being " productive," suggesting that he is more task-oriented now. The patient therefore appears to be more involved and more realistic than he was previously.

Summary Picture #14: The patient appears to be more involved, more planful, and more realistic about his work than he was before therapy.

PICTURE #15   Omitted

TAT PROTOCOL

ANALYSIS AND INTERPRETATION

PICTURE #16

There is a woman sitting on a bench at the right. The bench is in a rustic garden. The woman's gaze does not meet that of the person looking at the picture. She is a very attractive woman and wears a " Mona Lisa " smile. She married a man and bore him a son whom she is watching as he plays in the garden. The boy will always be the apple of her eye but she will never be able to return the love of her husband.

The patient is in a competitive situation with one of his children for the love of his wife. He feels that he does not get all the love he desires and he is apparently unable to share her. The data here support the interpretation made previously for Pictures #10 and #13, that although his relationship with his wife may be a positive one, it is not as satisfactory as he desires. The fact that he can be so threatened by his own son suggests the intensity of his needs in this regard.

The jealousy manifested here, it is suggested, may be related to the patient's own early development, in which he may have felt deprived of his mother's love and affection because his father or siblings may have interfered. Now in a new triangle he again feels threatened.

Summary Picture #16: Although the relationship with his wife may be a positive one, it is marred by the fact that he desires to be her only love object. This is frustrated because of his child.

TAT PROTOCOL

ANALYSIS AND INTERPRETATION

PICTURE #17

The subject has heard cheers from behind a high wall as though an athletic event were in progress before a large and partisan audience.

The subject here is separated from an event which is in progress and, as he tells us later, he would like to participate in this event. The audience is a "partisan" audience.

The structure of this story is similar in its major aspects to the preceding story. There, too, the patient was left out of an experience he would like to have and there, too, the audience was partisan, since the boy was favored. Since the setting here is different, it is suggested that it refers to situations other than those related to his wife. Specifically, it relates to those situations in which he sees others engaged in competitive, exhibitionistic activities, demonstrating their physical prowess or manhood, being accepted and getting approval for their efforts.

He becomes anxious to see what is going on and climbs a rope hanging from a building under construction. He wishes he were participating in the event. After looking on interestedly, he climbs down and redoubles his training efforts.

He has the desire to experience what the others are experiencing but doesn't feel quite adequate to compete. The inadequacy is inferred from the content of his last remark and also from the fact that the building is still under construction — i.e., the ego is still under construction.

His statement that the hero redoubles his efforts corroborates the material obtained previously, which suggested the effort and energy he is putting forth to attain his new role.

The fact that no conclusion is presented for this story reflects the patient's uncertainty as to whether he can realize his goal.

This story is different from the pre-therapy story. In the latter the patient was afraid of his instinctual drives and was escaping from a difficult situation. Here he is not escaping but moving forward. The fact that the patient is better able to deal with these drives, as indicated by the analysis of the previous stories, may be the reason why he now has more energy to devote to new goals.

Summary Picture #17: The patient does not as yet feel sufficiently adequate to engage in competitive, exhibitionistic, and manly activities in which he would attain acceptance and approval. However, he is still preparing himself to realize the satisfaction of such needs.

PICTURE #18 Omitted

TAT PROTOCOL

ANALYSIS AND INTERPRETATION

PICTURE #19

A severe winter storm has struck a fisherman's dwelling close to the sea. The house is covered with snow and ice. A strong wind is whipping clouds and water into grotesque shapes. Inside the house the fisherman and his family are warm and comfortable. The storm will subside in a day or so without resulting in any permanent damage.

The content of the story presented here is similar to the pre-therapy story. It differs in that the environment is not as intense as it was previously and also, while the individuals in the house were previously described in impersonal terms — " inhabitants " and " occupants," here they are described as a " fisherman and his family," thus reflecting more warmth in social relationships and probably also within the family.

As in the analysis of the pre-therapy story, the patient feels he has the capacity to withstand the difficult environment but as yet he has not become too active in doing so.

Summary Picture #19: The patient sees his environment as somewhat less threatening than before therapy and he also appears to be warmer in his family and social relationships. He feels he has the capacity to deal with his environment but is not active in this regard yet; neither does he avoid it.

PICTURE #20   Omitted

Final TAT Summary

Mr. A. C.'s post-therapy protocol differs from the pre-therapy protocol in several significant aspects. In the former he manifests a greater capacity to recognize his hostile and aggressive feelings as such, and he can accept and verbalize them. To be sure, his problems with regard to aggression are not completely resolved. He tries to control his hostile feelings and, expressing them, is not devoid of anxiety and guilt. However, since his aggression is no longer associated with such intense guilt feelings as were manifest before therapy, there is no longer the necessity for expending a great deal of energy in imposing controls and defenses against the aggression and consequently there is more energy available for constructive activity and better social relationships.

The patient is making a very concerted effort to utilize the knowledge he has gained during the therapeutic process and to build upon the changes that have taken place. There is a forced quality about his attempts to establish his new role which may be characterized by the motto: " I want to be an assertive, autonomous, and ' normal ' person and therefore I must behave in such ways as will be consistent with what I have learned in therapy." This suggests that the therapy is still in process, with the patient now assuming the role of the therapist for himself. New behavior patterns are neither completely integrated nor completely spontaneous but they are in the process of becoming so.

Mr. A. C. feels more adequate with respect to sex and his capacity to assume a masculine role. Here too his behavior is marked by a conscious effort to live up to the standards that he would like to attain. His need for love and affection is strong and when it is frustrated he becomes jealous and hostile. His relationship with his wife is more positive now than it was previously but it is not as happy as he would like it to be. To some degree this is a function of his feeling frustrated in the satisfaction he is able to obtain for his need for love and affection from her by virtue of the fact that he has to share her with the children. He feels that his love for her is not returned in the same degree. This may well be related to his early life experience, in which he also had to share his mother with others.

In social situations Mr. A. C. shows a greater capacity for warmth and assertive behavior. He is less impersonal with regard to people. His capacity to manifest his warmth may well be limited to smaller and more intimate groups at the present time (such as his family), but having gained some experience in this regard here, he may well be able to expand his scope later. If he is isolated he feels depressed and he now has a stronger desire for social interaction than privacy.

The patient also shows greater capacity to manifest assertive behavior. He is not as subservient to authority figures as he was previously and he has a stronger desire to be an autonomous and independent individual. The barriers to achieving such a role have been removed to some extent in the sense that he does not equate such behavior with aggression. But he does not yet feel completely prepared to engage in competitive activities. The desire to do so, however, is present, and he is preparing himself for such interaction. Another characteristic of his assertive behavior is that his desire to effect an autonomous role is so strong that he may not evaluate sufficiently all the factors which may make it necessary for him on occasion not to be assertive.

In his problem-solving behavior the patient is less concerned with details and more attentive to the over-all aspects of the situations with which he has to deal. He is more planful, more involved in, and more realistic about his work. He also has a stronger need for achievement than previously. In this regard it is suggested that the energy formerly utilized for controlling his aggressive impulses is now more channelized to constructive activities.

The patient's perceptions with regard to his parents have also undergone change. He is now capable of expressing hostility toward his mother and more capable of breaking his ties to her than before therapy. His father is now not as depreciated as he was previously and there is a growing tendency to perceive him as a more positive person. This is a new attitude which is not yet completely integrated.

The patient generally feels more certain about himself than he was before therapy. He has found satisfaction in various aspects of the new personality that he is trying to develop. His time perspective is broader now than it was previously. He feels less constricted now than before therapy. He is aware of the fact that he has not yet attained the capacity to manifest his feelings spontaneously and to gain satisfaction for his needs in social relationships. He is, however, still working on this, and he is optimistic that although it will take time he will achieve his goals.

Notes from the Case Folder

Mr. A. C. had two major problems that led him to seek therapy. First, his job was one in which he had responsibility for large numbers of people and he had numerous problems in administering them. He preferred to avoid people and he had difficulty in getting his ideas across. His second major problem was concern with his virility. During the course of his therapy it was learned that his father was a rather quiet, passive, and weak individual with whom he had a very restrained and distant relationship. His mother was a more aggressive person. She kept him close to her at all times. The patient was extremely fond of her but because she was rather restrained in her feelings his affectionate feelings were often frustrated. His relationship with her was also marred by a sibling who competed with him for his mother's affection. The pattern of his relationship — distant and nonassertive — with this sibling and with his father was repeated with his own children and subordinates. After the analysis his virility had improved, he had become more assertive in his position and less guilty about his aggression, he had begun to take a deeper interest in his family, and he had begun to socialize more with others.

INDEX

Abasement, 56, 177, 185
Achievement, 2, 50, 81, 85, 92, 95, 97, 106, 107, 110, 114, 192, 196, 197, 213, 220, 221, 222, 225, 327, 339, 347
Acquisition, 45, 50, 93, 94, 101, 108, 327
Additions, 65
Administration, role of psychologist, 34 ff
Administration time, 31
Affiliation, 46, 53, 106–107, 113, 150, 258, 282
Aggression, 2, 5, 13, 17, 22, 29, 46, 54, 86, 87, 94, 95, 101, 166, 170, 180, 182, 187–188, 190, 200, 201, 205, 216, 217, 227–228, 233, 236, 263, 291, 292, 298, 300, 310, 315–316, 326, 333, 335–336, 338, 339, 344–345, 348, 349, 350, 352, 354
Ambivalence, 101, 190, 196, 235, 266, 309, 327
Anxiety, 26, 40, 67, 68, 185, 191, 235, 352–354
Anxiety, and behavior during test, 62
Aron, B., xii
Attention to single detail, 66
Autism, 68–69, 180, 249, 254
Autonomy, 56 f, 88, 168, 170, 185, 190 f, 220, 262, 263, 313, 346–347, 351, 352, 360, 361

Beck, S. J., 202
Behavior, 42 f, 50–58
Behavior, during test, 62 f, 161 f
Behavior, level of expression, 60, 162
Blamavoidance, 57
Blind analysis, 40 f

Castration anxiety, 72, 73, 109, 200–201, 223, 224, 242, 243, 247–248, 291, 292, 302–303
Cathexes, 49, 58, 179
Change, 51, 151, 152, 360
Classification, 40
Cluster analysis, see Syndrome analysis
Cognizance, 47, 51, 106, 124

Condensation, 73
Conflict, 2, 6, 7, 10, 59, 85, 122, 173, 183, 193, 219, 256, 269, 288, 289
Construction, 51
Counteraction, 2, 51 f, 167, 168
Curiosity, 2, 9, 17, 72

Deference, 47, 57
Dejection, 5, 127, 128, 163–167, 171, 172
Dependence, 185, 186, 187, 203, 204
Diagnosis, assumptions, 41
Diagnosis, meaning of, 39 f
Displacement, 73
Distortions, 65 f, 170
Dominance, 2, 47–48, 55, 93, 94, 114, 178, 220–221, 239, 240, 256, 267, 269, 281, 333
Dymond, R. F., 160

Ego-alien, 98, 100, 103, 112, 334
Ego-boundaries, 130, 145, 343
Ego-ideals, 81, 83, 94, 95, 122, 327
Ego-strength, 123, 134, 135, 155, 157, 185, 202, 225, 245, 282, 284
Energy level, 15, 86, 100, 101, 236, 263, 329, 340
Environmental stimuli, 42, 44–50
Eron, L. D., 2
Evasiveness, xv, 75
Example, 48
Excitance, 52, 104
Exhibitionism, 25, 321, 322
Exposition, 48, 55

Family situation, xv
Fantasy, 2, 13, 14, 59, 146–147, 158, 184, 342, 352
Fleming, E. E., 2
Frank, L. K., xiii
Free association, 38, 231
Frustration, 28, 127, 128, 148, 158, 164, 166–167, 168, 173, 174, 184, 304
Frustration tolerance, 130, 173, 239, 240, 254